# COACHING SOCCER SUCCESSFULLY

## Second Edition

Roy Rees
Director of Coaching, Southwest Soccer Club

Cor van der Meer
Community Colleges of Spokane

Human Kinetics

**Library of Congress Cataloging-in-Publication Data**

Rees, Roy.
    Coaching soccer successfully / Roy Rees, Cor van der Meer. -- 2nd ed.
        p.   cm.
    ISBN 0-7360-4609-7  (soft cover)
    1.   Soccer--Coaching--United States.   I.  Van der Meer, Cor.  II.  Title.
    GV943.8.R356  2003
    796.344'07'7--dc21

                                                                                              2003000181

ISBN: 0-7360-4609-7

Text and illustrations on pages 68, 75, 76, 87, 89, 92, 93, 95, 99, 100, 101, 102, 103, 104, 105, 111, 112, 118, 125, 126, 127, 148, 151, 154, 156, 157, 159, 160, 161, 162, 163, 166, 169, 171, 172, 173, 174, 175, 176 reprinted, by permission, from Roy Rees, 1987, *The Manual of Soccer Coaching* (Spring City, PA: Reedswain, Inc).

**Developmental Editor:** Laura Pulliam; **Assistant Editors:** Alisha Jeddeloh and Carla Zych; **Copyeditor:** Scott Jerard; **Proofreader:** Jim Burns; **Indexer:** Cheryl Landes; **Permission Manager:** Toni Harte; **Graphic Designer:** Nancy Rasmus; **Graphic Artist:** Tara Welsch; **Art and Photo Manager:** Dan Wendt; **Cover Designer:** Kristin Darling; **Photographer (cover):** © Human Kinetics; **Photographer (interior):** Technique photos by Rick Harrison, all other photos © Human Kinetics unless otherwise noted; **Illustrator:** Brian McElwain; **Printer:** Versa Press

We thank Community Colleges of Spokane in Spokane, Washington, for assistance in providing the location for the photo shoot for this book.

Human Kinetics books are available at special discounts for bulk purchase. Special editions or book excerpts can also be created to specification. For details, contact the Special Sales Manager at Human Kinetics.

Printed in the United States of America       10   9   8   7   6   5   4   3   2   1

**Human Kinetics**
Web site: www.HumanKinetics.com

*United States:* Human Kinetics
P.O. Box 5076, Champaign, IL 61825-5076
800-747-4457
e-mail: humank@hkusa.com

*Canada:* Human Kinetics
475 Devonshire Road Unit 100, Windsor, ON N8Y 2L5
800-465-7301 (in Canada only)
e-mail: orders@hkcanada.com

*Europe:* Human Kinetics
107 Bradford Road, Stanningley, Leeds LS28 6AT, United Kingdom
+44 (0) 113 255 5665
e-mail: hk@hkeurope.com

*Australia:* Human Kinetics
57A Price Avenue, Lower Mitcham, South Australia 5062
08 8277 1555
e-mail: liahka@senet.com.au

*New Zealand:* Human Kinetics
P.O. Box 105-231, Auckland Central
09-523-3462
e-mail: hkp@ihug.co.nz

To my immediate family, particularly my wife, Ann, who typed and retyped the text as it took shape; and to my larger family, the many players whom I have had the honor of coaching.

—R.R.

To my most diligent teacher, the game; to the game's indulgent assistants, those who coached me; to the source of my rich memories and future challenges, my players; and to the best teammate I ever had, Sandra, my wife.

—C.v.d.M.

# CONTENTS

# Part IV  Coaching Tactics

# Part V Coaching Matches

# Part VI Coaching Evaluation

# FOREWORD

As soccer coaches, we expect much from our players. And they, in turn, should expect and receive much from us. That's the magic of the coach-player relationship.

Veteran coaches Roy Rees and Cor van der Meer know that this relationship begins with the coach. A prepared coach can meet this responsibility; an unprepared one cannot. *Coaching Soccer Successfully* covers all aspects of what it takes to be both prepared and effective in your role.

And who better to learn from? Roy and Cor have a wealth of education and experience to draw from—their own. They've coached youth levels to elite levels; men and women; school, club, and national teams. Their win-loss records are outstanding no matter who they've coached, and they are among the more highly respected teachers in our sport.

My own experiences as an author add to my appreciation of this effort. *Coaching Soccer Successfully* is both comprehensive and detailed. Part I (Coaching Foundation) is reason alone to buy the book. But there's more. Sections for teaching offensive/defensive skills and strategies are perhaps the highlight. From start to finish, you'll find valuable practice and game tips to improve how you work with your players as a coach.

Roy and Cor have done a great service to the profession of coaching soccer by sharing their wealth of knowledge in *Coaching Soccer Successfully*. Take the opportunity to read and learn from them. And keep the book handy on your office shelf for quick reference—and a better season.

Jerry Yeagley
Men's Head Soccer Coach
Indiana University

# PREFACE

The idea for the first edition of this book was discussed some years ago in Anaheim, California, with the American Sport Education Program. At first, the proposal was somewhat overwhelming. The scope of the book seemed too comprehensive. After some days, though, the awe and anxiety were replaced by feelings of excitement. Here, at last, was an opportunity to offer all those who love and coach our great sport a book that not only presents a fresh and contemporary approach to technical and tactical development of players and teams, but one that also dares to address all the other prerequisites necessary to coach soccer successfully.

After the few years it took to write the book, the concept became a reality. The goals that we set with the American Sport Education Program in the beginning were met. All coaches—and, in particular, those who coach at the junior high and high school levels—will find helpful and practical advice within the pages of *Coaching Soccer Successfully*.

Imagine then the significance of this, the second edition. The first edition was comprehensive to say the least; however, the second edition contains even more valuable and practical information. In particular, you'll find new, detailed explanations for understanding the principles of play and the tactical evolution of our beautiful sport.

Part I begins by showing the need for developing a solid coaching foundation, which includes a strong, consistent philosophy of coaching; practical methods of effective communication; and an understanding of motivation. Approaches to building a successful soccer program are also thoroughly discussed.

In part II, coaches can learn how to save time by following our suggestions for planning the season and preparing practices. Part III concentrates on how to coach basic defensive and offensive skills and techniques, whereas part IV deals primarily with tactics and the concepts behind them. Part V takes the coach to the field for some meticulous insights into effective coaching during matches, and part VI shows how success is perpetuated by courageously evaluating your players, staff, and program.

In the first edition we wrote: "Soccer is our life. It has been good to us. We have much to be grateful for. We hope that we are giving something back by sharing our experiences with dedicated coaches, so that they can in turn have a positive influence on America's greatest asset—its youth." The need for a second edition is therefore most gratifying.

# ACKNOWLEDGMENTS

My final thanks go to the players I currently coach and have coached. They have been my teachers. Their trust, integrity, competitiveness, honorable sporting behavior, warmth, ability, and performance have been and continue to be the joy of my life. I would like to mention my appreciation of all those players—from six-year-olds, competitive club players, college players, and professional players to World Cup players—who have helped shape my coaching philosophy. At times, I labored to find the right answers to problems, but now, with over 35 years of experience coaching players at all levels and from many countries and cultures, I find little that is "new." My deeply felt thanks to those thousands of players whom I have coached—I hope you enjoyed it as much as I did.

**—Roy Rees**

Again, in this second edition, I want to acknowledge the men and women who fought in the Second World War. They gave their lives so that I could live in freedom.

I'm grateful to so many other people—my mother, who instilled in me my competitive drive; my father, who died young but not before teaching me that displaying poor sporting behavior while winning results in an empty victory; my teachers, who taught me the value of education and curiosity; my coaches, who took endless hours to teach us youths the fundamentals—they all contributed to this book.

Later in life, other coaches generously gave their time to help me better understand our game. I will be grateful forever to people like Jimmy Gabriel, Bobby Howe, Tony Waiters, Clifford McCrath, Billy McNichols, Jan Smisek, Alan Hinton, Clive Charles, Karen Stanley, Betsy Duerksen, and so many others. They are the unsung heroes, the true pioneers of soccer in the United States. I have also learned much from the coaches who coached against me in our conference, in particular, from David Ryberg. I give special thanks also to Dr. Frank Smoll, who taught me that there is so much more to coaching than knowing how to play the sport. From a coaching perspective, the last 19 years have been exciting and rewarding, and I am thankful that my college and its athletic director, Dr. Maury Ray, created an atmosphere of trust, so conducive to a coach's growth.

All these people contributed to this book indirectly. The efforts of several others were more direct. I'm referring to the thoroughly professional people at Human Kinetics. In particular, I want to thank Karen Partlow, who started me dreaming about writing this book; and Ted Miller, who made me realize that the dream could come true. Most of all, I shall be forever grateful to Jan Seeley for the guidance, prodding, cajoling, and constant encouragement that I needed to not give up on the dream during the first edition. Also fond thanks to our developmental editor for the second edition, Laura Pulliam.

—**Cor van der Meer**

# Part I

# COACHING FOUNDATION

# Chapter 1

# DEVELOPING A SOCCER COACHING PHILOSOPHY

Your success as a soccer coach is totally dependent on the strength of your philosophy. Your philosophy is your plan, guide, and map to achievement. With your personal philosophy, you will find coaching to be exciting, challenging, and rewarding. Every soccer team needs a leader with a strong and realistic concept of direction. After all, no sport places more physical and psychological demands on athletes than soccer does. In fact, some call it a long, high-speed game of chess.

Soccer presents a particular challenge to new coaches. That challenge—your challenge—is that often your players will be fairly educated in the sport by the time they reach you. Unlike other sports, soccer has a well-developed club system in the United States. Millions of young athletes are now playing soccer, and they are doing so through the efforts of U.S. Soccer (and its youth branch, United States Youth Soccer), the National Soccer Coaches Association of America, the American Youth Soccer Association, Soccer Association for Youth, and many others. Because of these organizations, the players on your team have probably been playing for several years. They will have had access to well-structured player-development programs, and chances are, they will have had a fair amount of soccer knowledge and experience. The question is, are you prepared to coach them? If you don't think you are, don't despair. Help is available—this book.

This book is an excellent source of help for you, the soccer coach, as the leader of a young group of motivated soccer players who are ready to run, jump, dribble, and dive for an entire match. It is written for all soccer coaches, but it is written especially for the coach who will be working with experienced players. For those who would like more help or for those who may be working with less experienced athletes, your state youth soccer association can offer additional resources, such as literature, visual aids, and coaching clinics. If you live near a college with a varsity soccer program, you can call the coach there and ask for help. Most coaches are willing and able to assist you. In fact, it is to the advantage of these coaches to help you—that is, if they want you to prepare what will ultimately be *their* players for *their* future teams.

To be a successful soccer coach requires an eagerness to meet the challenges of coaching, and it requires that you have a thorough understanding of this often-misunderstood sport. Mastering the Xs and Os of soccer is just a small part of this great and complex sport. What is more important is that you have a plan for success. So let's get started.

# BUILDING A COACHING FOUNDATION

As a soccer coach, you will need several crucial ingredients to create a plan for success. To take the first step in building your foundation, ask yourself the following questions:

- What are my objectives as a coach?
- What objectives do I have for each athlete?
- What objectives do I have for the team?
- Why do I want to be a coach?
- Am I willing to give the time and effort to become the best coach I can be?
- Am I willing to put the needs of my athletes before my own needs?
- Which is of greater importance to me—the performance of the team or the outcome of the match?

The answers to these questions reflect your personal coaching philosophy. They come together to form one philosophy that ultimately serves as your guiding force for every coaching decision you make. How exactly does one arrive at such a philosophy? Coaches develop their philosophies from sources such as earlier soccer experiences (perhaps as athletes, or even as spectators), books, methods learned from other coaches, clinics, videos and films, and one's own personality.

## Personal Experiences

The experiences you had as an athlete and the lessons you learned from those who coached you will certainly carry over into your coaching methodology. For instance, if you had a lot of fun during your soccer-playing days, then I imagine that your players today probably have a pretty good time, too. On the other hand, if your former coaches were sticklers for skill development, then you, too, are probably such a stickler in your current regime. Likewise, if your former coaches were obsessed with winning records, you may currently think that winning is to be your players' foremost consideration. Regardless of the specifics, your experiences as a player carry over into your methods as a coach.

In other sports, many veteran coaches rely on only one educational resource—former coaches. If the former coaches had weaknesses, then the current generation of coaches probably have those same shortcomings. Unlike other sports, however, soccer has few (if any) role models for coaches. In fact, any sources of information about coaching soccer were (until recently) hard to find.

As a last personal consideration, you may even be one of the many soccer coaches who has had little or no playing experience. That is not a problem. In fact, you may even find it to be an unexpected benefit. As someone without experience, you will be starting with an open mind, unencumbered by preconceived ideas. You will be developing a coaching style that is uniquely your own, one that is unbiased and free of preconception.

## Books

Books are a great learning source, and soccer coaches can find many books about our great sport. Some, of course, are better than others, but I've never picked up a book on soccer that did not at least give me a few new ideas. I recommend that every coach take the time to read a book thoroughly, even if some of the sections are familiar. Somewhere in those pages may be the exact pearl of wisdom you have been looking for.

## Clinics

Simply stated, clinics are a must for every coach. Period. And I can already hear you say what many coaches say: "A clinic is only as good as the clinician." Not true. Even if the clinician leaves something to be desired, you, as a soccer coach committed to your players, can benefit by talking with and learning from the other coaches who are in attendance.

As coaches, we too rarely seek information from, or share experiences with, our colleagues. Here is a case in point: I used to finish my clinics with a question-and-answer period. I don't do that anymore. It usually ends up being a waste of time because in most cases coaches do not ask any questions. Instead, they either make a statement or simply fail to participate in the discussion.

Remember: Coaches are our greatest source of knowledge. If, as a coach, you want to increase your body of knowledge and wisdom, just ask questions. I'll say it again: Just . . . ask . . . questions. Some of the following are good ones:

- "Our opponent next week plays five men back. How can we beat it?"
- "One of my best players turns negative when things go wrong. Any suggestions?"
- "You have talked about a 3-5-2 system. Who supports the attack more, the outside or the inside midfielders?"
- "One of our parents has been behaving destructively during matches. How would you handle him?"

As coaches, we must make a conscious effort to tap this knowledge, whether by attending clinics and asking questions or by reading books such as the one in your hand. But remember, learn from many coaches; don't limit yourself to one. True knowledge comes from the collective wisdom of many, not just one.

## Of Apples and Oranges, or Coaches and Referees

When I was the program coordinator for the local youth sport association, I instituted two new programs, a weekly coaches' meeting and a weekly referees' meeting. The purpose was to provide an opportunity for coaches and referees to discuss their ideas or problems freely (and, I hoped, to learn through this communication). The first few meetings flopped, but the problem wasn't attendance. It was what the coaches and referees chose to talk about. They chose to focus their conversations on last Saturday's match, from the highs to the lows. Neither group, unfortunately, asked for help or advice.

I was about to give up on the meetings when a thought struck me and then inspired me to try out an idea. At the next meeting, I decided to give assignments to two coaches. One assignment was to explain how to beat an offside trap. The other assignment was to design a functional practice for forwards. I instructed the coaches to study the assignments and report at the next meeting. I then designed similar assignments for the referees. Future meetings became more successful because coaches took the time to prepare. Thus, they felt more comfortable discussing problems and issues.

On a final note about clinics, the one you decide to attend does not necessarily have to be soccer-specific to help you be a better coach. My advice to coaches is that they go to clinics that deal with a range of topics, such as sport injuries, sport psychology, nutrition, drug abuse, time management, risk management, sports law, motivation, and management skills. In fact, clinics dealing with other sports are great for picking up new approaches to our own game. In short, coaches should try to attend clinics—any clinics—that can help them better serve players, staff, and school.

## Videos

Films and videos are another great source of learning for soccer coaches and their players. Here is a great example of a scenario that is enhanced by the use of video. I often conduct advanced coaching clinics. When I do, I include theory that can be difficult to remember. To help the coaches assimilate the information, I use specific video from matches. When we cover different styles of play—Italian, German, South American, English, and so forth—I can show those styles to coaches, who can then more readily grasp the differences.

When I can show visual examples of a team executing a style of play, principles such as depth, balance, and support in the defensive third are much easier to convey. Through video, I can also demonstrate principles of attack and the effectiveness of various systems of play.

Because so much happens off the ball, I often watch match videos in slow motion. I recommend that you try it yourself. Watch it especially after a goal has been scored to figure out who caused the goal. You may be surprised at the way slow motion will change how you see a play—you may pick up on subtle nuances and movements that you didn't notice before. Videos are fun and educational when you try to see what's happening off the ball, and watching them in slow motion is the ideal way to do so.

## Credit Where Credit Is Due

One of my favorite video clips is of Marco van Basten's scoring a goal for the Netherlands in the 1988 Europe Cup match against Germany. We use this clip in clinics to test the coaches on who caused the goal. In the video, at about the 85th minute, the match is tied at 1-1. After a slow buildup in the back (which is typical of the Dutch), Ronald Koemans receives the ball. Koemans spots a wide-open Jan Wouters about 30 yards from the German goal. He passes to Wouters, who could have taken a shot from his position. Instead, he scans the field and sees van Basten on a lateral run, two steps ahead of his marking defender. Wouters crisply plays the ball in the space in front of van Basten, who then receives, pivots, and shoots, beating both the defender and goalkeeper Immel.

Most people like to credit Koeman's and Wouter's passing for the goal. After looking at the video in slow motion, you can see that when Koemans is in possession of the ball, teammate Ruud Gullit makes a brilliant run off the ball toward Koemans. With that run, Gullit draws no fewer than three defenders out of position, leaving Wouters wide open. Thus, the real credit should go to Gullit as a result of that one move.

## STAPLES OF A COACHING PHILOSOPHY

Earlier in the chapter, I asked you some questions so that you could get a feel for your coaching philosophy. Perhaps until reading this book, you hadn't given the matter much thought. In fact, maybe you never even considered the value of a sound coaching philosophy. If not, it's time to do so. And it starts with being yourself.

### Be Yourself

I have often dreamed of playing NBA basketball, but at five-foot-six, I know that Michael

Jordan isn't lying awake worrying about me. Then again, maybe I could be a quarterback. Do you think the NFL is looking for a 140-pound signal caller? Tony Banks, I think that you are safe. I guess I have to accept that I have limitations . . . as do you and every athlete. The key is to understand those limitations through honest self-appraisal. After doing so, you can then make the most of your potential.

All of us know coaches we greatly admire. We learn from them, and sometimes we use their ideas and methods as our own. There is nothing wrong with that, of course, but it is a mistake to pattern your entire style after another coach. Remember: A copy can only be second best. In the end, it is your personality that must prevail.

Among my friends and acquaintances, I count such coaching greats as Tony Waiters, former Canadian national coach; Lothar Osiander, former U.S. Olympic team coach; Anson Dorrance, who so brilliantly coached the American women to the World Championships; Roy Rees, who was the U.S. boys' under-16 coach and is coauthor of this book; and Clive Charles, the tenacious coach of the University of Portland and former Olympic team coach. All are successful, and all reach their goals—but, all use different methods to get to where they want to go. No one copies any other, and no two have similar personalities. All put distinct, personal stamps on the teams they coach. They are strong because they are themselves—always.

Coaches sometimes have difficulty defining their strengths. If that is true of you, ask your family, members of your coaching staff, and others close to you what they think your strengths are. Then work to enhance those strengths to become the best person and coach you can be.

## Lead by Example

"Do as I say, not as I do . . ." You know what? That won't cut it in coaching. To be effective, we as coaches must lead by example. If we want practices to start on time, guess what? We must be on time. If we want our players

to respect each other? That's right, we must show respect to our players, our assistants, and our superiors. If we want our players to perform with a positive attitude, we need to coach with a positive attitude. In general, we as coaches are probably not aware of just how much our attitude and expectations affect the teams we coach.

As the leader of our teams, we must set the tone. Think about the high and low points of your career. Now think about how you felt and acted at each point. Did the team's poor performance coincide with a temporary setback in your own life? Did the team's success happen at the same time that you experienced a positive plateau? Is there a pattern in your team's success as opposed to your personal life? If so, your awareness of these moods can help you prevent, or at least minimize, inconsistent performances of the team.

For a long time, I have had a sign in my office that says, "You get what you expect to get." I have since added a note at the bottom: "That goes for the coach also." As coaches, we have a strong influence on our teams. Keep your example and lifestyle in line with your expectations for the players, and you will see the team behave as you hoped it would.

## Keep Perspective

Early in my career I had some difficulty keeping things in perspective. I tackled my tasks as a coach with single-minded enthusiasm, and it often upset me when those around me would share my enthusiasm but not my single-mindedness. I've since learned the hard way that my priorities and someone else's may not always be mutual.

As coaches, we should not expect young athletes to be single-minded. Think for a moment of your players' personal commitments. They face pressure to achieve academically; some have part-time jobs; others are members of religious organizations; a few may even have special family obligations. We must respect them, their priorities, and their schedules if we expect them to respect us.

## To Prom or Not to Prom

When I was vice president of development for the Washington State Youth Soccer Association, I managed the Olympic Development Program in our state. One of the player-evaluation tournaments we conduct is the Big Sky Tournament.

During my tenure, I once received a phone call from an irate parent whose daughter was scheduled to play in the tournament. The parent's dilemma was that her daughter was required to leave for Boise (the tournament site) hours before her senior prom. The player's coach and the team's administrator had said that if the player did not travel with the team, they would not allow her to play in any of the matches.

I called the coach and the team's administrator, and we talked about perspective. The player went to her prom, flew to Boise on Friday night, played in all four matches, and was selected to a regional camp. Shortly after the camp, she received a scholarship from Coach Dang Pibluvich, then the coach at the University of Washington.

I am a stickler for rules. I know it is difficult to win without fair and consistent team discipline, but flexibility is an asset that every coach should have. Too few of us take the perspective of our players. We want them to be totally dedicated to our program, and when they aren't, we get angry. We then wonder why they don't turn up for the next season.

## Win on More Than the Scoreboard

The players' willingness to give their best and play to win is important. A lesser effort is dishonest, and it is a discredit to the sport, the fans, and the team. Every team should want to succeed, and every coach should encourage the team to go for the win. This philosophy doesn't mean that we must win every match. What it does mean is that we must at least try to win every match.

If players and coaches give it their all but fail, then they didn't really fail because they tried to succeed. Maybe the other team was just better. In that experience, players and coaches gain much more than is lost. But, if they lose a match from a lack of trying, regardless of the opponent, then that is a shameful loss indeed.

One season, in the quarterfinals of the playoffs, my team won 3-1. We then won the semifinal by the same score. In the final, we faced a team we had beaten twice during the season. I immediately knew we had a problem. Our players thought that the match was going to be a piece of cake; our opponents, however, were breathing fire.

After 90 minutes of listless play on our part, the score was 0-0. Five minutes into overtime, we scored. The players, viewing the outcome as inevitable, relaxed and lost their focus. The opponent scored two quick goals, and we went home as the runner-up. It took the team weeks to get over the disappointment. We knew that the other team didn't win the championship; we had simply lost it.

Three years later, we won our division and were seeded into the semifinals of our league championship. As defending champions, though, we paid the price. Throughout the season, each team played us hard and tough. The result was that we lost forward Joe Chadwell (who scored 12 goals in six matches) as a result of a broken tibia. In the last match of the regular season, we lost another forward, Adeeb Al-Dhain, with broken ribs. That left us with Nicolas Reep as our only healthy forward.

We eventually won the semifinal match 2-1, but we unfortunately lost Nicolas Reep with a crippling rolled ankle. By the time of the final, we were to face an extremely strong team, and we were to do so without any true forwards. But what a match it turned out to be. We ended up losing 1-0, but for 90 minutes the fans saw a tremendous demonstration of skill, honorable sporting behavior, and desire. Although we didn't win on the scoreboard, we did win on the field. We held our heads high, and we felt good about each other and ourselves.

Playing to win is important and should be any team's goal. However, to coach successfully, we must be conscious of the team's performance rather than the result of the match. If we can honestly and realistically evaluate our team's performance, we can always find ways to improve. And if we do so conscientiously, then the winning will take care of itself. Always.

## COACHING AS A MISSION

Dr. Rainer Martens in his book *Successful Coaching* says, "To coach, one needs the teaching skills of an educator, the training expertise of a physiologist, the administrative leadership of a business executive, and the counseling wisdom of a psychologist." Add to that sentiment the need to have a thorough knowledge of soccer, and what you once thought was an interesting pastime has suddenly become a demanding profession. But that's how it is.

None of us are born with all the qualities just mentioned. We do, however, have the opportunity to acquire them along the way because with each season, we can continually grow and get better. That's what makes coaching challenging and exciting. We are in a unique position to serve our players. We guide and travel with them through the entire emotional journey of a season—the practices, the matches, and everything else.

As coaches, we all have dreams of being carried off the field on the shoulders of our players while holding that huge, golden trophy way up high. Carrying the golden trophy is a great objective; every soccer coach wants to have a winning team. But you cannot build a house starting with the roof. In other words, you have to have a foundation and a framework if you and your team are going to shoot for such a successful season. And where exactly do you start laying this groundwork? You and your team's foundation is built during practices.

Encourage players to share the joy of achievement.

Before you begin developing your players' technical abilities, you must first be willing to spend the time developing their physical condition. Only after doing so can you worry about the team's tactical development. In addition, the development of any athlete is not complete without your building the athlete's confidence and self-esteem. This psychological aspect is particularly important for the soccer player.

Contrary to popular thought, soccer is not a coached sport. By this statement, I mean that the soccer coach does not have the luxuries that coaches in other sports have. For instance, in football, the coach often calls every play; in baseball, the manager flashes signals between every pitch; in basketball, the coach has several time-outs in which to adjust strategy, and the coach is even close enough to the play to direct it. But in soccer, once the opening whistle is blown, the players make all the decisions.

True, the coach may make some tactical adjustments, such as substitutions for players who are mismatched or having a bad day. The coach may even revise the game plan at halftime. Otherwise, that's about it. The secondary role of a soccer coach during a match is highlighted by the international rule that the coach may be seen but not heard during a match. This rule is being adopted in the United States, and before long, the coach's ability to make substitutions may even be restricted. Thus, in a soccer match, the players are the decision makers.

Players without confidence and high self-esteem are unable to make the necessary decisions, and they may sometimes hesitate before making them. Because soccer matches are played at lightning speed, such indecision is costly. To be successful as a coach and a team, we will therefore find the players' psychological strengths an essential component to work on. Only after developing the athletes mentally and physically can you as a coach realistically expect to have a team that can perform to the best of its ability.

Coaches can lead their players more than any other adult figure to be the best athletes, the best students, and the best citizens they can possibly be. With our guidance, our fairness, our impartial discipline, our honesty, our openness, and our work ethic, we can instill in our players the qualities needed to live happy and productive lives. That's coaching. That's our job. That's our mission. Let's get prepared!

## MAKE SOCCER FUN

Someone once asked me to define fun. I think it means to present young people with realistic challenges and then allow them, without interference, to overcome the challenges. Success at anything is fun.

Close to my home is a large sports complex. On Saturdays, it is packed from early morning until evening with youth soccer teams. On occasion, I go out and watch the young ones play.

One morning a father came to pick up his son shortly after the match. The boy, still excited from playing, rushed to his dad yelling, "Hi, Dad! We had fun." The dad came closer and said, "Hi, son. Did you win?" The boy looked confused, turned to the coach, and asked, "Coach, did we win?" The coach said, "Well, if you don't count their eight goals, we won one-nothing." At that point, the father appeared to lose interest.

Some years ago, in Vancouver, Washington, I watched an under-12 match that was pretty lopsided. Halfway through the second half, the blue team was ahead 6-0. I learned from one of the parents that the green team had never won a match. I wondered how the coach of the green team felt about their record. I positioned myself close to him so that I could hear his comments. Just then, the green team executed a perfect wall pass. The coach came unglued. "Did you people see that?" he yelled. "A perfect wall pass. For weeks, we have been working on that and they did it. They did it!"

What I thought was, here was a coach whose team had not won a match in its entire history, whose team was losing 6-0, but who was elated when they performed a skill they had practiced. I admire that coach.

Young players are not wrong for wanting to have fun, nor are fathers and mothers wrong for wanting their children to win. And the coach who went crazy over the wall pass is not wrong for wanting his players to be proud of their skill rather than the score. What I am saying is that these three qualities—having fun, playing to win, and striving to improve and develop skills—should all be part of your soccer-coaching perspective.

At this point, it is obvious that being a soccer coach means more than just knowing the sport. In fact, coaches must be capable of setting clear objectives for themselves and for their athletes, while keeping in mind that there is more to a young athlete's life than just soccer.

To help athletes reach their objectives, you must be willing to spend the time to get to know them and to let them get to know who you are and where you stand. If you want them to overcome weaknesses, you should not be afraid to expose your own shortcomings. The ability to laugh at yourself is an important asset.

## SUMMARY

The components needed to develop your coaching philosophy and thereby lay a foundation so that your players and team can perform at peak are as follows:

- Evaluate your objectives and your current qualifications to coach.

- Be hungry for knowledge. Read, attend clinics, watch and analyze matches, and talk with fellow coaches.

- Be yourself, lead by example, and keep things in perspective.

- Coach to succeed by focusing on performance rather than immediate result.

- Balance the need to succeed with liberal amounts of fun, laughter, and good humor.

- Respect the sport, players, fans, officials, opponents, and everything else associated with your team and program.

- Accept challenge and maintain an enthusiastic attitude.

# Chapter 2

# COMMUNICATING YOUR APPROACH

Success in any relationship depends on clear, effective communication. When any message is transmitted, both the sender and receiver should have a clear understanding of its content. The message should ideally be closed to any interpretation other than the one intended by the sender. Although such an objective may sound simple, relationships often break down as a result of ineffective communication.

Keep in mind that many communication styles are effective. For instance, you may be one who speaks rapidly and excitably, or you may be one who is calm and laid back. What matters is that the content of your message is logical and similarly interpreted by all.

Coaching, by its very nature, is communication. It is communication in its purest form. How you communicate is the essence of how you coach. The better you develop your communication skills, the more successful you will be with

- your players, on and off the field, about positive and negative subjects;
- your assistants and staff, about goals and progress;
- your superiors, about budgets and administrative policies;
- officials—before, during, and after matches;
- parents, with questions about their son's or daughter's playing time;
- faculty, to gain their respect;
- the student body, to entice them to come to matches;

- the community, for support for your program; and
- the media, to write and talk about your program.

These scenarios require that you have excellent communication skills. Of course, you will encounter many other situations—many of which you won't see coming—and they all will require that you use a unique and successful communication style to handle them effectively.

# KEYS TO EFFECTIVE COMMUNICATION

You must choose the right words to transmit your messages, but keep in mind that you do have other tools for effective communication. For instance, as coaches, we also receive messages. Our understanding of those messages depends on our ability to listen and interpret the content. Active listening is therefore one of the communication skills we must learn and continually work on.

Remember, too, that people transmit messages through gesture, body language, and voice pitch—in other words, they communicate nonverbally. In effective communication, nonverbal messages play a crucial role because they often indicate the sender's true state of mind. Like verbal messages, nonverbal messages need to be interpreted skillfully by coaches—that is, if they want to receive their players' genuine messages.

## Sending Messages

Even if a coach sends a clear and consistent message, how does one know it was received as intended? One simple way is to ask the receiver to repeat the message. But, if one is still unsure, the message sender can then ask a few quick and pertinent questions about the message. I encourage all coaches to use these methods with their players.

During times when we wrongly assume that athletes know how we feel about them, we need yet another form of reality check.

To meet this need, I include as part of my postseason activities a conversation with each athlete so that we can discuss the next season.

In his book *Sport Psychology,* Dr. Rainer Martens gives the following guidelines to sending effective messages:

- Your messages should be direct.
- You should own your messages.
- Your messages should be complete and specific.
- Your messages should be clear and consistent.
- You should clearly state your needs and feelings.
- Your messages should separate fact from opinion.
- You should focus your message on one thing at a time.
- Your messages should be supportive.
- Your verbal and nonverbal messages should be the same.
- Your message should be somewhat redundant.
- Your message should be appropriate to the receiver's language skills.
- You should obtain feedback that your message was accurately interpreted.

Reprinted, by permission, from Rainer Martens, 1987, *Coaches guide to sport psychology,* (Champaign, IL: Human Kinetics), 51-53.

An effective communicator will apply all, or most, of these rules.

## Receiving Messages

Receiving messages is as important as sending them. Sounds obvious, right? Well, this ability is a coach's most neglected skill. Fortunately, anyone can get better at it. First, your body posture alone can tell the athlete that you are ready to listen. When you are ready to listen, face the athlete. Maintain eye contact as the athlete speaks, and nod your head to indicate you are following the athlete's message.

Active listening requires your full attention, accurate interpretation, and constructive response. Such a requirement takes time that coaches on a hectic schedule often believe they don't have; however, we sometimes don't have time to listen because we are too busy correcting errors caused by earlier faulty communication. Let me give you an example to illustrate.

John Blake takes care of our travel arrangements. For one of our trips, he chartered a bus to pick us up at 10 A.M. on a Friday. A few days later, I told John that I wanted to leave earlier. The next day he handed me a slip of paper and said that the woman at the bus company needed to know what time the bus driver should report. So I told him: "8 A.M." The problem was that I never looked at the slip of paper—the slip of paper that had on it the name and phone number of the woman at the bus company. Obviously, John had expected me to call, and I had assumed that he would call. Guess when we departed. At 10 A.M.

Allow me to give you another reason you should learn to listen. An active listener is someone your athletes want to talk to. Players will open up to you more, sharing their dreams, hopes, and anxieties, and you will get to know them better. Remember, you can't coach an athlete you don't know.

### Keys to Becoming a Better Listener

- Face your athlete squarely, and lean toward him.
- Be relaxed.
- Assume an open posture.
- Maintain eye contact.
- Paraphrase messages with questions such as, "Are you saying that . . . ?"
- Listen with empathy; try to understand the sender.
- Don't judge the message until it is delivered fully.
- Don't judge the sender by appearance or reputation.
- Listen for main ideas in the sender's statements.
- Get rid of distractions.
- Actively practice your listening skills

## Nonverbal Communication

Coaches must be effective communicators, and fortunately, most of us are great with words. What is equally important is for us to realize that we send numerous nonverbal messages. By using our hands, body, and face, we can express—without uttering a single word—any emotion: disgust, disbelief, surprise, confusion, anger, joy, and so forth. In fact, we often express our emotions better through nonverbal messages than we do through the spoken word. If nonverbal messages don't correspond with verbal ones, senders and receivers will be guaranteed a miscommunication in the exchange.

---

## A Visit to Babylon

Some years ago, while still living in Vancouver, Washington, I had the opportunity to coach the Terriers soccer team. The Terriers represented the Washington School for the Deaf. That is correct: All my players were deaf. The question became, how was I going to communicate? I mean, I couldn't even sign. I did have my doubts about the situation, but after an awkward first session, the players and I actually started communicating effectively—and we did so without the use of the spoken word. We didn't need to speak. Our facial expressions, gestures, body language, demonstrations, and pure enthusiasm were all that we needed.

---

In our classes we do a little exercise to highlight the problem of verbal–nonverbal incompatibility. Try it sometime. Sit in a chair, put your head between your knees, and say loudly, "I feel great." Then, stand up tall, raise your arms way up, clench your fist, lift your head, smile, and say loudly, "I feel terrible." Doesn't sound very convincing, does it? I know these are extreme examples, but they are not much different from, say, telling an athlete you are interested in what she has to say while staring off in another direction once she starts to talk. Or suppose that during a game your left forward misses a shot at goal, and you throw your hands in the air as if to say, "Dear Lord, why me?" Do you think it does any good to follow it up with a half-hearted, "Good try, Jimmy." Not likely. As a coach, you can be truly amazed at how much can be accomplished without benefit of the spoken word.

Although you can communicate successfully through body language, nonverbal messages can be just as misleading and misinterpreted as verbal messages. A coach must be aware of, and be careful with, this form of communication. We should match our nonverbal messages with our spoken words.

# Haste and Waste

The end of one of our seasons was hectic. With two rounds of matches to go, four teams each had a chance at first place in the division. Our last two matches were back to back and out of town. Luckily, we won. However, that put us in a quarterfinal match on Monday in Portland, Oregon (600 miles away).

We got permission to fly to Portland, but unfortunately, I could take no more than 15 players, two coaches, and a trainer. It had been my intent to meet before the team meeting with the three players we had not selected, but time got away from us, and I didn't get it done. During the meeting I realized the error, and I asked the three players to stay after so that I could explain my reasoning.

One of the three was Tony Frieske. Tony had suffered an ankle injury most of the season, but he had come on as a substitute in the Pierce contest and was instrumental in winning the match. He did not stay after the team meeting. I have met with Tony since, and he accepts the reason for my decision. Although I believe that I have undone some of the damage, I can never make up for the pain I caused him. What I can do is simply never let it happen again.

# Open-Door Policy

Have you ever been in a situation where you thought you had a problem or needed counsel and the only one who could help you was your boss? Do you remember that it took some courage to walk into your supervisor's office and present your situation? Do you also remember how badly it hurt when your boss said something like, "I'm extremely busy right now. Can't it wait?"

When I first started to coach, the job consumed all of my time. I saw interruptions as major distractions. When someone interrupted me, I was often abrupt. I frequently asked the interrupter to come back some other time, and of course, they never did—and rightly so. I now know that a significant part of effective communication is simply being available. When I arrive at my office, I open my door and it stays open until I leave for the day. My staff and athletes know they can come in anytime. When a staff member or an athlete walks in, it's often because he has a problem or needs advice. If there's a problem, I want to know about it. I have so often learned that a minor problem becomes a major one if it's not resolved quickly.

I can hear many of you ask, "With that open-door policy, how do you get anything done?" I actually get a lot done because solving minor problems takes less time than solving major ones. I also get a lot done as a result of a little trick I learned from a former business associate. She told me that I should schedule in time for interruptions during my day. If the interruptions come, I am ready; if not, I have the luxury of a few extra moments to work on a task I would not have gotten to otherwise.

Simply stated, an open door shows that you are available and that you care. Keep it open, and note how it affects your relationship with your players and staff.

# Communicating With Players

Although your communication principles should never change, the style you use for communicating should change to meet the needs of the situation. For instance, the way you talk with your spouse differs from the way you talk to your boss. Likewise, each of the following situations dictates that you use a different style.

## Handling Confrontations

You can be far more direct in a one-on-one conversation in the privacy of your office than you can be in a situation when the athlete is with the entire team. Be careful not to say anything that will make the athlete look bad in the eyes of teammates. Athletes can accept negative statements in your office about their efforts, but they will never forgive you for making the same statement in front of their peers. Fellow athletes may even sympathize with the player who is being scolded; therefore, you lose all around.

Bottom line: If you have a problem with an athlete, handle it in private. Your athlete will thank you, and your conscience will, too.

Even in private, though, be careful of what you say and how you say it. Attack the problem, not the person. A big difference exists between saying, "Heather, you are stupid," and, "Heather, that was a stupid thing to do." The first statement attacks Heather personally; the second attacks something Heather has done. Athletes need confidence; humiliation destroys it.

In discussions with my players I like to use "I" statements instead of leading with the word "you." For instance, when a player hasn't been playing well, don't say, "You are playing terribly. Why?" Instead, try saying, "I think that you are far more capable than what you have been showing me. Do you feel the same way?" The first statement puts the player on the defensive, and it will make the player shut you out. The second statement doesn't accuse anyone; it puts the player at ease. The latter statement makes the player realize that you are there to help solve a problem. The conversation that follows a nonaccusing message is usually revealing and fruitful to both the player and coach.

Another method I like using, especially during a confrontational discussion, is to

Be clear and stay focused when dealing with confrontation.

start out with an agreement. For example, a player on the team may have some concerns about playing time. I would just ask the player whether she agrees with me that, with work and dedication, she can be an excellent player and a real asset to the team. After the player agrees, we can continue to work on the problem. This method shows the player that I am ready to help solve a problem. We establish common ground and can then move on to a rewarding discussion.

Remember, in all confrontations, stay focused on the problem. A player who makes a mistake, or even two or three, is guilty of bad judgment. Of course, no one mistake makes any player a bad person. The problem is that most people think that every confrontation must yield a winner and a loser. One person's will must prevail. That assumption is simply not true. An effective communicator tries to create a win–win situation. It can be done as follows:

- State the problem, preferably by using "I" statements or by making an agreement with the other person.

- Allow the other person to state her views and thoughts.
- Listen to what the player says or doesn't say.
- Restate the player's feelings and thoughts, making sure that both of you understand exactly how the player feels and thinks.
- Find the common ground in your feelings and thoughts.
- Find alternate solutions to any remaining problems.

## Communicating at Practices

Most coaches I have met and dealt with like the command style of coaching—or what I call "coaching down to their athletes." They think that the players are the students and that the coaches are the teachers who must be obeyed. I don't agree with this style of communicating, especially during practices. It doesn't enhance any player's self-esteem, and it disallows a player the opportunity to grow.

I prefer the "level" style of communicating with athletes. This style does not coach up, and it does not coach down. It communicates on an equal level. In other words, my players and I interact as if we were peers. And in many ways, we are. We're partners, working together to maximize our performance. The level style of communication allows me to be the facilitator in helping players solve problems on their own. Players' successfully solving problems on their own immensely raises their self-esteem. It is a skill well worth investing your time to teach.

## Communicating During a Match

During most international matches, a soccer coach may be seen but not heard. Many coaches in the United States are opposing that traditional restriction, but I favor the ban on touchline instruction during matches. Players' total concentration should be on their performance and on their opponent—not on their coach. Coaches shouldn't bombard their players, especially those who have possession of the ball, with instructions while they are on the field. That rule doesn't mean, however, that you can't offer an occasional comment to a player off the ball. Instead, coaches should be active observers during matches. They should bring their trusty clipboard and make notes about the things that go right and wrong. These notes are great cues for preparing the next practice, and they help a coach make tactical adjustments during the match or at halftime.

As a coach, remember that when you observe from the touchline, you need to control your body language. If you look irritated, upset, or uninterested, your players will play sluggishly. Conversely, if your gestures are positive, encouraging, and enthusiastic, your team will play with some zip.

## Communicating off the Field

As a coach, you have a great opportunity to influence your athletes through your communication with them off the field. This can consist of an occasional phone call during the off-season, a postseason meeting in your office, or maybe something as simple as a "hello" in a hallway. As a way to express an interest in my players, I check my calendar once a month to make sure that I remember to send a card so that it arrives on each athlete's birthday.

I really believe that you measure your success as a coach with the number of personal, long-lasting relationships you build with your athletes. You build those relationships off the field through simple gestures that show you care.

Sometimes we get so busy that even when we see a problem developing, we don't step in to prevent it; or maybe we think that somehow the problem will resolve itself. As a result, we wish we had another chance to help those who got hurt. Unfortunately, we too often don't get another chance. Communication mistakes that hurt are regrettable but sometimes unavoidable. If we learn from such mistakes, then they avoid becoming a lost cause.

## COMMUNICATING WITH OTHERS

As a coach, you work with two teams—the team that plays soccer on the field and the team that consists of assistant coaches, trainers, managers, program administrators, information directors, and so forth. Both teams must be focused on the same goals and philosophy, but they can only do so once they have played a role in establishing them. Sound, skillful play by the team on the field requires explicit communication. Suffice it to say that open communication between the coach and the support team is essential to overall success.

## Communicating With Assistants and Staff

You must communicate with your immediate staff—assistants, trainers, and managers—on a daily basis. Two-way discussions with the assistants may involve talking about progress to date, effectiveness of the daily plan, adjustments to the daily plan, the next practice, the next match, player progress, and player concerns.

Listen carefully to what your assistants are saying. You can determine whether everyone is pulling in the same direction by carefully considering their statements. They may even have suggestions for improvement. In many circumstances, some players actually find it easier to talk to an assistant coach than to talk to the head coach. This indirect communication between the team and the head coach via the assistants is extremely valuable in detecting problems in an early stage. If it weren't for your assistants, how else would you receive all this valuable information?

### The One Who Almost Got Away

We had three goalkeepers on our roster. Ryan Porter was one, and he saw a fair amount of action during his freshman year. During his sophomore year, he had to compete for playing time with two excellent freshmen. Ryan realized that he would see limited playing time, if any at all. Jim Martinson, my assistant coach, came to see me and told me that Ryan had indicated to him that he was quitting. I told Jim that I didn't want Ryan to quit because he had other assets that greatly helped our team. I knew Ryan was a positive person with a superb sense of humor. At the time, he was also an inspiration to the team, and he helped us keep things in perspective. I needed Ryan, so Jim and I decided to meet with him.

During the meeting, I explained my feelings to Ryan. I told him that it was true that he would not play much, but his contributions to the team culture, or team spirit, were as valuable as a stellar performance in goal. Ryan understood and he stayed. At the end of the season, he visited me and thanked me for talking him out of quitting: "I had the funnest time of my life."

Because your players' welfare is naturally of concern to you, you should maintain open and daily communication with your trainers. In my routine, I require a daily report about our injured athletes, and I discuss with the trainer the effectiveness of the rehabilitation plan. I also invite comments from our trainers about our physical conditioning program, and I solicit their suggestions on injury prevention.

Be aware of a certain potential problem in communication with assistants and staff. Never display disrespectful behavior toward or make negative comments about your own supervisor. As a head coach, you are

Discuss calls with officials calmly and effectively.

a supervisor, and you will quickly lose the respect of those you supervise if you disobey or bad-mouth your superiors. If you don't respect your supervisors, why should your staff or players respect you?

## Communicating With Officials

Over the years I have seen the quality of referees improve dramatically. But for every 10 referees recruited, 8 quit during their first year. Those who quit cite verbal abuse during matches as a major reason for their decision.

Coaches, players, and fans seem to think that a referee must make perfect calls during his first match . . . and then improve some more. Such an expectation is obviously unrealistic. Even the best referees make mistakes, just as coaches and players do. When the North American Soccer League (NASL) was still active, the referee was considered efficient if 85 percent of the calls were correct and if the ball was in play for more than 55 minutes. Thus, a 15 percent error rate was acceptable. That may be difficult to accept, but this fact is your reality.

For players and coaches the match is the ultimate teacher—and the same goes for the referee. The more matches a referee officiates, the better she becomes. If the referees can do these matches without the added stress of abuse from players, fans, and coaches, their decisions will naturally become better. As a coach, extend the same courtesy to referees that you do to your players. Try to control what you can—your players, your fans, yourself. You will never be able to control the referee's performance, so why waste the time trying?

If you do feel the need to discuss certain calls with the referee, that is certainly reasonable, but do so in a quiet, dignified manner. Don't put the referee on the defensive. Who knows? After the explanation, you may learn something.

## Communicating With Parents

I often hear coaches complain about certain parents, and in most cases, I find that the problem is a lack of communication. The problem is that the coaches don't communicate with the parents, nor do they invite the parents to communicate with them. These coaches usually interpret any parental inquiry as a disguised complaint, a nuisance, or an encroachment on their authority. This kind of attitude not only hurts your program but also your team.

As coaches, we have many valid reasons for being candid with parents. Just as the players have a right to know their exact status on the team, so do parents. For instance, if parents are left guessing why their son or daughter isn't getting more playing time, they may turn negative and become a problem. However, if they know exactly how you feel about the child and if they know your plans for the child's development, you may actually win those parents as your supporters.

With careful communication, parents can become an integral part of your program. Win them over so that they can become part of a sound social structure for you, your team, and your program.

## From Foe to Friend

Jeff and Amy Montgomery, brother and sister, played for us. Jeff had been successful with us, and his father was supportive of the team. After Jeff left, Amy joined us. At first, she had difficulty because she was not in match condition. I could see the chagrin on Mr. Montgomery's face when Amy did not get to play in the first few league matches. I decided to talk with him. I told him why Amy wasn't playing, and I assured him that Amy was a quality player. I also said that as soon as we had overcome the problem, she would be starting immediately. I then shared with him the training program we had for Amy. At that point, Mr. Montgomery became happy and supportive. At the end of the season, he wrote us a letter. I'd like to cite one particular part to illustrate what effective communication is all about: "Thank you for coaching our proud children, preparing them for a future life of successes and small failures, and teaching them to make the best of both."

## Communicating With the Student Body

Playing in front of a crowd of cheering fellow students—nothing is as exciting. Getting them to the game, however, is not always easy.

Your players need to be involved in student activities. They should certainly show an interest in the other school sports, and they should attend contests whenever possible. Simply stated, their behavior on campus and in classes must be exemplary.

One problem that often comes up, though, is that many students have a misconception or distrust of athletes and athletics, with the hardest assumption being that athletes get preferential treatment. What many students are unaware of is that athletes have to live with many rules that do not affect the rest of the student body, such as eligibility. Once the student body becomes aware of the academic pressure on athletes, the distrust practically vanishes. To defuse the misunderstanding, we as coaches use various tools to educate the student body. Eligibility rules are clearly displayed on all college bulletin boards. The grade point averages of our athletes are accumulated quarterly, and the averages (as compared to the college average) are published in school newspapers. We don't allow our athletes to wear team uniforms, warm-ups, jackets, sweaters, or other equipment to classes, and we encourage our athletes to be members of any one of the numerous campus committees.

With some effort, you can win the students over and get them to come to your matches. Remember to have the announcer thank them for attending and to thank them for demonstrating honorable sporting behavior.

## Communicating With Faculty

When it comes to athletics, every campus has two factions: those who enjoy sports and believe that they are an important part of human development, and those who think that academics are a school's only function. I totally agree with and appreciate the first group, of course, but I respect the second group because it is made up of dedicated, caring, and knowledgeable educators. Regardless of whether you fall into the former or latter group, you can earn the respect of all faculty through conscientious communication.

By all means, keep the faculty informed of the team's progress and specifically of their away dates. Check the academic progress of your athletes, and certainly don't play an athlete who is in trouble academically (even if it hurts the team to do so). And, no matter what, don't ever defend an athlete who is academically ineligible, and don't ever attempt to intervene between the athlete and the teacher.

## Classroom on Wheels

Matt Kinder, our captain, was scheduled to take an exam on one of our travel days. With the instructor's cooperation, we arrived at a simple solution that allowed Matt to go to the game and take his test. We left Friday at 7 A.M., with Matt in the passenger seat of the van I was driving. At 8 A.M., I promptly reached under my seat for a sealed envelope that contained the test, and I handed it to Matt. During the next hour and a half, Matt did the test—while we were traveling. After he finished, he handed it to me. I sealed it in an envelope and delivered it to the instructor on Monday morning.

## Communicating With the Community

I am grateful to live in a community that is sport- and youth-oriented. In fact, I maintain an active mailing list of community leaders, business people, and other supporters. When my team or anyone associated with my team experiences a significant event, my staff and I inform the community. In turn, when we need funds or equipment for a special occasion, we let people know and they are always ready to help us.

The support we receive from the community is truly awesome. Every one of our tournaments and clinics is fully sponsored by the community. Some years ago when we entered a team in the Cascade League during the off-season, we collected league fees, travel costs, and uniforms within 10 days as a result of community help. Whenever we get support from the community, every one of our players contacts the sponsors with letters of thanks. Over the years, I have visited many businesses that display these letters on bulletin boards.

We also contact coaches and physical education instructors in elementary, junior high, and high schools. If they attend one of our matches, they get to visit with our players. When they bring their team, we have some small gifts or mementos for the players.

## Communicating With the Media

One of our biggest challenges as coaches is to convince the media that soccer is newsworthy. Many coaches get angry that the efforts of their teams aren't reported properly, especially during a successful season. I share that frustration. That is, I get frustrated until I step back a moment and take a look at what is really happening. Then I change my attitude.

Most sports writers and broadcasters don't know soccer. I can't count the number of times I have had to explain the difference between a free kick and a penalty kick. Those in the media, who are human just like you and me, tend to talk about what they know best. Most, especially television sports broadcasters, have limited time and space in which to report.

My advice to those dealing with the media is to avoid becoming discouraged. I recommend instead supplying them with information as a professional. Provide them with your match schedules; highlights on some of your athletes; and any special honors you, your staff, or players have received. Report match results accurately and promptly, whether you win or lose. If asked for highlights, be sure to have some to report. And if your school has one, make sure you supply the sports information director with any pertinent information as well.

The media can be friendly, open-minded, and supportive. Coaches can't demand support, but they can earn it. As a coach and spokesperson for your players and staff, keep the media informed. Report news accurately and promptly, and be sure to present highlights. Be available when called on. Whenever a special event or an interesting story develops, call the media and share the story.

## SUMMARY

The following suggestions will help you to become a more effective communicator.

- Send clear and consistent messages. Invite comments.
- Become a better listener. Listen actively, and determine whether you are interpreting messages accurately.
- Be congruous in your verbal and nonverbal communications.
- Make sure that communication with your assistants and staff are two-way discussions.
- Communicate respectfully with officials and superiors.
- Keep parents, faculty, student body, community, and media informed.

# Chapter
## 3
# MOTIVATING PLAYERS

Wouldn't it be great if we had a simple word or a magic button to motivate each of our players? What about a five-minute, "pride of the team" speech at orientation; a "do it for the Gipper" prematch pep talk; a fire-and-brimstone half-time sermon; or an "If you win, the pizza's on me" approach? These motivational methods may work in certain situations, but they aren't the ultimate answer. In fact, they often backfire.

Some coaches question the methods of motivation I am going to talk about. They may still think that fear is a great motivator, but I'd rather coach a team of happy, risk-taking, innovative, and motivated athletes than a herd of psychological cripples.

## WHAT IS MOTIVATION?

Some athletes pursue their dreams and fully expect to achieve them through hard work and dedication. They see each obstacle as a challenge, and they interpret each setback as a call for a renewed effort to improve. They are self-motivated; their motivation to succeed comes from within. This kind of athlete is a joy to work with. All this player needs the coach to do is provide an environment conducive to concentration, supply tools for development, and give help with setting realistic goals.

Most athletes, however, lack the belief in the dream or the willingness to spend the endless hours of hard work to achieve it. For these athletes, the coach needs

additional tools of motivation. These athletes first need to believe that they can succeed. Second, they need to accept that only hard work will lead to success. These athletes are extrinsically motivated, and they need outside forces to help them achieve.

Years ago, a reporter asked me what I thought was the most difficult part of coaching. I don't remember how I answered, but the question has always stuck with me. I know what my answer is now: "To make athletes believe in themselves and each other."

## A Famous Halftime Talk

One of the finest gentlemen I know is C. Clifford McCrath, coach of soccer at Seattle Pacific University. SPU is a soccer powerhouse, with much of its success being attributed to Cliff's tremendous motivational powers. At a dinner one night, he told the following story that truly illustrates how influential he is.

SPU was playing on the road, and they found themselves behind 2-0. At halftime Cliff gave the team one of his trademark speeches. When he was through, the players were so fired up that they burst out of the dressing room. But there was a problem. The dressing room had two exits, one to the playing field and one to the swimming pool. Guess which door the players burst out of? It so happens that between the door and the pool was a deck about three feet wide. This incident became the first one in history to include half of a soccer team spending halftime in a swimming pool. It must have worked, however. According to Cliff, they won 4-2.

## MOTIVATIONAL TOOLS

Extrinsic motivation has no simple, standard approach. What turns on one athlete may turn off another. Some of your players may have low self-esteem, whereas others might have inflated egos. Even those who are cocky and who display much bravado may actually be covering feelings of self-doubt. Athletes with true self-confidence are rare.

Athletes perform in a competitive environment where challenge, risk, and uncertainty are facts of life. Succeeding in sport competition takes courage, confidence, high self-esteem, and trust in oneself and teammates. Motivation must therefore start with the development of these personal qualities. To help me succeed in instilling such confidence in my players, I rely on several tools:

- Relaxation
- Imagery
- Self-talk
- Goal setting
- Reinforcement

The most enjoyable part of coaching is motivating players. It is rewarding to see a timid, self-doubting, mediocre player turn into an assertive, confident, well-functioning athlete. By using these tools, you as a coach will find it easy to promote positive changes in your players.

## Relaxation

Among the numerous relaxation techniques I have experimented with, I have found that progressive muscle relaxation (PMR) seems to work best for athletes. To perform it, the athletes lie down or sit in a comfortable position while a prerecorded cassette tape instructs them to tighten and relax major muscle groups in a certain sequence. After the muscles are relaxed, the tape instructs the athletes to concentrate on the feeling of relaxation.

The benefit of this exercise is the ability to control tension and anxiety. When players are alert, they can make decisions more quickly and more accurately during a match. My own team does PMR as a group before each match.

## Imagery

When players have a low opinion of their collective or individual abilities, they will find themselves unable to compete successfully. To help players see themselves more favorably, I recommend they practice positive imagery techniques. Through imagery sessions, athletes can improve their performance substantially—that is, if the exercise is specific and if the athletes are in a state of total relaxation. When players are relaxed, they can use imagery to rehearse a variety of aspects, such as focusing on overcoming a weakness, embracing strengths, or mentally preparing for a match. Allow me to take you through a typical imagery session.

After relaxing through PMR, players imagine themselves in action on the soccer field. They picture the scenes vividly. They hear the fans, the whistle of the referee, the shoe hitting the ball; they smell the grass, the popcorn's aroma coming from the concession stand; they see the colors of the uniforms, the sky, the buildings in the background; they feel the warmth of the sun, the tug of the wind. Still in their mind's eye, they enter the scene and play. They focus on the positive, and they eliminate the negative.

Imagery sessions lasting 5 to 15 minutes per day can cause dramatic changes in athletes. After a few weeks, you yourself will even notice your athletes experiencing increased intrinsic motivation. With it, they begin to realize that their dreams can come true.

### Imaging Specific Performances

Once your athletes have developed the habit of imagery, they can start working on their specific problems. For example, they can work on their shooting, heading, passing, ball control, or any other soccer techniques. The more specific they are, the better.

### Imaging the Match

As a result of our location, we must travel no less than 300 miles to most of our away matches. I think it is important to have the time and opportunity to visit the opponent's field and its surroundings, so when possible, I like to have the team arrive a day early. Our visit lasts about half an hour. We walk the field, and time permitting, we pass the ball around a bit. This walk-through makes our imagery about the next day's match more vivid and therefore more effective. We are more comfortable and motivated on match day because by that time we have already played on their field—in our minds.

## Self-Talk

I often tell my players, "Listen to what you're saying to yourself." I give them this instruction as a means of making them more aware of what they're thinking about themselves, whether positive or negative.

Like you and me, athletes talk to themselves all the time. This self-talk influences their emotions, mental pictures, physical states, and behavior. How they are functioning is a product of what they think. Sad to say, many athletes think of themselves negatively and their self-talk reflects this poor self-image. Like an unchecked infection, these types of negative self-statements fester and spread throughout each athlete. These put-downs serve no other purpose than to reinforce pessimistic attitudes, low self-concepts, and eventually, resignation.

### One Forward's Affirmation

Jerry Havens, an outstanding forward, had trouble with his shooting. His shots were erratic. In a one-on-one conversation, I asked Jerry what he thought of, or what he said to himself, directly before the shot. Candidly, he said that he feared missing the shot and that he communicated that fear to himself. We then designed an affirmation for him: "I can make this shot." I asked Jerry to affirm that message to himself repeatedly, especially during practices before taking the shot. Over the next few weeks Jerry's shooting accuracy, speed, and power improved steadily. After leaving our school, Jerry was recruited by Gonzaga University, where for a long time he held the record for most goals scored in a season.

Once players have become aware of the importance of positive self-talk, however, they can begin to regulate it. They can listen to themselves, catch the negative self-talk, challenge it, and change it into a positive conversation. It isn't easy, but it can be done. Once mastered, the results are astounding.

When I help players improve their self-talk, I like using an exercise designed by Tom Kubistant, author of *Mind Pump*. It's a simple exercise. Many scoff at it, but to these skeptics I say, "Try it, what have you got to lose?"

During the first 12 days of practice, we give the players one basic affirmation each day. They memorize the affirmation and then repeat it to themselves as many times as possible. At the end of the 12 days, they must be able to recite all 12 affirmations. Afterward, they use the recital regularly, almost like a mantra.

1. Every day, in every way, I am better and better.
2. I like myself.
3. I am the captain of my ship; I am the master of my fate.
4. I trust my abilities.
5. I am relaxed.
6. I forgive my errors.
7. Sure I can.
8. I enjoy what I do.
9. I am on my side.
10. I always do the best job I can.
11. I am proud of my efforts.
12. I can do anything I choose to do.

Adapted, by permission, from Tom Kubistant, 1988, *Mind pump,* (Champaign, IL: Leisure Press), 105.

## Goal Setting

One of the most effective tools to motivate athletes is goal setting. When used correctly, this form of motivation allows an athlete to create a well-defined plan for improvement with measurable results at each step to promote personal peak performance. If used incorrectly, however, it can set up the athlete for failure.

Coaches should ideally schedule a goal-setting session at the beginning of the season. Remember, athletes involved in a team sport such as soccer deal with two sets of goals—their individual goals and their team's goals. As coaches, we should first help the players set their individual goals.

Many players have long-term, individual goals. Some may want to attend a college with a highly competitive soccer program; others may want to play professionally. Although setting long-term goals is beneficial, they won't do much to develop a player unless she establishes a set of realistic intermediate goals. Improving physical condition, ability to finish, maintaining possession under pressure, enhancing tactical awareness—those are intermediate goals. When I first start to help my athletes set goals for themselves and the team, I tell the following story.

A young child has just learned how to crawl. To help the child become accustomed to stairways, the father shows the child a large sucker. He then puts the sucker at the top of the stairs and tells the child that he may have the sucker if he crawls to the top. The child is enthusiastic and starts his climb. He climbs the first step with difficulty, but he is undaunted and attacks the second step. It is more difficult, and some of his determination vanishes. Nevertheless, the sucker beckons. He goes for step number three. He tries and tries but doesn't make it. Soon, large tears roll down his face, and he gives up. The father takes pity and rewards the child with the sucker for the good try.

This kind of goal setting obviously does more damage than good. The child has been set up to fail. He also learned a negative truth: You don't really have to succeed to be rewarded.

It would have been much better if the daddy had put a small sucker on the first step. He could have told his son that if he climbs the step, the sucker would be his. The next day, he could have put a sucker on the first and the second step, and so on.

Realistic, intermediate, attainable goals are essential for success. Each player and I decide whether the intermediate goal is attainable. If it isn't, we simply determine a different goal. In either case, our next step is to determine what needs to be done to reach the impending, intermediate goal.

Keep in mind that players, or coaches for that matter, have no control over outcomes. If a player sets a goal to be the leading scorer this season yet did not score one goal last season, then the player is setting herself up for failure. But if the player's goal is to improve herself by spending 20 minutes before or after each practice to work on shooting, she may not become the leading scorer but she will certainly improve.

When goals include tasks over which the athlete has complete control, they are called *performance goals.* Such goals include, for example, to improve scoring by spending 20 extra minutes each practice, to be physically and mentally prepared for the match, and to agree to play at one's individual best. These performance goals are critical in that they allow players to focus on important and controllable aspects of their matches.

After the players have set their individual goals for the season, you will find that they all share some common ground. From this collective pool of goals, develop the team's goals and review them regularly.

## Reinforcement

The most important principle of motivation is reinforcement. The idea of reinforcement is that rewarded behavior increases with frequency, whereas neglected or punished behavior decreases and eventually stops. Here is a list of questions you need to answer to use reinforcement effectively with your players:

- What do you reward?
- What do you discipline?
- When do you reward or discipline?
- How do you reward or discipline?

Many coaches, myself included, find it easy to focus attention and praise on our star players and to be impatient and neglectful with those who are less skilled. To overcome this habit, we have to remind ourselves that everyone on the team, not just the stars, must be motivated to play the match successfully. In addition, we need to remember to not only distribute rewards equitably, but to be consistent in what behavior we reward, and when and how we reward it. This task is easy to do if rewards are based on effort, as opposed to performance or outcome. Even though your players may have vastly different skill levels, each one of them can demonstrate a sound work ethic. For the coach, effort becomes easy to judge, and you will eventually find it easier to be consistent in your praise.

At times you may want to praise a player in front of the team for his effort. This notion is especially true when most of the team seems to be giving less than 100 percent. Remember, however, that some players feel uncomfortable when they are singled out. You might instead call the player out of the practice or wait until after practice to tell him you appreciate the hard work. I find these short one-on-ones invaluable. Try it for yourself. You're likely to find that after receiving your praise, the player works even harder.

# Coach's Role in Motivation

Your role as coach should be to bring out the best in each player you work with. To do so, you must create an environment that satisfies each athlete's basic needs. Some suggestions for doing so are the following:

- Get to know your players.
- Offer security.
- Show you care.
- Develop a positive team culture.
- Have fun.

## Getting to Know Players

Get to know your players. Find out how well they take care of themselves. Are they being taken care of in their home life? If their means are inadequate for day-to-day survival or if they have to worry about their basic needs, they won't be able to reach their athletic potential. Maybe you can find them a part-time job or get them involved in a work-study program.

## Showing You Care

Players need to know that you care for them. They will work and play hard for you if they know that you're concerned with them not only as athletes but also as human beings. If you show them that you care, they'll probably care more and as a result try to meet your standards.

---

### It's the Little Things That Are Important

James Jasso played for us for two years and was an exceptional attacking-stopper. In one of our matches, James looked out of it. I subbed for him, then took him to the side to ask what was wrong. James said he felt uncomfortable because I had neglected to talk with him privately before the match.

I knew the talk James was referring to. It was a habit of mine to say just a few private words to each starting player before the match. Our conversations are simple words of encouragement just to let them know that they are not alone. It also gives me an opportunity to make literal contact with them. It might be my hand on their shoulder, a high five, a handshake, or a pat on the back.

I assured James that my neglect was caused by a meeting with officials that went longer than expected. I simply ran out of time. James smiled, went back in, and did his usual superb job. All he needed to know was that I cared.

---

Once your players have their basic survival needs met, once they feel secure, and once

they know that you care for them, you can begin the task of improving their self-esteem, confidence, and feelings of self-worth.

## Offering Security

Provide your players with an understanding of their roles on the team, and make sure you do it with an assurance that their roles won't be diminished because of one bad performance. The easiest way to make players feel secure is to discuss with starters and nonstarters, individually, how you foresee their best contributing to the team. Make them believe that they can add to the team's success and that you consider each player important.

## Developing a Positive Team Culture

Nothing motivates a player as much as a positive comment from a teammate. From

When all players are focused, success is imminent.

the moment training starts until the final match, our coaches freely praise outstanding effort, and we encourage our players to do the same. When I hear one of our players make a positive comment to another player, I immediately take him aside and thank him for the contribution he has made to the team's positive attitude. Soon all players begin to realize that we reward positive comments, and praise becomes the rule rather than the exception. At the same time, we squelch all negative comments the moment they are made.

## The "I'm OK, You're OK" Game

At times friction may develop between players, and at other times players may have deficient self-esteem that rears its ugly head in the form of bad performance or low morale. When such an incident occurs, I like playing a game I call, "I'm OK, You're OK." I admit the title isn't very original, but it works.

To play the game, all players gather in our meeting room before or after a practice. I ask them to say something positive about every one of the players. A captain usually starts the game. To do so, she describes a quality she likes about every player in the room. For example, she may say, "Becky, I like your positive attitude," "Jen, I wish I could volley like you," and "Heather, I appreciate it when you encourage me after I make a mistake." She continues until she has made a positive comment about each player. When she is finished, the next player compliments everyone. The game continues until every player and every coach has had a turn.

The purpose of the game is to force the players to think positively about each other. During this time, a player finds out that her teammates really appreciate her. A player may even discover that her teammates notice qualities in her that she was not even aware of herself.

## Having Fun

If athletes did not have fun, sports wouldn't exist. In fact, the reason most athletes cite for quitting is that the game is no longer fun.

At one of my seminars, I asked the coaches when soccer should stop being fun. One coach answered, "When they start playing select soccer." How sad, I thought. Curiously, this same coach has a new team each year; his old players just don't want to come back. I wonder why.

Take a look at yourself as a coach. I've done so. I'm a coach because I'm having a ball doing it. If it weren't fun and exciting, I'd quit. How about you? Are you having fun? Yes? If you are entitled to have fun, shouldn't your players have the same right? Of course.

Recall my definition of fun. I think that it means to present realistic challenges to young people and then allow them, without interference, to overcome the challenges. Success at anything is fun and motivating.

Sometimes even silly things can motivate players. I'm still trying to forget my personal aftermath of winning a conference championship. You see, halfway through the season, in a moment of madness, I told the team that if they won the championship, I would get my hair cut into a Mohawk. Well, we won. Two days later my team came to visit me in my office, and they physically transported me to a nearby barber, who in 20 minutes managed to turn me into one of the most ugly human beings on this planet. When I came home that night, my dogs barked at me. Three months later my wife moved back in. Well, I may exaggerate a little. But I sure did look ugly.

## DISCIPLINE

A soccer team is a small society, and like all societies, it has laws, rules, and regulations. How those laws, rules, and regulations are established is important. Some rules (such as eligibility rules) are clear-cut, and the punishment is spelled out. Those rules are beyond the control of the team and the coach. Other rules can be controlled by the coach and the team, particularly those concerned with behavior on and off the field.

When a player on your team breaks a rule or regulation, deal with it fairly, firmly, quickly, and calmly. Before anything else, make sure you have all the facts, and give the player an opportunity to explain. After an explanation, a player typically realizes that discipline is in order, and the two of you can then determine what form of discipline should be administered. The disciplinary measures you apply should be constructive. Humiliation, for example, is destructive, and the player will never forgive you if you use it. I also recommend avoiding physical punishment, such as running laps. After all, that kind of exercise is part of their conditioning program, and conditioning, especially in soccer, should be enjoyable for the players. Better methods of discipline include having players provide a certain number of hours of community service, attend a referee clinic, or take part in a substance-abuse class.

When discipline issues come up, judge each infraction on its own merits and be flexible. Remember that at times anyone can have extenuating circumstances. If you are firm, fair, and consistent, your players will remember you for it and they will be grateful for it.

## Discipline on the Field

I was taught that if you can break the other player's concentration, then you have a better chance of winning. Soccer is a game that requires total concentration. A player who loses focus may as well come out of the match. Focused players, on the other hand, are less likely to be bothered by opponents' words or actions or by the calls of the referee.

To me the most serious loss of concentration occurs when teammates attack each other. Sometimes players are not willing to accept responsibility for their errors, and they therefore blame others—their teammates. Such players have totally lost focus, and the player who receives the blame will be less effective as well. Before long, everybody is at each other's throat unless you catch it in time.

Be observant to such incidents, and rely on the captain to make you aware of problems. You are usually too far away from the players to hear what is being said, so you will need to rely on your players to keep you informed. Indications that you should make a substitution include temper flare-ups, gestures of frustration, facial expressions, and other negative body language.

As a coach, you will need to establish some rules that deal with the issuance of red cards and perhaps even the issuance of yellow cards. You must immediately deal with your players' receiving cautions, especially for dissent and dishonorable sporting conduct. The player who receives one has lost some control and should come out for a little while to cool down. If all your players, including your stars, know that on receipt of a caution they will be substituted, your team's number of yellow-card cautions will go down—guaranteed.

## The Cost of a Red Card

Kevin Scuderi played for our school as a wing forward. He was quick and real feisty—too feisty. After being tackled hard in one match, he came up swinging. His punches missed, but the referee didn't and promptly ejected him. After telling Kevin that his behavior was totally unacceptable, I sent him to the dressing room with instructions to meet me in my office directly after the match. I learned that before meeting with me, he bragged about his red card to his teammates. In my office, he was in for a surprise—he had forgotten a team rule that states, "Any player ejected from a match for violent misconduct or foul and abusive language may not play again until he has performed 10 hours of community service." I handed Kevin the address of a local youth center where he was to report the next day, a Sunday, at 7 A.M. for a day of cleaning windows. I never heard him brag again. By the way, we don't get red cards.

A red card, or being ejected from a match, is serious business and is in my opinion completely uncalled for. The ejected player not only damages the reputation of the program, but also lets his team down. Players have no excuse for an ejection.

The assumption that the referee must control the match is incorrect. The referee applies the laws of the game. That's it. In the end, the coaches are the ones who are responsible for the behavior of their players, the spectators, and certainly their own conduct.

## Discipline off the Field

The success of your program depends a great deal on the goodwill of administrators, faculty, community, and the student body. On campus, the athlete is forever on display. All athletes should therefore realize that on- and off-campus behavior reflects on the entire team and the program. Dr. Maury Ray, our athletic director, points out that when an athlete is arrested, the newspaper will not say, "Jim Williams was arrested." It will say, "Jim Williams, a soccer player at Community Colleges of Spokane, was arrested."

We ask our athletes to behave exemplarily, and we also ask them to police each other. I ask the sophomores in particular to help me catch problems early. They know that I deal with problems fairly and that I never reveal my sources. I never ask for specifics because

as long as I know that a problem exists, I can help solve it. No matter what it is.

Consistent and fair discipline motivates players because it gives them a clear set of boundaries that are the same for everyone on the team. Discipline shows you care, and every one of your players on some level recognizes it and appreciates it.

## SUMMARY

Motivating athletes is a demanding but rewarding job. To make the task easier and to motivate your players more effectively, try using the following suggestions:

- Understand what motivation is, and learn how to turn extrinsically motivated players into intrinsically motivated players.
- Schedule time to use the motivational tools of relaxation, imagery, self-talk, goal setting, and reinforcement.
- Understand your role in motivating your athletes. Get to know your players, offer them security, show them that you care, create a positive team culture, and allow them to enjoy themselves.
- Be consistent, flexible, and fair when applying discipline both on and off the field.

# Chapter
## 4

# BUILDING A SOCCER PROGRAM

I was hired as the first varsity soccer coach at the Community Colleges of Spokane (CCS) in the spring of 1984. Our college is a member of the Northwest Athletic Association of Community Colleges (NWAACC), where 21 members offer varsity soccer for men and 17 offer varsity soccer for women. In 1987, we made it to the championship match. Since then, we have won the championship twice; we were runners-up four times; we captured third once; and we have been divisional champions seven times.

Because we have a successful program, I'm often asked to share my secrets. I regret to say I have none. I can't draw a map for success, nor can I supply a proven plan or a magic formula. I believe we are successful because we have been willing to invest an inordinate amount of time fine-tuning the program. We have certainly worked hard to put an exciting product on the field by developing not only our players but also our ability as coaches, trainers, and managers. We have carefully cultivated support for our program from faculty, students, media, and community. We have identified our feeder system, and we have established rules and policies that make the program run smoothly and effectively, all while creating an environment conducive to the development of team pride.

Building a successful program depends much on the personality of its builder. No single plan will work for everyone; I can only write about the things that worked for us. If some of my personal experience can work for you, by all means use it. Don't forget, however, that our country has many successful soccer programs, and the coaches who make them work may use methods of their own.

## DEVELOPING A STYLE

When you as a coach build a soccer program, one of the earliest and more difficult decisions you have to make is what style to adopt. Errors we sometimes make include deciding on a style of play before becoming familiar with that style and not being flexible enough to make changes when needed. We need to be reminded that what works for one team may not work for others.

Rinus Michels coached the Dutch national teams that made it to the finals of the World Cup in 1974 and 1978. He was credited with creating the "total soccer" concept, although he prefers to call it "high-pressure soccer." In later years, he tried to use that style when he coached Barcelona. Much to his frustration, it didn't work. He analyzed the differences between the Dutch national team and Barcelona, and he observed that high-pressure soccer requires athletes in superb condition who have a high work ethic. The Dutch satisfied that need; Barcelona did not. For the style to be successful, the team had to have an outstanding leader on the field. For the Dutch, the great Johan Cruyff filled that role, but Barcelona wasn't so fortunate and thus lacked any such leader. Being the brilliant coach that he is, Rinus Michels decided to create a style of play specifically based on Barcelona's strengths. The style worked, and the club became a major power. As an ironic twist, Barcelona was later coached by Johan Cruyff.

Not only do coaches have different styles, but soccer as a game has many styles. The Brazilians refer to it as the "beautiful game"; Germans play with vigor, discipline, and speed; Italians exhibit tenacious defense with rapid counterattacks; and the French are known for their midfield magic, especially during the days of Platini. As we saw earlier, the Dutch invented the total soccer concept, whereas the English like to bring the ball up quickly. Although all these styles appear to have little in common, all of them are dictated by conditions prevalent in their particular parts of the world. The development of a country's style depends on a number of environmental factors, particularly climate. In colder climates, players like to run with the ball, whereas in hot climates, energy preservation is important—that is, players pass more, letting the ball do most of the work. Subsequently, field conditions are important. In wet climates, such as England, the field may be muddy and heavy, making play on the ground almost impossible. Fields that are dry and hard, however, allow more play on the ground, and the game sees more short passes.

## Chiliburgers and Casseroles

A few years after coming to Spokane, I was interviewed for the head coaching job at a high school. One of the athletic director's first questions concerned the style of play I intended to use. I told him I couldn't answer that question. He looked disappointed, and I knew the interview was over. What he didn't realize was that I was just as disappointed. I wasn't disappointed because I couldn't answer his question; I was disappointed because he asked such a question. As athletic director, he should have known that no answer to his question was the best answer.

After I started coaching at the Community Colleges of Spokane some years later, I met him again. He lamented that I would have had the job at his school if I had just answered his question. At that point, I told him one of my favorite stories.

Let's suppose that I'm hungry and that I decide to fix myself a chiliburger. I need a bun, some hamburger, and some chili. When I open the refrigerator, I find only potatoes, sauerkraut, and sausage. No way am I going to make a chiliburger, but I can make a truly delicious casserole. In other words, regardless of what I want, I don't know what I am going to cook until I know what ingredients I have.

He laughed, and we shook hands. Two years later he gave me a superb compliment. The coaching job at the high school opened up again, and the athletic director promptly hired my assistant.

In the development of style, the physical condition, technical level, and tactical understanding of the athletes come into play. What are also certain to be determining factors are the personalities, temperaments, and cultural backgrounds of not only the athlete but also the viewing public.

We all have favorite styles. As a coach, you may find it difficult to compromise the desire to force a team to adapt to your favorite style. Predetermining a style of play sets you up for disaster—that is, unless you know your players, the field conditions you have to work with, the time you have to spend with the team, your opponents, the level of officiating, your assistants, the support you will receive, and so forth. The style you choose must depend on the assets you have. Once you choose a style, you should then allow for adjustments.

## How Systems Work

The system of play you select depends significantly on outside factors. You must not only adapt the system to the strengths and weaknesses of your team, but you must also consider the system used by the opponent and the strengths and weaknesses of their individual athletes. For instance, if the opponent plays with only two forwards, do you really need four players back? Might you strengthen your midfield by playing only three back in a 3-5-2 system? If the field is narrow, could you use a 4-3-3 system?

Making changes in your system of play is difficult. You must always weigh the advantages of a change against the vulnerabilities it causes elsewhere. Regardless of how you change a system, you must be sure that the gains outweigh the losses. What is more important is that you have the players who understand the changes and can adapt to their new assignments.

When choosing your system of play for a particular match, you may find the following exercise helpful. Start with a 3-3-3, which will give you solid player distribution, then ask yourself where the 10th field player would serve the occasion best.

Regardless of what style or system you adopt, you also need to consider your viewing public. Our philosophy at CCS is that we owe our fans an exciting match. We take chances, we attack, and we play to win. Our philosophy is unlike many teams who are simply coached not to lose. Some teams use as many as six players back to keep the opponent from scoring while hoping that they may get that one breakaway to give them a 1-0 victory. How dull!

## Gaining Support for Your Program

After each of our seasons, the college schedules a banquet for our teams. Anywhere from 400 to 500 people attend. Among the guests we usually find our chief executive officer, our three presidents, vice presidents, athletic director, program coordinators, faculty, classified staff, our trainers, players, parents, and friends. We definitely couldn't be too successful without those people. We truly rely on their support.

Our need for support goes further than just those who attend the banquet. We also need the support of suppliers, sponsors, equipment managers, groundskeepers, ticket takers, security personnel, and concession workers. A program suffers when a match worker is rude to one of the fans, so we count on everyone having a positive attitude about their contributions to the program. Nothing makes people feel better than when they realize that they are appreciated. A few kind words, a thank-you card, a handshake, or a pat on the back goes a long way to say to a person, "Hey, I'm glad you're part of our program. It couldn't work this well without you."

## Administrator and Faculty Support

You and I coach a team sport. Our teams are successful only when our players support each other. In turn, our programs are successful only when we generate the support of our schools. What that translates to is a need for an adequate budget, playing facilities, travel and meal allowances, equipment, and acceptance. Administrators and faculty are the ones who can satisfy our needs and allow us to operate a classy program.

Coaches can receive backing from administrators and faculty by letting them know that their support is important. As a coach, communicate with them frequently. Make them aware that you are willing and available to cooperate by serving on committees, and take advantage of the many opportunities you have to discuss your program at informational meetings. But keep in mind that although the soccer program may be of extreme importance to you, your communications should indicate that the school is always the first priority.

Support from administrators, faculty, and staff is essential to the success of any program. Although most administrators are not involved in soccer directly, many of their children are and many of their children attend our camps. If their children have enjoyed themselves, if they have learned something, and if they have been treated with dignity and respect, they will carry the message home.

Support from the many members of your program is the result of effective communication, cooperation, respect, an understanding of others' feelings and philosophies, and a readiness to help. Practice these tenets, and you will feel your program become embraced by those who agree with its mission.

## Student Support

Nothing motivates your athletes more than being cheered on by a large group of fellow students. Getting that kind of support isn't always easy, but you and the entire team working together can create vibrant student support specifically for your program.

To achieve solid student support, the team must earn the respect of the student body. The athletes can accomplish such a goal by exhibiting maturity, dignity, and class. They must respect their instructors, their classmates, each other, and most of all,

The team needs to work together on and off the field.

their school. In addition, they must be willing to become involved with the activities of other student groups.

As a coach, you will have many opportunities to talk with student groups. When students do support your program, let them know that you and your team appreciate it. One way to thank them is through in-house news bulletins that many schools publish. When one of the compilers offers to interview you, see it as a golden opportunity to let the student body know how you feel about them and their support at matches. Let them know just how important they are, and don't forget to express your pride in the school.

When it comes to gathering student support, I often think of one particular area that is easy to tap. It never fails to surprise me how few soccer players are willing to watch a basketball game, or how few baseball players attend a softball game, or how few tennis players go to a volleyball game, and so forth. And it's not just the students. I don't see coaches cross-attending either. What

I am trying to say is, go to an occasional game—and encourage your players to do likewise.

## Thanks, Irene

One of the coaches I truly admire is Irene Matlock, our volleyball coach. She was hired about the same time that I was. She has built a program that has received national recognition. In 1994, Irene was voted national coach of the year by the American Volleyball Coaches Association (AVCA).

Some years back, our men's team played a must-win match at Shoreline Community College late in the season. It was a dreary day, rainy and cold. We had few supporters, and we were struggling. At the half, the score was 1-1. Unbeknownst to us, the volleyball team was playing in a crossover tournament at Shoreline. A few minutes before the second half started, Irene, her staff, and the entire volleyball team seated themselves behind our bench and began to cheer us on. Our morale got an immediate boost, and we decided that we were not going to let them down. We played an inspired second half and walked away with a 3-1 victory.

I don't know how many sports are played at your school, but at our college we offer 15 sports involving more than 400 students. Wouldn't it be nice if at every home match, you could have a base group of 400 cheering fans? That's precisely the reason why we make sure that our players attend other teams' home matches. One's attendance makes all the difference in the world.

## Media Support

If you can somehow get press coverage, your soccer program can really receive a boost. Doing so isn't easy, however, because soccer is the relatively new kid on the block to most U.S. sportswriters and broadcasters. The intense coverage of World Cup 2002 certainly helped, but coaches and players still find it difficult to get the coverage we think we deserve.

Fortunately, our program has seen its coverage increase year by year. Every one of our matches gets some space in the newspapers; and if broadcasters have time, they even mention us on the air. I truly believe that the accuracy and the quality of the information we supply have earned us their respect and attention. A reporter who writes a story about soccer in general, or your program in particular, likes to color the story with easily available information. Reporters find it helpful when supplied with such information before the season starts. Although it may not always be used, the reporter is more apt to write a story if spared the time on the phone tracking you down and soliciting information. My advice to coaches is that, shortly before the season, they should prepare an informational packet that includes a roster, player highlights, a brief history of the program, highlights of the preceding season, and a schedule. And be sure to include phone numbers.

Directly after a match, I call our local papers and broadcast stations. I do so whether I am at home or on the road, and I do so regardless of the outcome. My report to the newspapers includes who and where we played; the final and halftime scores; the order of goals scored, who assisted and at what time; shots at goal and shots on goal; saves made by both goalkeepers; our season record, our league record, and the opponent's record. I conclude with some highlights of the match. I report only the final score and our record to the broadcast stations, and I may also mention any of our players who had an outstanding match.

In the beginning of your coaching career, your reports may be ignored, but don't give up or become angry. Persist and always be courteous. Reports on your team will soon start to pick up, especially on slow news days. Make sure that at the end of the season you submit a season wrap-up, and don't forget the thank-you notes. The media can be of great help to your program. Respect them, and they will reciprocate.

## Community Support

During a normal year, coaches have many opportunities to meet people in the community. Each of these opportunities gives you a chance to talk about your program. Remember that you have a family physician, a dentist, and an accountant, too. Invite them to matches as your guests. The guy who fixes your car, your barber, your grocer—invite anyone you meet. Accept opportunities to talk at Kiwanis, Optimists, Lions, Eagles, and other get-togethers; then invite them to your functions and games. Invite as your guests the people who supply your uniforms, balls, audiovisual equipment, and goal-repair services.

## Special Match

We dedicate one of our conference home matches to youth in general, and five-a-side players and campers in particular. We usually pick a Saturday night match. All youth players wearing a team jersey or a tournament T-shirt are admitted free. These nights have become quite successful. Kids bring their parents, and it is truly spectacular to see all the colors in our stands. Many even return to see subsequent matches.

All high school coaches who attend receive our schedule with invitations for them and their teams. As a return gesture, we get invited to visit their practices. In the spirit of reciprocation, local youth soccer associations are another source of community support to consider. Coaches should help them with coach-and-player clinics, lectures, workshops, and wherever else they may need you. In return, one's program would certainly see a boost in attendance as a result. The message of all of this outreach, however, is simple. Actively seek the support and enthusiasm of the community, and your program will thrive.

You can also stage events that attract large groups of people, such as tournaments and camps. You can then use such opportunities to promote your program. In the spring, we run a five-a-side tournament where over 400 teams compete. During the two weekends of the tournament, the players and our staff get to talk with many coaches, parents, and others who like soccer. Our summer soccer camps have also become popular, and again, we talk to as many people as we can. If our schedules are ready, we distribute them. If not, we take names and add them to our mailing list.

## IMPLEMENTING THE PLAN

After developing your plan and after laying the foundation for obtaining support, you can start thinking of how to implement the actual plan. Consider the following points as you start the building process.

## Feeder System

Make sure that you have your own feeder system in order. If you are coaching varsity at a high school team that has a junior varsity team, for example, then make the coaches of that team aware of the kind of players you need. Likewise, if the JV team needs help, you and your staff should be available to help them.

As previously mentioned, another resource to consider are the youth soccer organizations that are in almost every community. Share your thoughts and goals with those coaches. They, too, are members of your staff, and with your help and suggestions they can feed quality players into your program. If youth coaches and junior high coaches know what kind of player you want and if you help them develop that kind of player, then players will enter your program with the basic skills in place. You can then immediately start building on those skills instead of spending endless hours coaching players out of their bad habits.

My staff and I have met and worked with many of our area's high school coaches. We give them guidance in camps and clinics; we go to as many of their matches as possible; and we frequently host them at our matches and practices. Our players even visit the practices of youth teams, junior varsity teams, and varsity teams. During their visits they help the coach with teaching a certain technique or tactic, or they simply talk to players to encourage them to work hard.

During our visits with coaches, we have the opportunity to answer questions, but we also have the opportunity to let the coaches know about our program, philosophy, goals, preferred style of play, and the qualities we look for in players. These coaches are our partners. If they respect our program, they will direct players to our college. Although not all coaches agree with our philosophy and not all players come to CCS, they at least all know who and what we are. They also know that we respect them for their abilities, and we show our appreciation by being available to them when they need us.

## Establishing Rules

Like any organization, a soccer team needs rules. Many schools have set rules regarding drinking or using drugs. Of course, neither the coach nor the team can control these aspects absolutely, but they should endorse them whenever possible. What often happens, however, is that those rules are usually applied *after* an offense. For my team, I want them to make the decision not to commit these offenses in the first place, not after the fact. Another thing that I do not want is for the team to determine specific disciplinary actions when a teammate commits an offense. Schools already recommend procedures for certain infractions. All other infractions should be punished after the offender has had a chance to explain her actions.

As a coach, you should supply a list of subjects for the team to discuss, set policy on, and vote on. The list may include the following:

- Curfews
- Drugs
- Smoking
- Dress code
- Punctuality

Add any reasonable item to this list as you see fit. The players will sometimes ask how other teams have voted on these subjects, and there is nothing wrong with sharing that information. In fact, returning players usually set the tone for the meeting and the voting, anyway. Nevertheless, the final vote should be on a secret ballot so that all players have the opportunity to express themselves honestly without fear of reprisal.

Once we tabulate the votes, we publish and share them. Again, I like to impress on the players that these are their rules and that in the end it is their responsibility to enforce them. Coaches are often uncomfortable giving this kind of responsibility to young athletes, especially those of college age. I disagree. I think that if I show my trust in them, they will go to great lengths to maintain that trust. I've never been disappointed. It is also interesting to see that the rules never vary much from team to team.

### Curfew

We play most of our matches at 1 P.M., so most players typically get up around 8 A.M. to enjoy an adequate and healthy breakfast. Because eight hours of sleep usually satisfies the average player's need, the team usually establishes an 11 P.M. curfew on nights before a match. When we are on the road, the curfew is the same with the provision that lights must be off at midnight.

### Drugs

Drugs are illegal. Period. This rule includes steroids and so-called socially accepted drugs such as marijuana. I have never had a team that was not adamant about this rule.

Regarding drinking, my staff and I spend some time with the team on the subject long before the team actually votes on a no-drinking rule. After all, the stereotypical, college-aged player is a drinker. But again, I have found this conception not to be true with our athletes. In addition, I'm blessed with excellent help from people in our department. Torrey Landers, our nutritionist and health and wellness expert, and John Troppmann, our strength trainer, work with teams through easy-to-understand explanations and demonstrations that show how badly performance is affected by the use of drugs and alcohol. After their presentation, the team invariably votes to abstain.

## Smoking

Smoking has also fallen into disfavor as of late, and my teams always vote against it. We once had a problem with players picking up the habit of chewing tobacco, but the team called its own meeting and voted against its use by any player. It therefore stopped.

## Dress Code

When the team starts to discuss the dress code, some of them don't see it as an important subject. At this point, the returning players always seem happy to explain that it is difficult to have pride in your team if the individual players don't take pride in themselves. That means that when the team represents the college or city, players are expected to be well groomed and properly attired. The team usually votes to wear sport shirts and clean jeans when in public places. The team does not permit players to wear outrageous T-shirts or any clothing with holes in it, and baseball caps are also to be removed in public places. The final rule about dress is that all players must wear their full warm-ups to matches.

Related to attire, however, is an issue that often comes up during the season. For some reason, many soccer players like to wear their hair long. (That trend is probably a result of their soccer heroes' rather strange and lengthy coiffures.) Our team doesn't rule out long hair as long as the hair is clean and combed. Again, players are school and city representatives, and their appearance must reflect a positive self-image.

## Punctuality

I've only recently added punctuality to the list of subjects that I want the team to vote on. It isn't because it is a big problem; in fact, only an occasional player is lax. I put it on the list because I want all players to under-stand that if they are not punctual, it isn't just the coach who is upset. They are doing a disservice to the entire team.

As I have stated before, once a team has set the rules, I like to put the rules in contract form and have the players sign the contract. These rules are their rules, and this contract is their contract with their team.

I should mention the evaluations of the program that the players do at the end of the season. One of the questions on the evaluation is, "Did the coach use discipline fairly?" I was thrilled when my athletic director informed me that one of the players had answered, "Yes, he treats us like adults, so we behave like adults. Besides he allows us to set our own rules. I never broke any of them. I didn't want to be the only child on the team."

Yes, I do treat them as adults because I have many other expectations of them. Not the least of these is exemplary behavior when we travel. For example, the players understand that people who work in restaurants and motels have difficult, low-paying jobs. Those people don't need a group of smart alecks to louse up their days. We are always welcomed at the motels and restaurants we frequent. We know that after our visit our hosts think highly of us, the college, our city, and yes, soccer.

# TEAM PRIDE

We often talk about athletes needing strong self-esteem. It should follow that teams need high team-esteem, or team pride. It is one of those intangible characteristics that spell the difference between success and failure. It is the quiet confidence that players have in each other, the coaching staff, the supporting crew, and the school. It is the characteristic that gives the team vitality and spirit.

It may sound somewhat corny when we say, "One for all and all for one," or, "The strength of the wolf is in the pack, and the strength of the pack is in the wolf." However, much truth resides in these statements. The coach needs to create an atmosphere in which each player knows that each member of the team is ready to help him. If every player knows this unspoken understanding, every player then becomes willing to contribute to the overall efforts of the team. If this objective can be accomplished, then the coach is halfway home to creating excellent team pride. Players should therefore be reminded of the proud history of the program. They should rejoice when goals are reached. They should be complimented when challenges are met. They should be allowed to grow to be the best they can be through positive instruction and encouragement.

The coach sets the tone for the development of team pride. Your love for the job, your pride in your school, your players, and your staff will set an infectious example. Young people need standards and ideals to believe in. Your program can provide such an atmosphere.

## SUMMARY

To build a successful soccer program, you will need to give attention to the following subjects:

- Give careful thought to the development of style and system of play.
- Learn to assess your personnel and environment.
- Be willing to adjust your style and system of play.
- Gain support for your program from administrators, faculty, students, media, and community.
- Create a plan and implement it.
- Evaluate and nurture your feeder system.
- Carefully establish rules covering subjects such as curfews, drugs, smoking, dress code, and punctuality.
- Develop team pride.

# Part II

# COACHING PLANS

# Chapter 5

# PLANNING FOR THE SEASON

About one month after a season ends, we begin planning for the next season. We carefully prepare a budget; we inventory equipment such as uniforms and balls; we place orders (if necessary); we evaluate facilities; and then we put desired changes out for bid.

A month after season's end is also a good time to assess the efficiency of our medical screening, medical examinations, insurance settlements, and handling of injuries. Although the past season is still fresh in our minds, we may feel a need to alter our methods of conditioning players and finding ways to make off-season conditioning and nutrition more effective and rewarding. We also use the results of the preceding season to reevaluate the methods used in practices and matches. If we can make any improvements to develop the team technically and tactically, we begin our planning. We coordinate the next season's schedule; we propose travel arrangements and find tournaments; and most important, we evaluate how we can improve our athletes' self-esteem, competitiveness, sense of fairness, and ability to function successfully in society.

Your planning list should include the following items:

- Budgets
- Equipment and facilities
- Medical screening and insurance
- Medical care

- Staff planning
- Conditioning players
- Preseason planning
- Travel

## BUDGETS

Decisions concerning the budget are ones that should be made early. I like to refer to our budget as a "wish list" that consists of four categories:

1. The services category includes items such as printing and promotional materials, referees, and so forth.
2. The goods and equipment category is divided into three sections:
   - Supplies used up yearly, such as training and first-aid supplies, field paint, video- and audiotapes, training uniforms, and practice and match socks
   - Supplies used up in two to four years, such as practice balls, nets, and corner flags
   - Supplies purchased on a rotation system, such as uniforms, warm-ups, and travel bags
3. The travel category includes transportation, meals, and motels.
4. The miscellaneous category includes items that are not essential, but they are ones that help us function more efficiently as a team:
   - Shirts for the coaching and training staff
   - Extra rain gear
   - VCR or camcorder
   - Cassette player
   - Ball-shooting machine
   - Additional goals

## EQUIPMENT AND FACILITIES

We are a state institution, and all orders for goods and equipment that cost more than $300 must go out for bid. This bit of red tape can present problems unless you are specific in preparing your orders. For instance, if you list 24 white Umbro jerseys, suppliers will bid for the least expensive white jersey Umbro has available. That generic request may not satisfy your need for a better-quality uniform, so be specific. Include the model, the sizes you need, what kind of screen process you want, and the height and font of the letters and numbers on your jerseys. The more specific you are, the more likely you will get what you really want.

I recommend that you buy equipment from well-established dealers and manufacturers so they will be available when you need to replace a broken or torn item. I also recommend buying the most current style. Some manufacturers discontinue production of items after a certain time frame, making it impossible to find a replacement. We donate items that we no longer use but are still in good condition to the intramural program, such as uniforms, balls, and other equipment.

## Uniforms

"Dress for success." I'm sure that you have heard that saying before. It doesn't apply only to business people; it also works for soccer teams. A well-made, clean, and colorful uniform instills pride and confidence in players. As one would expect, proud, confident players tend to play better. When purchasing your team's uniforms, remember to get ones of good quality because they have to last three years. We follow a rotation schedule to help minimize cost. For example, in year one, we buy the away uniform; in year two, we buy the home uniform; and in year three, we buy warm-ups and travel bags.

## Footwear

Your team, like ours, probably plays on a variety of surfaces. Our region is usually dry, and our surfaces are often hard. Our players therefore tend to wear a multicleated shoe. On the West Coast, where we play most of our away matches, it rains often, so players need a six-cleated shoe. On occasion, we have to play on artificial turf, which requires a turf shoe. Naturally, our budgets can't handle 60 pairs of shoes per team, so athletes are responsible for purchasing their own shoes.

## Balls

Most balls are guaranteed for a year although a quality ball should last at least two years. Cost is always important, but quality is essential. You certainly can't expect players to improve technically if the ball they are using is of poor quality, improper weight or size, or not inflated properly. Another point to consider is that FIFA's spread of approved circumference and weight of a number-five ball is rather large. A big difference exists between a 27-inch ball and a 28-inch one, between a 14-ounce ball and a 16-ounce one. A smaller, lighter ball is more difficult to control, but it is livelier and will travel faster and farther. For high school play I recommend a 28-inch, 14-ounce ball.

## The Ball Game

When I was coaching Team Vancouver in Washington, we played in the Pacific Northwest Conference. Several of our opponents were NASL (North American Soccer League) teams, among them the Seattle Sounders, Portland Timbers, and Vancouver Whitecaps. The NASL-approved ball was the largest size and weight allowed by FIFA, and it was inflated to the highest limit permitted for matches. The ball we decided to use was an 18-panel Mikasa, which was small, light, and lively. When the Timbers came to our stadium, they immediately complained about the ball. In fact, they blamed our upset victory entirely on the ball. Two weeks later, we played them on their home field, Civic Stadium in Portland. After our warm-ups, a Timber ball boy had inadvertently taken all of their balls, including the match balls, to the locker room. When we kindly offered one of our balls to the referee, Portland's captain, Pat McMahon, ran off the field and brought out the match balls. He looked over at me and said, "You're not gonna do that to me again." We didn't win that second match; we tied 1-1. Darn!

Although most balls are stamped "FIFA approved," all that means is that the materials used to manufacture the ball were approved by FIFA (Fédération Internationalé de Football Association). It may not necessarily mean that the ball is a quality one.

Don't compromise on the quality of your soccer balls, and don't differentiate between practice balls and match balls. Players who have been practicing with a certain kind of ball often find it difficult to play well with a different ball during matches.

## Training and Match Facilities

By carefully planning your training and match facilities, you can save yourself and your team significant time. Our match facility is a stadium that seats approximately 8,000. The playing field is 75 by 115 yards. It is lighted, and we play most of our matches there. We also use it for 11-on-11 practices.

Our training facility includes a grid area, a conditioning area, and two fields. One field is 75 by 115 yards; the other is smaller at 55 by 100 yards. We use the small field for practice on the days before playing an away match against an opponent whose home field is small. All fields are clearly marked, and all have portable aluminum goals. We use 12 goals: 2 in the stadium, 2 on each training field, and 6 in the training grid.

The training grid is an area of 40 by 60 yards. We divided it into 10-yard squares, 4 squares one way and 6 the other, or 24 squares. The team has 1-on-1 and 2-on-2 practices in a 10-yard square; 2-on-2 and 2-on-3 in a 10-by-20-yard square; 3-on-3 in a 20-by-20-yard square; and 5-on-5 sessions take up the entire 40-by-60-yard grid. The system saves a lot of time because you are not forever setting up areas with cones. It also keeps many practices off the playing field.

Another advantage of the grid system is that no one has to stand around wasting time. Once a technique or tactic has been demonstrated, the team can break into small groups and practice. Assistants and captains oversee the practice, and I wander from group to group. Because the grid has a goal on each 40-yard line and two goals on each 60-yard line (thus six goals), it is ideal for shooting practices and goalkeeper practices.

If your team doesn't have the luxury of space, you can use areas on your playing field to accommodate your various practices (see figure 5.1). For instance, penalty areas are ideal for working 4-on-2. For 4-on-4 or 5-on-3 practices, use the area between the halfway line and the penalty area line (from the touchline to halfway across the field). You can create an ideal space for 7-on-7 or even 8-on-8 practices by moving the goals to the top of the penalty areas.

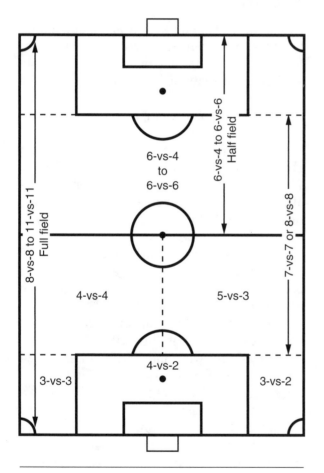

**Figure 5.1**   Practice areas.

# MEDICAL SCREENING AND INSURANCE

Our players report for orientation in mid-August, the day before we begin practices. At that time, players must view a risk film, which points out the dangers of participation in a contact sport. Before any ball hits the field, the following papers have to be filled out, signed by proper authorities, and submitted to the athletic secretary:

- Recruiting disclaimer
- Health history
- Medical examination results
- Athletic insurance information form
- Explanation of medical policies form
- Explanation of athletic policies form
- Informed consent form

You may joke about all the paperwork; however, these are important steps designed to protect your athletes, your school, and you.

## Medical Examinations

The most important papers you need to file are the ones with the results of the medical examination and the physician's approval to participate. Keep in mind your school's deadlines. Our conference doesn't accept these documents if the exams occurred before July 1. To accommodate our players, we bring in a physician the evening of orientation day, and he examines them for a nominal fee.

## Insurance

Information on insurance coverage is another important issue to be aware of. Most athletic department insurance is secondary insurance, which pays only after an athlete's personal insurance has been billed. This kind of insurance covers the athlete only when participating in supervised practices or matches. If the student athletic insurance or parental insurance does not cover the charges or if it denies a claim for any reason, the athlete and the parents are responsible for the bill.

The school must have a parental consent form on file. That form authorizes the school, the coaches, or qualified medical personnel to make decisions in case of medical emergency situations. The trainers and the coach should have copies of this document.

## MEDICAL CARE

Injuries occur—no matter how careful you are or how conscientiously you train. It's tough on you; it's tough on the team; but most of all, it's tough on the injured player. Thank heaven for the trainers, the unsung heroes of the team. Trainers are an important part of your staff. Their ability can differentiate between your player being out for the season or having the player back on the field in just a short while. I'm fortunate to have at our college one of the finest I have ever met, Phoebe Duke.

If injuries are treated quickly and properly, the severity of the injury can be reduced and the recovery time can be shortened significantly. Although most injuries to soccer players deal with the knees and the ankles, on occasion you may be faced with fractures or injuries to the back, neck, or head. Having someone present who is thoroughly trained in handling these medical emergencies is of immediate benefit to the injured player. The player benefits physically and, more important, psychologically.

I don't want to make it seem that by having a trainer in attendance you are relieved of responsibility, because you are not. Even if the trainer is certified, the final decision in any medical emergency is still the responsibility of the coach. Having a trainer also does not relieve you or anyone on your coaching staff from having to be versed in first-aid procedures and cardiopulmonary resuscitation techniques. In addition, you and your staff need to have at least some knowledge of blood-borne pathogens.

Our trainers keep a daily journal on all injuries. Once a player is in rehabilitation, I require a daily report about the recovery. I need to know whether the player is conscientiously following the trainer's instructions. To declare a player fit is a decision that must be mutually agreed on by the trainers and me. I refuse to use a player whose injury may be aggravated, no matter how important the match.

## The Fastest Response Ever

Two years ago, late in one of our practices, Brandon Trowbridge, a midfielder, was clipped going up for a header, and he came down headfirst. He was unconscious, and both the trainer and I suspected a serious neck injury. The trainer, Tory Carl, immediately called 911 on his cellular phone. Before he had finished giving the address, two emergency medical technicians from our fire department came running onto our field and with Tory's help, they immediately started to work on Brandon. Several minutes later, emergency vehicles appeared, and Brandon was soon transported to a hospital.

After the ambulance left, I had an opportunity to chat with the two emergency technicians. I wondered how they got to our practice field so fast. It turns out that the two men had been playing tennis on the courts next to the soccer facility at Spokane Community College, but they had left their radios on. It truly was the quickest response we had ever had. Although Brandon did not have a neck injury, he did have a concussion and eventually returned to practice a few weeks later.

When players are injured, they need to be referred to a physician, whom most schools have on staff. The athletic trainer typically makes the player's first appointment with the team physician, and the team physician may then choose to refer the athlete to another doctor.

Although our trainers handle nearly all our injuries, they are never overconfident. If they suspect anything out of the ordinary about a specific injury, they make a same-day appointment with the team physician. Our team physician happens to specialize in sports medicine. He may make some recommendations, but in most cases, he simply confirms the trainer's diagnosis and approves the prescribed treatment.

Our procedure of injury care does have two exceptions, however. The first occurs when we think that an injury is life threatening, in which case we seek immediate emergency medical help. The other exception deals with the coach's responsibility. If you think that an athlete needs to be seen by the team physician, even though the training staff assures you such a visit is unnecessary, it is your right and responsibility to overrule the trainers.

## STAFF PLANNING

The success of any program depends on the hard work and dedication of all the people who are directly involved with the program. Determine your immediate staff early in the season—especially your assistant coaches and managers—so that you have ample time to prepare them and get them qualified.

## Coaching Staff

Many of our former players and assistant coaches coach the local high school soccer teams, and some of them even coach at the college level. Because I encourage our assistants to find new challenges and further their careers, I find as a result that we have a continual turnover of coaching personnel.

New assistants must be thoroughly trained; but more than that, they must understand and subscribe to our philosophy. The college and our conference also require that new assistants have certain qualifications. They include the following:

- USSF or NSCAA coaching license, or expression of intent to pursue it
- Valid driver's license
- First-aid card
- CPR card
- Proof of having attended a class dealing with blood-borne pathogens
- Willingness to submit to a police background check

- Passing an exam regarding the understanding of conference policies, rules, and codes

These certifications take time. Your assistants therefore become a significant investment of your time and energy. Your relationship with them must be open because you will want them to confide in you and give you early notice of their intent.

## Managers

It takes several diligent people to get ready for a season. Fields and practice grids have to be groomed and lined. Goals need to be netted, and balls need to be pumped. Other equipment has to be repaired and checked for safety. Uniforms need to be issued. Audiovisual equipment has to be cleaned and checked; travel arrangements and motel reservations have to be made. The list goes on and on.

Our college employs full-time and seasonal managers, who perform a range of important tasks and duties for our athletes. For instance, one of our college's program managers makes travel arrangements for all 15 of our athletic teams. His job is to reserve vans or buses for a specified time and date, to make motel reservations, and to deliver a check to the head coach to cover meals and motels. Another program manager is an administrative assistant. He checks the eligibility of our players and their academic progress; he arranges for excused absences when players have to miss class time because of travel; he oversees the design and printing of promotional items; he does still photography; and he supplies visual aids during matches. The audiovisual production manager, the field manager, and the equipment manager are present at all practices and home matches. For matches at home, we use a statistician and a spotter. We also use a greeter who meets the opposing team on their arrival and takes care of their needs.

We treat our managers with respect and dignity, and we make them feel part of the team. In turn, I expect them to do their jobs promptly, correctly, and cheerfully.

# CONDITIONING PLAYERS

Soccer has three major components: fitness, technique, and tactics. If a soccer player is not fit, his technique suffers (especially late in the match). If players are not proficient with their techniques, their working on tactics (no matter how simple) is a waste of time. Each component affects the other; there's no getting around it.

Players need to realize that physical fitness has many advantages that can improve their game. If a player is fit, the player's vision, awareness, instinctive reactions, adaptability, inventiveness, composure, skill, confidence, decision making, and hardiness all benefit. In addition, fit players are much less likely to be injured; and when injured, they tend to recover more quickly. All athletes, particularly soccer players, must develop physical fitness long before anything else.

Soccer players should have a balanced fitness program as part of their lifestyle. The moment a player has indicated his intention of trying out for us, I provide our fitness program to him. Although many athletes understand the importance of fitness and are willing to train during the off-season, they find it difficult to get match-fit without pressure and competition. When they report for the season, they become somewhat discouraged to realize that, even after their hard work, in-season conditioning is still an agonizing experience. Keeping that in mind, you might as a coach want to put in more time planning your off-season conditioning for your players. To begin, you should encourage the players to condition in as large a group as possible. A group atmosphere introduces the element of competition. You should provide them with a workout program that is challenging but achievable, enjoyable but rewarding, and intense but interesting. The program should also be one that gives them a means of measuring their results.

Because soccer players need such a variety of components, laying out an interesting and challenging program is not difficult. The physical demands of our sport require that soccer players work on all five components of health-related fitness. Although cardiovascular endurance and muscle endurance rate high on the list, you can't overlook the significance of muscle strength, ideal body composition, and flexibility.

## Cardiovascular Endurance

Exercises for cardiovascular endurance may include running, power walking, aerobic dance, stepping, jumping rope, cross-country skiing, swimming, and cycling. When designing cardiovascular endurance programs, most fitness experts like to refer to the "training pyramid," where each stage builds to the next (see figure 5.2).

The first stage, called the *base phase*, consists of 3 to 5 workouts per week to build endurance. The workouts may vary, from running to stair climbing to cycling. The theme should be duration, not intensity. Players should exercise for 30 to 60 minutes per session.

The *build phase* has three workouts per week at higher intensity. They can include mile repeats or 800-yard runs. The theme is to go faster, but the players should not cut back on the actual time of the session, which should be at least 30 minutes. Another build workout of particular interest to soccer players is fartlek training, a continuous tempo run that is interrupted with short bouts of faster running.

The third stage is the *peak phase*. Players are now approaching their competitive season so running workouts must be short, but high in intensity. This stage includes sprints of 10, 20, 40, 60, 80, and 100 yards. The normal work-to-rest ratio starts at 1:3. For example, if the first 100-yard run takes a player 15 seconds to run, then the player will take a 45-second rest before the next 100-yard run begins. One month before the season starts, reduce the ratio to 1:2, and at

| | Jan | Feb | Mar | April | May | June | July | Aug | Sep | Oct | Nov | Dec |
|---|---|---|---|---|---|---|---|---|---|---|---|---|
| Base—aerobic | ■ | ■ | ■ | ■ | ■ | | | | | | | |
| Build—intervals | | | | | | ■ | ■ | | | | | |
| Peak—sprints | | | | | | | | ■ | ■ | | | |
| Maintenance | | | | | | | | | | ■ | ■ | ■ |

Base phase—build aerobic base, longer bouts 30 to 60 minutes
Build phase—change to shorter bouts, higher intensity, intervals
Peak phase—short duration, high-intensity sprints (10 to 100 yards)
Maintenance—maintain by practicing sport and high-intensity sprints

**Days per week for cardiovascular training**

Base phase—3 to 5 days per week
Build phase—3 days per week
Peak phase—2 to 3 days per week (prior to lifting or on nonlifting days)
Maintenance—3 days per week, arranged around competitive schedule

**Figure 5.2**   Yearly cardiovascular periodization schedule.

two weeks before the season, make it 1:1. A full set of sprints consists of 10-yard sprints (20); 20 yards (18); 40 yards (16); 60 yards (14); 80 yards (12); and 100 yards (10).

The *maintenance phase* takes place during the season. The activities scheduled in daily practices will maintain cardiovascular fitness, but I recommend that you still schedule at least one or two sessions of intense running workouts per week to truly maintain cardiovascular fitness throughout the season.

If training time is lost, players suffer a definite decrease in aerobic conditioning. Every week of lost training causes a player to lose approximately 10 percent of conditioning. Injured players should keep such a statistic in mind and maintain an aerobic exercise program that doesn't use the injured part of the body.

# Muscle Strength and Endurance

To jump for a high header, to get off a hard shot, to stay on the ball when being charged takes muscle strength. Although you may not have given much thought to the need for developing muscle strength in soccer players, this kind of exercise is quite beneficial, especially for the goalkeepers. True, soccer players shouldn't train for bulk, but their tone and strength are essential. Players can develop muscle strength through activities such as working with free weights, weight machines, rubber bands or tubing, gymnastics, and calisthenics.

Although muscle strength is significant, muscle endurance is of the utmost importance to the soccer player. Athletes can enhance this kind of endurance by working with lighter weights or resistance and by increasing the repetitions of the exercises used to build muscle strength. Muscle endurance also benefits from any long-distance aerobic activity—such as running, cycling, fast walking, or lap swimming.

Our strength trainer, John Troppmann, has designed strength and endurance training exercises just for soccer players. They include "the matrix" and metabolic training for legs and chest. The matrix is a combination of 72 movements using dumbbells. The movements must all be performed between 90 and 120 seconds. Most players start with five-pound dumbbells, and they increase the weight once the time goal has been achieved. The theory that supports the need for the matrix is that although a soccer player needs endurance, she nevertheless works in spurts of high intensity. At those moments, her actions are explosive. The matrix therefore duplicates those explosions of energy during training.

### The Matrix

6 × overhead press

6 × sagittal press

6 × rotational overhead press

6 × alternating curls

6 × alternating upright rows

6 × alternating upper cuts

6 × alternating lunges

6 × alternating side lunges

6 × alternating back lunges

6 × alternating lunges to overhead press

6 × alternating side lunges to overhead press

6 × alternating back lunges to overhead press

### Metabolic Training for Legs and Chest

Metabolic training develops the muscles used during moments of explosive action and the ones needed for strength when in possession of the ball. The following exercises duplicate the energy expansion a soccer player experiences during matches.

Metabolic training for the legs:

Body weight squats (20)

Alternating lunges (20)

Alternating step-ups, 18-inch box (20)

Jump squats (20)

Metabolic training for the chest:

Push-ups (20)

Band bench presses, alternate stance after 10 repetitions (20)

Band flys, alternate stance after 10 repetitions (20)

Ballistic push-ups (20)

## Body Composition

The capabilities of the human body are truly awesome. Think for a moment of all the intricacies the body must go through when a player receives a ball, controls it, turns, sees that space is available, attacks the space, avoids a tackle, views an open teammate, passes the ball, continues the run, receives the ball back, looks what the goalkeeper is giving, shoots, and scores. In those few seconds, hundreds of muscle contractions have occurred; thousands of chemical reactions have taken place; energy has been expended; and calories have been burned. To perform each task, our bodies need three elements—air, water, and food. For all of us, and particularly for the athlete, the amount of water must be adequate and the food must be of high quality. After all, would you build an expensive race car and drive it with little coolant and cheap fuel?

Few soccer players drink enough water, yet water is the very thing that regulates the body's temperature, affects the blood volume, aids in the body's chemical reactions, and carries off waste. Because the body's thirst mechanism lags way behind the body's need for water, players can't depend on their thirst when maintaining their hydration. Soccer players should learn to force themselves to hydrate their bodies by drinking 8 to 10 glasses of water per day.

Hydration is a task in which they can easily check their status. If they urinate in large volumes and if the urine is clear and colorless, they are probably drinking enough water. If not, they need more.

Food is our body's energy. The body's preferred source of energy is carbohydrates. Fat and protein can also be converted into energy, but the conversions are slow and inefficient. For optimum performance, an athlete should eat a great variety of foods but give preference to pastas, whole-grain breads, potatoes, cereals, fruit, vegetables, and beans—all of which are high in carbohydrates.

## Flexibility

A soccer player can improve flexibility by performing activities such as yoga, static stretching, light swimming, or any other light activity that puts major muscle groups through a full range of motion.

A few cardinal rules apply when stretching for flexibility.

- Stretch the muscles on both sides of the body.
- Do not exceed the threshold for discomfort or pain.
- Do not bounce or jerk; gradually induce the stretch.
- Maintain each stretch for 20 to 40 seconds.
- Be aware if one side is more or less flexible than the other. It could be the result of structural difference, recovery from injury, or the possible development of an injury.
- Do not squeeze the knees. Be careful not to put too much pressure on the knee joint, especially when stretching the quadriceps.
- Stretch the muscles after a brief warm-up.
- Stretching after a workout helps speed recovery for the next workout.

## PRESEASON PLANNING

During the month before the players report for the first practice, my coaching staff and I meet at least once a week. The purpose of these meetings is to prepare a plan for the upcoming season. The plan is somewhat general at that time because several things are still unknown. What we do know are the abilities of the returning players; and of course, we have seen and met with the recruited players. Until we have gone through several practices and until we have seen all the players under the pressure of a match, we do not know how we are going to create the team culture necessary to play successfully with this new group. As a result, whatever we plan, we need to be flexible.

Our conditioning- and technique-development program doesn't vary that much from year to year, but our tactics do. They may even change during the season. The changes we do make are based on observations made during the preceding season, which include the effectiveness of our tactics and the tactics used by our opponents. And although we have many unknowns, I have to say that much of the plan is consistent from year to year.

As a coach, make sure that everyone on your staff contributes to the plan. Once you establish the plan, all should be thoroughly familiar with it. Because my entire coaching staff contributes to the plan and helps with scheduling, all of us are well prepared for the start of practice. This preparation makes practices efficient and varied.

Without a plan, or with the wrong one, you set up both yourself and the team for failure. Success is not a chance happening; you plan for it.

## Scheduling Matches

Like most college teams, we are restricted in the number of matches we may play during a season. We may have as many as 20 conference matches, leaving us with 3 matches and 2 scrimmages to schedule on our own.

We schedule these matches carefully so that the competition is challenging but not overwhelming.

After the official start of our conference season, we don't have time to play nonconference teams. We schedule all the extra matches during our preparation time because I don't want to set us up for unnecessary injuries. We used to play four-year schools, but with the numerous NCAA restrictions, to do so now is becoming increasingly difficult. As far as preseason matches, I believe those are best scheduled against teams that are competitive yet evenly matched with your team's level of talent.

Played at any level, soccer is exciting for the players. But soccer played against a vastly superior opponent can demoralize your team. Likewise, playing against a weak team provides no satisfaction at all, and your team will learn little from such a contest. I recommend that as a coach, you therefore schedule your matches wisely to complement your team's best interests.

# TRAVEL

Traveling can be exciting, educational, and enjoyable . . . or it can be pure misery. It really depends on the behavior of the players. Before a trip, remind the team of their responsibility to their college, their city, and each other. I like to point out to them that I enjoy being a coach, but I am quite the temperamental baby-sitter.

When our team stays at a hotel, each room has a room captain. That captain is responsible for behavior in the room, which includes adherence to curfews, lights-out, and cleanup. We usually don't have problems when we travel, but I have to admit that I don't believe this is because of the room captains. I believe our players behave well because from the day they first arrive, we cultivate team pride.

# SUMMARY

Planning for the season is hard work, but following these suggestions may make the task less overwhelming.

- Prepare your budgets carefully; include some contingency funds to cover the unexpected.
- Check your equipment and facilities thoroughly, and, if replacements are needed, order early.
- Assess the efficiency of your administrative processes, such as medical screening, examinations, insurance, and injury care.
- Reevaluate and strengthen your conditioning plan, in particular your off-season program. Include nutritional information.
- Review and prepare, as much as possible, your plan for technical and tactical development of both players and team.
- Plan your training and match schedules, including possible tournaments, and make the travel arrangements.
- Analyze your program in its entirety to make sure that all who are involved have a chance to grow.

# Chapter
## 6

# PLANNING AND CONDUCTING PRACTICES

In soccer, all the hard work is done at practice. It is in practice where we must work on the players' physical and mental condition while also developing them technically and tactically. Naturally, we as coaches should plan our practices carefully. Each one of our practices should emphasize one or more specific components of soccer in an order that allows for gradual improvement.

For my teams, I like to work off of a master plan that lists every component that needs attention. From the master plan, I can then create my daily practice plans. I try to emphasize economy in my daily practice plans by combining as many components as possible. One of my favorite ways to do so is through the use of small-sided, conditioned games.

Remember that for practices to be effective, they must be challenging, and they must be enjoyable. But they must also provide each player with a certain amount of success. A practice without success is simply a waste of time.

## PRACTICE EMPHASIS

I mentioned earlier that I expect the players to report in good physical condition for the first practice. I know that a player's concept of physical fitness is frequently not the same as mine, which ultimately means that we devote significant time on physical conditioning during the early part of the practice season.

Because we cannot start practice (per our conference) until the third Friday in August, physical conditioning is a challenge for both the players and the coaching staff. Our first conference match is scheduled in mid-September, so we have a time constraint that allows us fewer than four weeks to prepare. Conditioning specialists will tell you that eight weeks is ideal for achieving optimal conditioning and that six weeks is workable. The challenge then, as a result of our time limitations, is to get the players ready without causing injuries. At the same time, you must devote energy and a part of the schedule to develop your players technically and teach them tactics individually and as a team.

Figure 6.1 gives you a picture of how I schedule the three major components of soccer. When practice starts, we spend the majority of time on conditioning with little time on tactics. As we go along, the time spent on conditioning decreases, and the time spent on individual tactics increases. By the end of the season, we spend almost all our time on team tactics with little time on conditioning. Of course, we're also working on technique improvement throughout the entire season.

I don't believe in long practices. As a result of our short time to prepare, however, we start the practice season with two sessions per day, and we maintain that schedule for 10 to

Start of practice                      End of season

**Figure 6.1** Scheduling the three major components of soccer throughout the season.

14 days. The length depends on how well prepared the players are when they first report. Each session lasts about two and a half hours, which includes an hourly water break and time to warm up, stretch, and cool down.

Each session, especially during the first 14 days, includes hard physical conditioning. You must take care not to have your players overtrain during that time. Every hard day of physical challenge should be followed by a day of lesser intensity. I have also found it better to schedule the purely physical work at the end of the practice. This way the players aren't as tired and have better concentration during the technique and tactics phases.

## Master Plan

In our master plan, I list all the components that we need to work on during our practices. Once we do so, it is not difficult to lay out the daily practice plans. See the sample master plan shown in figure 6.2.

## Daily Practice Plans

At the beginning of the season, prepare daily practice plans from your master practice schedule. Once the match season starts, you can prepare practice plans that are based on a review of the last match and on a scouting report for the upcoming match. Remember that every practice, no matter what time in the season, needs to include conditioning and technique development. The team should ideally peak physically, mentally, technically, and tactically late in the season, when fatigue and play-off pressure start to take their toll.

Figure 6.3 shows a typical daily practice plan for a session during the preseason. (This schedule is more detailed than it appears on our personal plan so that you can make the necessary adjustments that work for your team.) We typically spend the first 30 minutes on stretching and warming up the muscles. By choosing one of the components on our master plan, we use the next 20 minutes working on technique. For the day illustrated in figure 6.3, we chose passing. I

## Sample Soccer Master Plan

| Goalkeepers | Offense | Defense | Midfield |
|---|---|---|---|
| Shot stopping<br>Punching, deflecting<br>Jumping<br>Diving<br>Cutting out crosses<br>Support of defense<br>Distribution | One-versus-one<br>Support<br>Balance<br>Depth<br>Tactics for the sweeper<br>Tactics for the stopper<br>Tactics for the marking defenders<br>Compactness<br>Transition | One-versus-one<br>Support (angle, distance)<br>Width and depth<br>Combination plays<br>Crossing plays<br>Takeovers<br>Mobility<br>Creativity<br>Compactness<br>Transition | Slow buildup<br>Quick attack<br>Width and depth<br>Redirection<br>Compactness<br>Transition |

| Team development | Conditioning | Technique | Set plays |
|---|---|---|---|
| Laws of the game<br>Player evaluations<br>Team evaluations | Physical<br>Psychological | Ball control<br>Passing<br>Tackling<br>Heading<br>Dribbling<br>Shooting | Kickoffs<br>Goal kicks<br>Corner kicks<br>Indirect free kicks<br>Direct free kicks<br>Penalties<br>Throw-ins |

**Figure 6.2** Sample soccer master plan.

think that passing in triangles helps a team immensely because it simulates game conditions by forcing the players to turn their hips toward the target. Players don't develop this habit when they pass in twos. After the water break, we work on another item from the master plan, support on defense. For this exercise, we use a number of grids and go for 30 minutes. We then use another 30 minutes to practice support on offense, again using the grid layout. We finish the work session with a strenuous conditioning exercise called *horseshoe running*. After that, we warm down with an easy, around-the-field jog and a stretch to cool down.

## PRACTICE PRINCIPLES

Because practice is so important to soccer, I check every practice plan to see that it satisfies the principles I believe are needed for an efficient and effective practice. Practices must be economical, and they must combine the three major components of soccer—conditioning, technique, and tactics. Small-sided, conditioned games usually satisfy that principle. The practice must be challenging, but at the same time, it should also allow the team and each player to achieve at least some success in overcoming challenges. Of course, as a final prerequisite, the practice must be enjoyable.

# Sample Daily Practice Plan

**15 min**       **Warm-up with ball and partner**

From the goal line partner #1 sprints out about 30 yards. Partner #2 yells "turn" and serves the ball. Partner #1 receives and controls the ball, then dribbles it back. When partner #1 crosses the goal line, partner #2 runs out.

**15 min**       **Stretch**

**20 min**       **Technique**

Pass in threes while moving. Maintain shape of the triangle. Pass in both directions, using the inside and outside of the left and right foot. Pass for 10 minutes with the ball on the ground, and do 10 minutes of chips.

**10 min**       **Water break**

**30 min**       **Support on defense**

*One-on-two.* Use a 30-by-10-yard grid and one goal. One attacker starts attack at the top of the grid. Two defenders start at the goal line. Lead defender must communicate intent to commit to the ball. Lead defender must close down the attacker quickly without overrunning. Watch lead defender's body position and patience. Supporting defender must watch angle and distance of support. Supporting defender must communicate.

*Two-on-two.* Use two attackers; otherwise, same as above. Supporting defender's role is to support the defender challenging for the ball but in such a position that if the ball is passed to attacker #2, the supporting defender can close down #2.

**30 min**       **Support on offense**

*Two-on-one.* Same grid as above. Two attackers with the ball start at the top of the grid. One defender starts at the goal line. Coach the attacking players. Player with the ball should not put the defender between the ball and partner, and should force the defender to commit before passing. The supporting player must provide a passing angle at a reasonable distance. Encourage wall passing and takeovers.

**20 min**       **Horseshoes**

Each player has a partner. Partner #1 sprints at full speed from the near goal to the intersection of the halfway line and the right touchline, then around the far goal to the intersection of the halfway line and the left touchline, and back to the near goal. When #1 enters the six-yard box, #2 runs while #1 rests. When #2 returns, #1 goes again until each player has completed five horseshoes. Do three sets.

**15 min**       **Cool-down and stretch**

**Figure 6.3**   Sample daily practice plan.

## Economical Practices

Soccer is not a coached game. Once the opening whistle in the match sounds, coaching stops. Except for injury, tactical substitutions, and halftime instructions and adjustments, coaches best serve their teams by observing calmly and confidently. The quiet confidence gets transmitted to the team. If the coach gets nervous or uptight, the players get uptight and their performance suffers. In addition to setting a calm, confident example, coaches can also benefit by using the observations made in the match to set the schedule for the next practice.

Because coaches are not permitted to coach during a soccer match, a team's practices should duplicate match conditions. Practices should highlight a technique or tactic that needs attention. The method is often referred to as the *whole-part-whole method.* That is, observe the whole, see the problem, isolate the problem, and design a realistic game that allows the players to work on the problem. Once the players master the problem in the small-sided game, they can take it back into the match.

The best coaching tool is often in the form of small-sided, conditioned games. When using them, the coach determines the number of players that will be involved on the basis of the component she wants to improve. For example, to work on defensive support, the coach may begin with playing one attacker against two defenders. She could instruct the second defender in achieving the proper distance and angle of support while giving information to the first defender.

The coach can also choose to put conditions on the game. For instance, if the team is practicing combination plays in a three-on-three game, the coach may specify that every goal will count. The conditions, however, can include such rules as the following: a goal scored after the execution of a wall pass will count for three; a goal resulting directly from a through pass will count for two; or a goal resulting from a successful takeover will count for two. In a heading practice, goals

scored directly off headers will count for five. Remember to avoid making the mistake of not counting goals scored by means other than the condition. You certainly don't want to take away options.

What is also great about small-sided, conditioned games is that they are match-related. They allow your players to practice a technique or tactic under matchlike pressure. A small-sided, conditioned game includes an opposition, a counterattack, and a goal. Small-sided games can involve as few as 2 players or as many as 10. In 1-on-1 games, you can coach players in individual technique and tactics, both offensively and defensively. In a 2-on-1 game, you can coach the attackers to beat the lone defender by dribbling or by passing. In this type of game, you can work on wall passing, through passing, back passing, and takeovers. The lone defender can be coached on positioning and marking space.

In a 2-on-2 game, you can also coach overlaps, space seeking, and isolating one of the defenders to create a 2-on-1 situation. The defenders can work on support on defense. In 3-on-2, you can then instruct the offense to create width and depth while applying all the technique and tactics of the earlier games. The defenders work on support, space marking, and role switching.

Keep in mind that the 3-on-3 game calls for mobility and innovation by the attackers and the defenders, in addition to good communication by the defenders. Also remember that everything that happens in an 11-on-11 match happens in a 3-on-3 game. In a small-sided game, however, players touch the ball more often, and the situations you want to work on occur more often as well. This kind of game is much easier to coach.

Games that are arranged 4-on-3, 4-on-4, 5-on-4, and 5-on-5 allow the players to work not only on the technique and tactics of the other small-sided games, but also on position-related specifics, width, depth, player distribution, compactness, and transition. Games that have numbers higher than 5-on-5 lose the economy presented by a small-sided game.

## Successful Practices

Nothing motivates athletes as much as mastering a realistic challenge does. Each one of your practices should present realistic challenges to the team and to the individual players, and each practice should conclude with a player's achieving a reasonable amount of success. At times you may present a challenge that somehow doesn't seem to work, but don't give up on it. Evaluate it. Did the players understand what you wanted? Did you demonstrate it clearly?

When an exercise, challenge, or small-sided game falls apart, one of the following scenarios usually applies: you are performing in too small an area; too many people are involved; or the basic technique is inadequate to overcome the challenge. Therefore, increase the space; use fewer players; or ease up on pressure to give more time to work on technique faults. Not having success at a certain endeavor is a coaching problem, not a player problem.

Practices can be challenging and fun, or they can be pure drudgery. When you present players with realistic challenges and allow them to have fun overcoming them, you will have a hard-working, enthusiastic team that gets things done. If your practices are purposeless and dull, the team will be discontented and tired. Your preparation, your effective use of time, your positive attitude, and your ability to praise and compliment even minor successes will create a fun and successful atmosphere.

To make the practices enjoyable for the players, you and your staff should keep the following in mind:

- Plan and be prepared for every practice. Make a schedule for all elements of the practice, and stick to it.
- Vary your practices. Don't work a subject to death; you can always go back to it.
- Make practices economical by keeping everybody involved. Work in grids so that several games can be played at the same time.
- Make sure that each challenge you present provides some success, not only for the team, but also for the players.
- Explain the purpose of each practice to your athletes. Encourage your players to communicate their feelings of success or confusion about the practice.
- Keep things positive and lighthearted. It will put players in a receptive spirit when it is time to do the serious coaching.
- Make sure you are enjoying yourself. Be rested, enthusiastic, caring, and compassionate. If you are having fun, players will too.
- Keep things in perspective. Soccer is a game, not a war.

It is my job to help players reach their potential and to coach the team to success. I know that in soccer the only opportunity to do so is in practice. Thus, I can best serve the team by thoroughly planning the practices and conscientiously executing the plan.

## SUMMARY

An important part of your job is planning your practices. The following suggestions help to make them successful.

- Emphasize what you want to achieve in the practice.
- Develop a detailed master plan. Extract your daily practice plans from this plan.
- Keep your practices varied and challenging.
- Don't give long explanations that try to anticipate every possible problem.
- Combine conditioning, technique, and tactics in your exercises so that your practices use time economically.
- Make sure that each practice attains some level of success and enjoyment.

# Part III

# COACHING SKILLS AND TECHNIQUES

# Chapter
## 7

# MASTERING THE BASICS

The success of the team depends on each player's ability to execute the basic techniques and tactics under the pressure of a match. What helps your team considerably then is to design practices that are intense, realistic, and match-related. Although conducting drills that serve no specific purpose may improve the players' technical abilities, they don't do much to improve the team's overall performance in a match.

Your job as the coach is to observe and identify those aspects of the game that need attention and then design a realistic practice that highlights those aspects. I recommend that you observe the practice closely to see that the players respond to the challenge successfully. Although your players may need some motivation to help them enjoy the challenges, they will truly enjoy the challenges if you allow them the opportunity to succeed on their own with you as the facilitator. Remember, what you do in practice carries over into the game. If you want them to solve problems and exploit options, you must allow them to do so during practice. The team's performance will then improve when you gradually introduce every element of the game in practice:

- A ball
- A defined area
- A target or goal
- A defined direction of play

- The rules
- Their teammates
- A realistic opposition
- Personal decision making

When introducing a defensive technique or tactic in a practice session, you can certainly give every player a ball. However, they must play within a defined area while trying to achieve a target or go to goal. The laws of the game must be observed at all times (except when the coach wishes to ignore the offside law). As the practice develops, teams can then be introduced, and an appropriate-sized area can be marked out with one group of players defending one end while attacking the other end (and vice versa). The wise coach will create "problems" to be solved and will encourage players to identify the cues in the play that forewarn them of these problems. Once these cues are identified and once the likely problems that inevitably arise are understood, then players can take appropriate measures to ensure corrective action. Remember that practice does not make perfect; practice makes permanent.

## PLAYER VERSATILITY

Ball possession determines everything. It is the first and foremost important thing to consider in soccer. Once a team has lost the ball, its first consideration should be to (of course) regain it. This objective suggests that a team cannot be rigidly divided into the positions of attackers and defenders. When a team loses possession, every player must immediately become a defender, whereas most of the opposing team suddenly become attackers.

The developmental trend in modern-day soccer demands that every good player must have the versatility to attack and score goals, plus the desire and ability to defend. Quality players, when attempting to regain ball possession, read and anticipate attacking moves, immediately pursue and chase the ball back, cut down the attacking space, smother the opponent's "perception-action"

time, intercept passes, block shots, steal the ball back, or use their bodies to separate attackers from the ball. Exceptional attacking players, on the other hand, adapt and succeed, even under intense pressure from opponents. They can react in a split second. They collect or control a ball with comfortable ease, and they can initiate and complete passes, runs, dribbles, shots, and feints to our complete surprise while performing completely unpredictable moves.

Scenarios always exist, of course, when a team risks losing ball possession, especially if there is an opportunity to shoot at goal. In other words, the closer the play is to the opponents' goal, the more a team is justified in taking such a risk. Conversely, the nearer the play is to a team's own goal, the fewer the risks that should be taken.

## BASIC DEFENSIVE POSITIONS

Let's first look at the players' defensive responsibilities. Defensive duties and responsibilities are assigned not only to the goalkeeper, sweeper, marking backs, and stopper, but also to wide midfielders, attacking midfielders, and forwards. Therefore, I can't stress enough that every player needs to have defensive skills. Players in certain positions, of course, need specific attributes to be effective, but each player on a soccer team must have basic defensive skills.

### Goalkeeper

As the last line of defense—and as the only player on the team allowed to use hands and arms to control, propel, or stop the ball—the goalkeeper deserves special attention. To have a successful team with a below-average goalkeeper is virtually impossible. The goalkeeper is a special case in the team yet also a vital team member. The goalkeeper is expected to rescue the team with saves when defensive lapses have occurred while at the same time being an integral part of the defense by organizing the players in front of the goal.

## Goalkeeper Skills and Attributes

In my experience, I have found that all top-class goalkeepers have the following attributes:

- They are fearless.
- They relish body contact.
- They have quick reflexes and reactions.
- They are agile.
- They are above average in height.
- They have a dominant personality.
- They have excellent eye-hand coordination.

If the goalkeeper is missing any one of these seven critical attributes, then the goalkeeper is unlikely to excel. I have known hundreds of promising goalkeepers who looked the part but were deficient in one or more of these attributes.

The goalkeeper also must be an effective communicator because he is in the position of being able to see the other 21 players on the field. The goalkeeper must convey vital information to the nearest defenders so that they can organize themselves effectively and thus prevent shots on goal.

Goalkeepers should have well-developed skills in the following areas:

- Positioning
- Stopping shots
- Punching and deflecting
- Crosses
- Distribution

**Positioning.** In saving shots on goal, the goalkeeper's distance from the goal line and the angle from the near post are critical. A goalkeeper who is only a few inches out of position may concede a goal.

Goalkeepers must invest significant time perfecting their positioning. Many of the world's top goalkeepers are the oldest players on their teams. We too often find goalkeepers in the youth leagues and high school programs who concentrate their practice time on fitness or agility. Their coaches should instead focus on perfecting their positioning.

*Low shots.* Figure 7.1 illustrates the basic set position in stopping low shots. This position is a classic set position from which the goalkeeper can thrust sideways to make a save. The goalkeeper must establish this basic set position a split second before the opponent shoots, with feet motionless at the desired distance from the goal line while at the correct angle from the near post. The goalkeeper's weight should never be on the heels; instead, he should carry the weight on the balls of the feet for balance, agility, and spring. By being on the heels, goalkeepers often fall backward when the shot is taken, presenting a much smaller target. The goalkeeper should at all times lean into the shot.

The goalkeeper's distance and angle are largely dependent on what is happening on the ball and what options are available to the opposing player on the ball. If an opponent is about to take a long-range shot from 25 to 30 yards, the goalkeeper's first priority is to be close enough to the goal line to prevent the ball from going over him and into the goal.

**Figure 7.1**  The basic set position.

*High shots.* In preparation for saving a high shot, the goalkeeper should adopt a modified basic set position a split second before the shot is taken. The goalkeeper should bend the knees only slightly, should have a slight forward lean at the waist, and should hold the hands high in preparation for saving what will probably be a high shot.

If the opponent on the ball has the opportunity of "chipping" it, the goalkeeper should understand the personal optimum distance from the goal line. The goalkeeper should recognize that chipping a fast-rolling ball is difficult unless it is coming directly at the chipper. A stationary or slow-rolling ball is much easier to chip. The goalkeeper must take a position from the goal line where it is still possible to recover and save shots that would have gone into the goal just under the crossbar.

*Recovery movement.* Goalkeepers can use the recovery movement to get into position to save a high shot that is going over the goalkeeper and into the goal. We too often find goalkeepers moving directly backward to the goal, which makes it difficult to get height in their vertical jump. The goalkeeper's recovery movement should instead be a sideways one. In saving a shot that is going high over the left shoulder, the goalkeeper should take a quarter turn to the left, take the left foot back, and lift the right knee to cross the legs by planting the right foot just left of the left foot, thereby enabling the goalkeeper to thrust upward off the right foot. The goalkeeper should keep an eye on the ball, then swing the right arm upward and backward to propel the ball over the crossbar (see figure 7.2). To save a shot going high over the right shoulder, the goalkeeper should use a recovery movement that is a mirror image of the previous description.

**Stopping Shots.** Of course, the keeper should stop all shots using any part of his body. Ideally, he should stop the shot with the ball solidly caught in his hands, but that is not always possible. Shots just inside the post or under the bar may have to be deflected, while balls played into a crowded area may need to be punched away. Also, many reac-

**Figure 7.2**   Recovery movement.

tion saves have been made with the legs or feet. No matter what kind of shot stopping the keeper selects, each method has its own technique that needs to be practiced.

*Low shots.* I cannot stress how important it is that the goalkeeper be in the basic set position a split second before the shot is taken. This preparation allows the goalkeeper to push off either foot and extend the body in a sideways-on position. The goalkeeper should never dive with the chest to the ground. In the sideways-on position, the goalkeeper should raise the upper arm high enough so that he can see through the "window" made by both arms.

The greatest fault in saving low shots is probably the goalkeeper putting weight on the heels in the basic set position and then falling down backward, thus taking his face away from the ball when the opponent shoots. This action means that the goalkeeper is blocking the least amount of space, and it almost always results in a goal.

*High shots.* Again, the goalkeeper needs to be in the basic set position. For a high shot, the goalkeeper (from the semicrouched position) pushes vigorously from the feet, swings both hands upward to add momentum to the lift, then throws both hands up so that the thumbs and forefingers form a W shape. The goalkeeper should try to get both hands behind the ball, and the eyes should be on the ball from the moment it leaves the opponent's foot.

**Punching and Deflecting.** For the goalkeeper to try to catch the ball in a crowded goal area is risky business. The goalkeeper might be wise to instead punch the ball, particularly if unable to get a clear run to the ball because of a congestion of players. When punching the ball, the goalkeeper should punch it high, far, and wide.

Another point goalkeepers need to learn is that a hard shot under the bar or just inside a post can often be reached with only one hand. The goalkeeper should be well practiced in deflecting those shots over the bar or around the post, thus giving up a corner rather than a goal.

**Crosses.** Dealing with crosses is probably the greatest difficulty for most goalkeepers. We too often find goalkeepers who are adept at dealing with crosses from one side of the field but who have problems with the other. The cause of the problem is usually starting in a position where it is difficult to move to the near- or far-post areas. The goalkeeper should take a position to deal with crosses by turning to face the opponent who is most likely to cross the ball. Such a maneuver allows the goalkeeper to make a rapid and decisive movement to the ball if it is played into the near-post area. If the ball is crossed to the far-post area from the right wing goal, then the goalkeeper should follow the flight of the ball and make a cross-step movement toward the ball. If the ball is catchable, the goalkeeper should attempt to catch it. But if there is any doubt, the goalkeeper should go ahead and help it along on its flight path.

**Distribution.** With possession of the ball, the goalkeeper can mount an immediate counterattack by distributing the ball with either the feet or the hands. In most instances, the goalkeeper should throw the ball one of the following ways.

*Underarm roll pass.* If the goalkeeper has the opportunity of playing the ball to an unmarked teammate within a 10-to-30-yard range, the best means of distribution is often the underarm roll. This pass is generally made to a wide player and is seldom played straight down the field.

*Overarm throw.* The most common throw made by goalkeepers is the overarm throw. Holding the ball in both hands, the goalkeeper takes it backward in the palm and fingers of the throwing hand until the throwing arm is straight. The goalkeeper then swings the arm vigorously upward and forward, releasing the ball off the tips of the fingers. The advantage of the overarm throw is that it can be used to pass the ball over the heads of opposing players. With practice, the goalkeeper can also impart spin on the ball by "cutting" it off the fingers. To do so, the goalkeeper pulls the little finger toward the ground a split second before release.

# Sweeper

When faced with opposing forwards, most defensive units assume a shape, such as a triangle or a diamond. In either case, an uncommitted player helps teammates form these defensive shapes. This uncommitted player, the sweeper, is just that—uncommitted, with no assigned marking duties. The sweeper is the last defender because she plays mostly behind the marking backs. From this position, the sweeper is the ideal person to direct the marking backs and the other players who are helping on defense. For this reason alone, the sweeper should be an above-average player.

Besides directing the defense, the sweeper is also responsible for providing cover to the player challenging for the ball and (if the situation warrants) double-teaming an opponent with a marking defender. The sweeper guards against through passes behind marking backs, unmarked players coming through, and combination plays such as a wall pass that might beat the marking backs.

## Sweeper Skills and Attributes

Most outstanding sweepers have the following attributes:

- They are good "readers" of the game, with uncanny ability to anticipate the opponent's next move.
- They are intelligent, with excellent analytical skills.
- They are well organized, both on and off the field.
- They have leadership qualities and often take the role of team captain.
- They are effective communicators.
- They have proficient ball skills.
- They can kick the ball well with either foot.
- They are precise headers of the ball.
- They have excellent speed.

The sweeper is a key player in any defense and should take charge of the organization (and reorganization) of the team's defensive unit. The sweeper should constantly communicate with the marking backs and stoppers so that the defensive organization remains finely tuned throughout the match. The sweeper should also be a levelheaded player. A sweeper who loses his temper easily, or is one who retaliates, can be a liability because he often works close to (or in) the penalty area. A sweeper's misbehavior could result in costly free kicks or penalties.

# Marking Backs

The job of marking just one player during a match may seem easy, but being a marking back is one of the more difficult jobs a soccer player can have. Knowing when and where to mark takes a reasonable amount of intelligence and tactical awareness; reading an action before it happens is yet another skill. The marking back should know when and how to contain an opponent, how to stop the opponent from turning, and if turned, how to tackle the ball away.

## Marking Back Skills and Attributes

The best marking backs will have the following attributes:

- They are fast.
- They are aggressive and competitive.
- They are strong, and usually tall.
- They relish body contact.
- They can concentrate on a task for a long time.
- They can kick the ball well with either foot.
- They are precise headers of the ball.

Positioning (relative to the immediate opponent and the ball) is by far the most important skill for any marking back. Most of the top marking backs, such as those in the Italian Serie A League, have their positioning worked out so that they can get to their immediate opponent just before that player receives the ball. Yet they can also do so while being close enough to other opposing players so that they can offer a degree of cover to the nearest defender. Marking backs should also be willing to take direction and submit to the leadership of their sweeper and goalkeeper. Although marking backs' problems virtually end when they prevent their immediate opponent from receiving the ball, their problems just begin if they allow that scenario to happen.

## Stoppers

The role of the stopper is to fill the space in front of the defense and to cut off the supply of passes to the opposing forwards. By offering defensive cover, the stopper can also act as a sweeper behind the midfield.

### Stopper Skills and Attributes

Most of the better stoppers have the following attributes:

- They are disciplined.
- They are fiercely competitive.
- They are extremely mobile with excellent speed and endurance.
- They are quick into the tackle.
- They are comfortable when the ball is in front of them. They play better when facing the opposing goal.
- They are sound passers.
- They are proficient headers, meeting most punts or goal kicks by the opposing goalkeeper.

The stopper can often be thought of as the sweeper's foot soldier. The stopper should respond to the sweeper's instructions and fill the space in front of the marking backs, thus cutting off the supply of passes to the opposing forwards. Stoppers are sometimes described as defensive midfielders, although defensive midfielders' responsibilities are not always restricted to the regular responsibilities of a stopper. The overwhelming function of a stopper is to stop passes and opposing players, particularly opposing dribblers.

## Wide Midfielders

Many coaches place their weakest players in the position of wide midfield. This strategy is often a mistake and can hurt the team both on attack and on defense. On defense, these players are isolated from any immediate defensive cover so that the opponents can mount offensive moves down the flanks. If the outside midfielder has been beaten, the marking back and sweeper find themselves in serious trouble. They may now have to contend with superior numbers on the flank and overlaps. Every coach has to make a decision where to place the weaker players. Regardless of where a weak player is placed, strong players should always be in front of and behind him.

### Wide Midfielder Skills and Attributes

The wide midfielder must actually fulfill the requirements of three different positions in the same match—wing back, wide midfield, and winger. Although they may confuse their roles at times, they should always remember to first concentrate on the defensive aspect of each position. The best wide midfielders have the following attributes:

- They mark goalside and inside when opponents have possession.
- They have great speed and endurance.
- They take up strategic covering positions when the opponents have possession on the opposite side of the field.
- They are adept long passers.
- They can close down opponents without overcommitting.
- They know when to challenge and when to delay.

Wide midfielders defend a long and narrow space on the side of the field, some 70 to 80 yards long and 10 to 20 yards wide. If they can, they should try getting into a good defensive position—goalside and inside—immediately before their team loses the ball. Wide midfielders are normally required to cover a large area of the field, so they must maintain a high level of speed and endurance.

## Attacking Midfielders (Playmakers)

I am reluctant to use the term "attacking midfielder" because this term often presupposes that such a player does not defend. On the contrary, every player on the team has an obligation to work hard to regain ball possession. I too often find so-called attacking midfield players and forwards standing around expecting others on the team to win the ball back.

### Attacking Midfielder Skills and Attributes

The best attacking midfielders have the following attributes:

- They share in their team's defensive organization.
- They can force the opposition to play down the channels.
- They are extremely fit.
- They are psychologically tough.
- They can tackle and take tackles without protestation.

The greatest defensive skill that an attacking midfielder (playmaker) will show is the ability to calculate whether the forwards should press and harass to regain ball possession, or whether they should drop back and regroup with the other members of their team.

## Forwards

According to the coaches of the world's top teams, the forwards are a team's first line of defense. A great deal of merit resides in this belief because a soccer team can more easily defend against a team that is forced to play down one channel of the field. If the forwards can harass the opposing defensive players and prevent them from passing the ball back and forth across the field, then all

the players behind the forwards can more easily work out the channel where the ball will likely be advanced. All the players behind the forwards—midfielders, stoppers, marking backs, sweeper, and goalkeeper—can adjust their positions depending on how the forwards force the play.

### Forwards Skills and Attributes

Top-class forwards have the following attributes:

- They are prepared to help their team on defense.
- They know how to challenge and when to commit.
- They know how to position themselves to take away the opponent's options.
- They know how to mark space.
- They know how to delay.
- They anticipate well and have excellent reaction speed.
- They have the ability to disguise their defensive intentions.

Forwards are expected to score most of their team's goals, but in the modern game they are also expected to play their part in defending.

## UNDERSTANDING DEFENSIVE RESPONSIBILITIES

I usually concentrate on coaching all the players on the team to think defensively without the ball. Forwards should understand that they are the first line of defense, and all marking and covering positions behind them are dictated by their defensive posture (or lack of it). Forwards should also recognize that the way in which they force the play dictates to a large extent the positions that their defenders take in marking and covering.

All players must understand that when the ball is lost, the opposing player in possession has only three options—shoot, dribble, or pass. If your team loses the ball in your attacking third (their defensive third), a shot at your goal is highly unlikely, which leaves but two options—dribble or pass. Defenders are taught not to take risks in their defensive third of the field, so an attempt at dribbling through (with the possibility of being stripped of the ball) is also improbable. The only option left is to pass the ball. Defensive positioning in this area can play a vital role in winning the ball back. That is, if players cut off the passing lanes, they increase their chances of reacquiring the ball. In other words, if the player with the ball has three passing options and if your players take away two of them, then the next touch on the ball becomes predictable. Your players may be able to intercept the ball easily; if not, they can put immediate pressure on the targeted player.

In my opinion, defensive positioning is the most significant defensive skill you can teach. Defending players should know where to place themselves relative to opponents, teammates, and the ball at any given time. Sadly, positioning is not often thoroughly understood, and therefore its teaching is neglected.

In most instances, the position of a defending player should be goalside and inside the immediate opponent. Goalside is a position between the immediate opponent and the defending player's goal; inside is a position between an imaginary line drawn from goal to goal and a line drawn from the immediate opponent toward the defending player's goal. Most young players understand what you mean by being goalside of their opponent, but many have difficulty in understanding what you mean by being on the inside line. In my experience, I find that most young players mark too tightly, too soon.

Another key factor in defending is the distance between the defending player and the immediate opponent relative to what is happening on the ball. The defender should take up a position based on these factors: How far away is the ball? Who has the ball? Which way is the player in possession facing? In general, the farther away the ball, the greater the distance between the defending

player and the opponent; likewise, the nearer the ball, the closer the distance between the defending player and the opponent.

Overlaps, late runs, and combination play easily penetrate a flat defense. Defending in a triangle, or a diamond, avoids those dangers. It is crucial for the defense, especially the sweeper, to be able to adjust the depth of the triangle (it all depends on the opponent's skill to penetrate).

## Triangle

The sweeper, the marking backs, and the forwards all have defensive responsibilities. The sweeper and the marking backs should understand the need for defending in a triangular shape, whereas the forwards must realize that their defensive actions dictate the actions of the rest of the team.

The optimum defensive shape for the sweeper and the two marking backs is a triangle with the free defender—the sweeper—forming the apex of the triangle (figure 7.3). Defenders should get into a solid defensive shape before their attackers lose the ball. We too often find defenders watching the game, waiting until their team turns over the ball before organizing their defensive positions; by then, it is usually too late. The goalkeeper and the sweeper should, of course, take most of the responsibility of organizing the two marking backs into an optimum defensive shape.

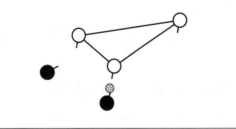

**Figure 7.3**  The triangle.

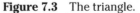

Closer examination of the positions adopted by Black 7 and Black 11 in figure 7.4 shows that when players take up triangular positions, they increase their passing possibilities. The more the positions form a wide triangle, the greater the passing possibilities

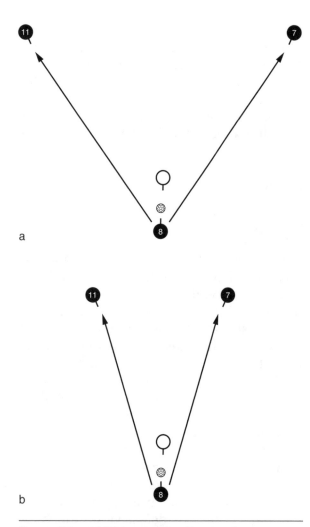

**Figure 7.4**  *(a)* Wide triangle offers good passing angles. *(b)* Narrow triangle increases interception possibility.

(figure 7.4a); conversely, the narrower the triangle becomes, the more likely the pass will be intercepted (figure 7.4b).

## Distances and Angles

In a double-team situation, the distance and angles between the challenging player and the covering player are critical. If they are too far apart, then it is possible for the opponent to evade the challenger (or even stumble) yet still have time to recover and take on the covering player. Conversely, if the distance between the challenging player and the covering player is too tight, then it is

possible for the opponent to beat both players with the same move or dribble.

The sweeper (covering defender) naturally has a bigger role in the team than merely double-teaming. The sweeper's biggest problem arises when an unmarked opposing midfield player has the ball and is running at the defense. The sweeper can resolve this crisis in one of two ways, either by coming forward to challenge the opposing midfielder or by instructing one of the marking backs to step forward to challenge while the sweeper steps up to mark.

## BASIC OFFENSIVE POSITIONS

For every defensive aim or objective, the offense will have an equal or opposite aim or objective; therefore, every player should have a role in the offensive aim or objective. It may be that you require the team's principal defenders—goalkeeper, sweeper, marking backs, and stoppers—to deliver early penetrative passes over and behind the opposing defense when they are pushing up too far and playing square across the field. This scenario would allow the team's forwards or attacking midfielders to run onto the passes in the space behind the opposing defense. On the other hand, perhaps the team should look for overload situations along the wings in which the wide midfielders take on the opposing player in one-on-one confrontations; or perhaps the central midfielders could overlap on the wide midfielders. Such situations should create numerous opportunities to cross the ball across the face of the opponent's goal. But perhaps the most overwhelming offensive aim or objective is to control the setup area nearest the opponent's goal to create frequent goal-scoring chances (see figure 10.4 in chapter 10).

Each player on a soccer team has attacking responsibilities when in possession of the ball. Coaches therefore need to take a look at the general attributes needed to launch a successful attack, and they need to examine position-specific skills as well.

# Forwards

Teams use three, four, five, or six players to try to control the setup areas. This arrangement usually means that they will play with three, two, or one forward. When a team plays with one forward, that forward is regarded as a primary striker. Most successful teams have a primary striker and a withdrawn striker. A team with two primary strikers and no withdrawn striker will have difficulties in developing attacking combinations. Similarly, a team with two withdrawn strikers and no primary striker will have difficulties in penetrating the opposing defense.

## Forward Skills and Attributes

Here are some of the skills and attributes of successful forwards:

- They have the creative genius to work out any weakness—bad marking, poor covering, lack of speed, and so forth—in the opposing defense, and they can exploit it.
- They can play with their backs to the opponent's goal, yet they will know precisely the position of every player on the field.
- They have great ball control.
- They are wonderful dribblers.
- They have a burning desire to score goals.
- They have the nerve of a bullfighter, and they are icy cool when in goal-scoring positions.
- They gamble on getting in behind the opposing defense.
- They have an uncanny knack of timing runs to escape their markers.
- They can shoot accurately with either foot.
- They are excellent headers of the ball.

The primary forward is often regarded as the most important player on the team. She is expected to lead the offense and score the majority of the team's goals. When a team has a successful primary forward, it usually will enjoy great results. The primary forward needs to be able to do each of the following.

**Stay up on the line of the sweeper.** The easiest way to beat any defense is to make a penetrative pass into the space behind the opposing defense. The forwards who do not stay up close to the line of the sweeper will be handicapped in the race for any through pass into the space behind the opposing defense. The forward should seek to gain every possible advantage by playing in a position that is almost offside. No matter how many defenders are deployed in the opposing team's defensive lineup, the forward will be required to outrun only the farthest one back, usually the opposing sweeper.

**Make runs behind the defense.** The most difficult run to make is the one behind the defense. That run should begin with a slow jog across the face of the defense, and it should then turn into a sudden sprint into the space diagonally behind the defense, just before the ball passer plays the ball. The forward should always maintain eye contact with the ball, never turning her back to the ball passer. The forward's objective is to be able to run diagonally into the space behind the defense while turning the head to view the ball.

To develop proficiency at making runs behind the defense, the forward should practice making runs for the ball on northwest, northeast, southwest, and southeast directions. The forward needs to avoid running in the east or west directions (across the field). The reason is that the defenders remain goalside in such situations, and the forward will end up receiving the ball while facing the touchline. The forward should also avoid running directly north because doing so makes it difficult for a teammate to pass accurately to the forward (and it would also be difficult for the forward to keep eye contact with the ball passer). Running directly south, or straight at the ball passer, presents difficulties as well because the forward will have her back to the defender and thus have greater problems choosing the next move.

**Avoid being outnumbered.** Getting a quick glance over the shoulder when coming to the ball will better inform forwards when they make their next decision. Doing so allows them to see the exact positioning of the defenders.

**Show quickness with excellent ball control.** One of the most important attributes of quality forwards is that they are quick with sound ball control. They need not be fast over 40 yards or more, but they should be quick from a stationary position to a point 5 to 10 yards away. They need proficient ball control to go with a burst of acceleration. They must also learn to ease into a ball-receiving position and decelerate to maintain a balanced posture.

**Anticipate well.** Without question, the most important attribute of good forwards is that they anticipate well and have an eye for goal-scoring opportunities. Many mediocre forwards stand and wait for their chances to score, whereas the best forwards go to the ball and make their chances happen.

# Withdrawn Striker

That some of the most famous players in the history of soccer were withdrawn strikers is no coincidence. Pele, Maradona, Platini, Baggio, DeStefano, Puskas, Keegan, Dalglish, and Cruyff are but a few that have played as withdrawn strikers. The demands of playing such a role are high, but a player who emerges with the talent necessary is usually stunningly successful.

### Withdrawn Striker Skills and Attributes

The attributes and skills required of a withdrawn striker are as follows:

- The withdrawn striker must be totally aware of all other players, teammates, and opponents, not only in the line of vision but also in the space behind him.
- The withdrawn striker attempts to exploit the space behind the opposing team's midfield.
- He must have an uncanny knack of timing runs to positions where and when teammates can pass the ball to him. The withdrawn striker is likely to be heavily marked.
- The withdrawn striker must be able to turn quickly over either shoulder and accelerate, usually preceding the turn with a fake.
- The withdrawn striker must be a supreme ball passer.
- He should be an adept dribbler and should be able to hold up the ball in crowded situations.
- The withdrawn striker should be an accurate shooter.
- He must recognize one-three opportunities, often called third player running combinations.

In short, the withdrawn striker exploits the space between the opponent's midfield and defense. Because that is the space that gets stretched out, especially by teams that make slow transitions, the use of the withdrawn striker can be quite effective.

# Midfielders

Soccer demands that midfield players have several attributes for success, and it is unlikely that any player will adequately fulfill all the requirements. For instance, in a 3-5-2 system, the midfield might play with two stoppers (or defensive midfielders) and one attacking midfielder (playmaker), or they might play with one stopper (defensive midfielder) and two attacking midfielders (playmakers). The demands made on a single stopper are different from those made on a stopper who is playing alongside another stopper. Similarly, the demands made on a single attacking midfielder are different from those made on an attacking midfielder who is playing alongside another attacking midfielder. Regardless, the demands made on the wide midfielders are fairly consistent, no matter how the center midfield is organized.

## Stoppers

When an opposing midfielder takes possession of the ball in front of the defense, any sweeper or marking back faces enormous problems. A player in this position can either play penetrative passes into the space behind the defense or run at the defense with the ball at her feet. The stopper's primary role is to prevent such a situation from developing. She does so by defending the space in front of the marking backs while providing defensive cover to the midfield. Effective stoppers need to be alert and need to anticipate dangerous developments early. Much depends on the stopper's performance because the stopper is in a position to be constantly involved in the heart of the game.

### Skills and Attributes of a Single or Double Stopper

All the attributes of the single stopper should be present in the double stopper. Furthermore, a double stopper should learn to play with her co-stopper and should share defensive and offensive responsibilities.

- The stopper should have sound positional sense to cut off the passing lanes to the opposing forwards.
- The stopper should be an effective leader and should communicate with players in front of her to ensure that the team takes a solid defensive shape.
- She should relish defensive responsibilities and should be prepared to anchor the midfield.
- The stopper should be a precise header of the ball.
- She should be a reliable and safe ball passer.

The stopper is really a sweeper behind her own midfield. Any player who is coming into (or any ball that is being played through) the stopper's space is her responsibility. If the position is played correctly, the stopper can relieve much of the pressure from the marking defenders and sweeper.

## Attacking Midfielders (Playmakers)

Intelligent, skillful attacking midfielders are a nightmare to opposing defenses. Their daring one-on-ones can leave a defense outnumbered, and their accurate penetrating passes into the scoring area can create scoring opportunities galore. They are the generals of the attacking forces. Fans love the excitement and thrills they bring to the match.

What is great about attacking midfielders is that they can adjust to the demands of the position, should the system of play change. For example, in a 3-5-2 formation, a team might play with either one or two attacking midfielders. In a 4-4-2 formation, one of the two central midfield players will be designated as the attacking midfield player, or they will pivot on each other while sharing defensive and offensive responsibilities.

### Attacking Midfielder Skills and Attributes

No matter which formation or system of play you use, attacking midfielders should have the following attributes:

- They should be incisive front-foot, outside-of-the-foot passers of the ball into the areas behind the opposing defense.
- They should be able to turn quickly, using feints and changes of speed. It is more than likely that these players will be below average in height, with low centers of gravity.
- They should possess a quality shot from either foot.
- They should be efficient dribblers of the ball and should always be prepared to go at the opposing defense.
- They should be adept at playing one-twos or give-and-goes.

- They should have the ability to ghost in behind defenses.
- They should be effective communicators, and when possession is lost, they should instruct the players in front of them to force the play to a particular side of the field.

## Wide Midfielders

Wide midfielders are the workhorses of the team. They usually attack and defend in a relatively narrow area of the field, but the area is ever so long (from goal line to goal line).

In reality, the wide midfielders in a 3-5-2 system have to play three positions during the same match. Depending on who has the ball, where the ball is, and what is likely to happen next, they might have to play fullback, wide midfielder, or winger. Wide midfielders in a 4-4-2 system, however, do not have such stringent demands placed on them because they have the luxury of having a defender in the space behind them.

### Wide Midfielder Skills and Attributes

The main attributes of wide midfielders are as follows:

- They should take up wide marking positions that are dependent on where the opponent is and where the ball is.
- They should instruct their forwards where to force the opposing defense when they are in possession of the ball.
- They should have the speed and endurance to cover the length of the field.
- They should be able to cross the ball well.
- They should relish opportunities of running their immediate opponent in one-on-one situations.
- They should anticipate runs to the far-post area for any long crosses.

## SUMMARY

Simply put, soccer has three major components: physical condition, technique, and tactics. A player who is not physically fit will have a difficult time mastering the fundamental techniques of soccer. Without technically developed players, time spent on tactics will be wasted time.

Fundamental technique development is a dynamic process; it is forever ongoing. No matter how skilled players are, they always have room for improvement. Fundamental technique development must therefore be part of each and every practice. When planning and conducting your team's practices, keep the following in mind.

- Give special attention to positioning. It is the most important aspect of all defensive play.
- Emphasize that every player on the team without the ball should think and act defensively.
- Make it clear to the forwards that they are the first line of defense. Teach them to work in groups of two or three, rather than on their own.
- Work with the forwards to further develop their explosive speed, ball control, and ability to anticipate what's going to happen next.
- Spend extra time with your withdrawn strikers. Emphasize improving vision, improving awareness, and exploiting the space behind the opponent's midfield.
- Develop the positional sense of your stoppers. Make sure the stopper communicates constructively. Work on heading and passing skills.
- Contribute to the effectiveness of your attacking midfielders by developing their awareness and leadership skills. Also work on dribbling, passing, and shooting.
- Teach the wide midfielders to recognize transition early.

# Chapter 8

# TEACHING DEFENSIVE SKILLS AND TECHNIQUES

For a team to develop offensive skills to a high level without first encountering a stern defense is impossible. The offense need only be slightly better than the defense for the offense to succeed. The better the defense, the better the offense has to be.

Every coach should therefore spend as much time on teaching defensive skills and techniques as he does on offensive skills and techniques. I have observed other coaches in practice sessions, and I am amazed at how they persevere with coaching offense when there is little opposition or none at all. Introducing new techniques and tactics with little or no defense is surely necessary, but the ultimate test is whether the players can succeed against a good, solid defense.

---

### Tips for Teaching Defensive Skills and Techniques

- Constantly reinforce the belief that some of the world's greatest soccer players have been defenders—Bobby Moore, Franz Beckenbauer, Franco Baresi, Paulo Maldini, Carlos Alberto, and so forth.

- Insist that all players take their part in any defensive plan.

- Spend at least 50 percent of practice time on defensive skills and tactics.

- Introduce practice activities and competitions whereby the winners are the ones who do the best defensively (e.g., concede the fewest goals).

- Reward players and teams who have been the most successful in accomplishing defensive tasks.

## MARKING AND COVERING

No player can become a solid defender unless she understands the positional requirements of marking and covering an opponent. In most cases, the player will need to mark in a goalside and inside position. The farther the player is away from the ball, the "looser" the player's marking position will be. That is, the player must be able to see the ball and the immediate opponent (as well as any other dangerous opponents), in addition to any teammates the player can communicate with. In figure 8.1, White 2 is the farthest player from the ball and can take up a loose marking position, goalside and inside of Black 11. This player is in a position to encourage White 5 and White 6 to tighten their marking positions on Black 9 and Black 10 because the whole field of play can be seen

from the position adopted. This player can also encourage the sweeper, White 4, to take up a covering position on White 6.

Defenders sometimes mark in a straight line between the ball and their goal, particularly if the ball is being played down the center of the field. Consider the situation presented in figure 8.2. If the attacker turns his back on the defender and if the defender positions out of sight and out of touching distance, then the forward will have little awareness of the defender's next action. This defensive position is often taken by defenders when they confront a fast forward who has weak ball skills. The defender can then close down the attacker after the latter has received the ball. This situation is one whereby the stopper can challenge the player with the ball from the other side—in other words, "sandwich" him (see figure 8.3).

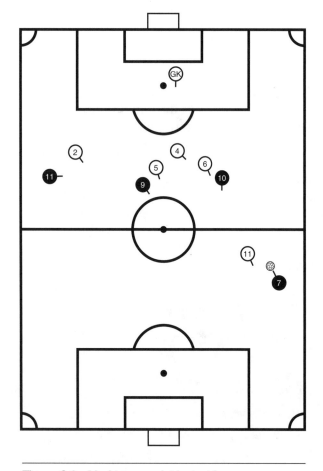

**Figure 8.1**   Marking—goalside, inside.

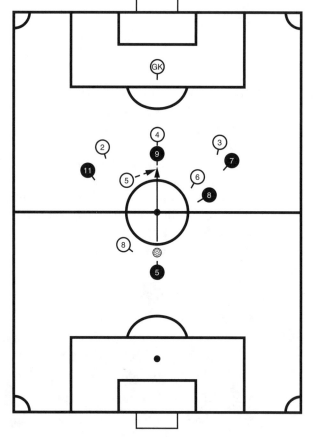

**Figure 8.2**   No awareness.

**Figure 8.3**   Sandwich.

At other times, defenders mark shoulder to shoulder or slightly in front of their immediate opponent, particularly if they are confident that a covering player will cut off any through passes behind them (see figure 8.4). In figure 8.5, White 2 is not only failing to mark goalside but is also taking up a position on the outside of Black 9. This marking position is often taken up by defenders who know that Black 9 is not a fast forward and is one who prefers to "come to" the ball, rather than run into spaces behind the defense. This modification of the usual marking positions of goalside and inside is noticeable at many defensive throw-in situations (see figure 8.5). In figure 8.6, Black 2 is marking White 11 goalside and outside with a confidence that Black 6 is in a covering position to prepare against the ball that is being thrown inside of White 11.

The following small-sided games are useful for developing marking and covering skills.

**Figure 8.4**   Marking shoulder to shoulder.

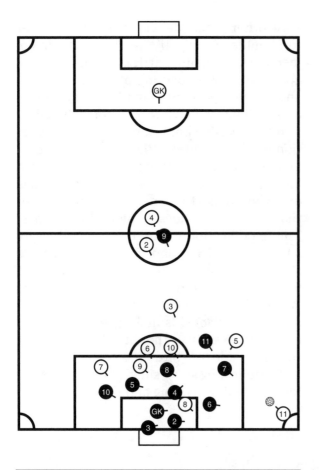

**Figure 8.5**   Marking—front and outside.

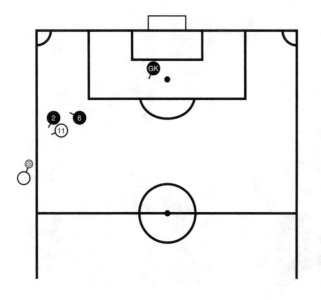

**Figure 8.6**   Marking at throw-ins.

# On Your Own

**Purpose:** To increase understanding of marking and covering.

**Procedure:** One-on-one, plus goalkeeper in each half of the field (40 yards by 20 yards). All players are restricted to their own half of the field. A goalkeeper serves the ball to his defender, who is allowed to play it unopposed to the attacker in the other half of the field, who is closely marked by the opposing defender (see figure 8.7).

**Coaching Point**

• The coach should focus on the defensive player in the half of the field without the ball to help prepare that player for when the ball is played into his area. This defensive player should fully understand the strengths and weaknesses of the immediate opponent:

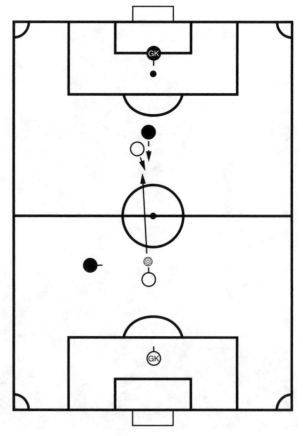

**Figure 8.7**   On your own.

- Is this opponent fast?

- Does this opponent look for passes behind the defender, or is this a player who comes to the ball? Does this opponent have a favorite move?

- Is the opponent right- or left-footed?

- Which way does this player like to turn with the ball?

If the defensive player knows the answers to these questions, then he can take up an appropriate defensive marking position to nullify the opponent's strengths through either interception of the pass or through challenge and containment (jockeying).

# Us and Them

**Purpose:** To develop concept of marking and covering.

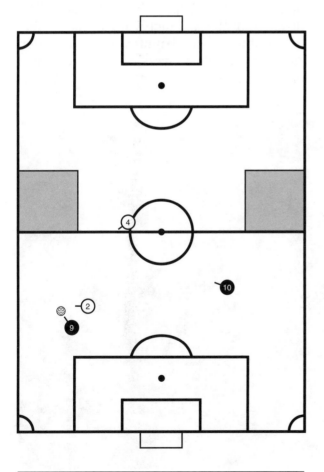

**Figure 8.8** Us and them.

**Procedure:** Two attacking players with a ball try to beat two defenders to take the ball under control into either shaded area (see figure 8.8).

**Coaching Point**

- The coach should encourage the challenging defender White 2 to force the play toward either corner of her grid square (shaded area). White 2 should adopt a defensive position that restricts the Black 9's possibilities to either pass to Black 10 or to dribble. In this situation White 2 has decided to cut off the pass by forcing Black 9 to dribble into White 4's covering position in the shaded area.

# Group Cover

**Purpose:** To develop concept of marking and covering.

**Procedure:** Four defenders and a goalkeeper against three attackers in a half-field (see figure 8.9). The coach provides multiple soccer balls. Three defenders—White 2, 4, and 6—mark on a player-to-player basis while White 5 plays as a covering player (sweeper).

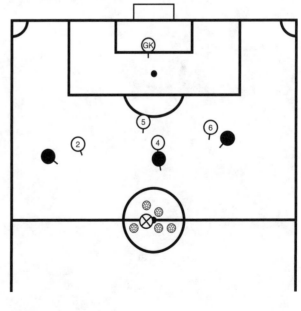

**Figure 8.9** Group cover.

### Coaching Points

• The marking defenders should be encouraged to mark so that they can either intercept, challenge, or contain.

• The sweeper should be encouraged to figure out when and where to double-team and when to stay in a covering position.

## INTERCEPTING PASSES

Whichever type of pass is made to the forwards, the principles involved in the earlier practices still apply. Defenders should almost always position themselves between their opponents and their goal, and where possible they should intercept, challenge, or contain when their immediate opponent is likely to receive a pass. Defenders should also ensure that forwards never have the opportunity to collect the ball in the space behind them. Thus, if an attacking player is served a through ball to run on to, the defending player should ensure a position so that he can get to the ball before the attacking player (see figure 8.10). The defend-

ing player can then either pass it back to the goalkeeper to clear or personally clear the danger by putting the ball out of play. On no account should the defending player attempt to turn with the ball. If a defender takes an unnecessary risk in his own penalty area, then the defense becomes unsafe.

A penetrative pass, which is played deep into the heart of the defense, can cause defenders major problems because most goals are scored from within the space behind the defense. Every defender must therefore be continuously alert to prevent the immediate opponent from running on to a through ball passed into the scoring area. The method of overcoming this problem might be a contradiction of our earlier coaching points. A defender that is marking an opponent who may receive a through ball should not mark skintight; rather, that defender should be in close contact with the immediate opponent on a line between himself and the goal. The distance of this contact will vary according to the ability and attributes of the defender. As a general rule, players can use a distance of one or two yards.

**Figure 8.10**   Intercepting a pass.

In figure 8.11, White 5 is expecting Black 9 to receive a through pass. White 5 lays off Black 9 sufficiently enough to ensure that, should a through pass be made, White 5 will have a one- or two-yard start on Black 9 when the ball is played through. This distance of one or two yards also ensures that White 5 can stand back to get a clear view of the events as they unfold; that is, White 5 is not too far away in the event that Black 9 decides to check back to collect a short pass. If alert, White 5 can still move up quickly enough to prevent Black 9 from turning with the ball.

Coaches need to suggest ways in which defenders can cope with two-on-one situations. Defenders should know that two main courses of action are always open to players in possession of the ball that will cause them any real concern: first, when the forward with the ball dribbles past her, and second, when the ball is passed to the second forward to take on and shoot. If either of these movements are performed successfully and quickly, then the forwards have a solid chance of scoring. The defender's first concern, therefore, is to slow down the attackers so that her teammates have time to get back to cover. Merely retreating toward her own goal may prove to be sufficient

enough to slow down the two attackers. The defender can also slow down the attackers by encouraging them to pass early so that two or more passes might be made before the defender has to commit to a challenge. The more passes the forwards make, the greater the chance of their losing control, thus the more time they will take in getting past the defender.

Sound advice for any defender caught in a two-on-one situation, especially if quick off the mark, is to get position in such a way that only one course of action is left open to the ball player. For instance, in figure 8.12, White 5 has established position in such a way that it is difficult for Black 9 to make a quality pass to Black 10. White 5 is practically inviting Black 9 to attempt to beat him, knowing that he stands a good chance of tackling Black 9 when the attempt is made. White 5 is already half-turned to make a quick start for the ball if it is pushed past him. White 5 also has the advantage of knowing that Black 9 has farther to run. Therefore, all White 5 has to do is kick the ball to safety.

Again, the defender might decide to establish position in such a way that would make it difficult for the Black 9 to beat him. In this case, White 5 would invite Black 9 to pass the ball to the Black 10, then White 5 could

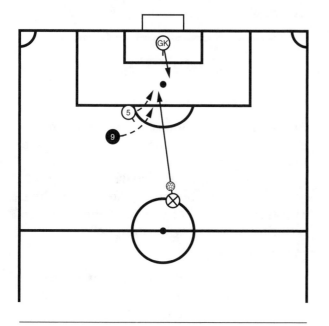

**Figure 8.11** Feed the runner.

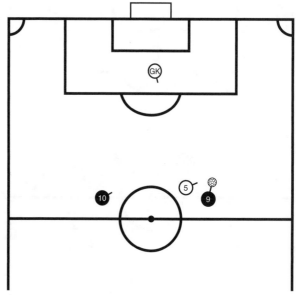

**Figure 8.12** Cut off the pass.

quickly move across to force Black 10 on the left foot and away from goal (see figure 8.13). White 5 may very well get away with this course of action, especially if Black 10 is technically weak and has a poor first touch; or if Black 9's pass is too strong for Black 10 to take in stride, thus making the ball go out too wide to the left of Black 10.

The best possible advice that can be given to a defender placed in a two-on-one situation just outside the scoring area is this: Prevent such situations from arising in the first place. Do not go for the ball with a desperate, lunging tackle, but invite the forwards to pass to each other and then cut off the passing lane to force the ball handler to dribble.

In the two-on-two situation illustrated in figure 8.14, solid defenders adjust their play by having White 4 take up a defensive covering position that allows an interception of any bad pass from Black 6. Thus, White 4 prevents a return or through pass from Black 8 to Black 6.

At the same time, White 10 resists the temptation to follow the pass. White 10 therefore concentrates on tracking down Black 6 if she makes a forward run. If need be, White 10 should turn to face Black 6 and run with

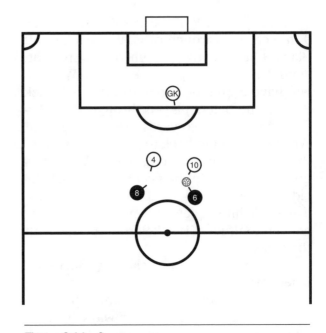

**Figure 8.14**   Cover.

her, even at the expense of losing sight of the ball. This tracking down action by White 10 forces Black 6 to run wider and farther to get into the space behind White 10.

"Stay with the runner" should therefore be an essential coaching message for any defender in a two-on-two situation. To help players focus on this aspect of defense, the following small-sided game provides a quality practice at intercepting passes.

## Under Siege

**Purpose:** To improve defensive techniques.

**Procedure:** The game is played in an area of 50 by 20 yards with goals. The area is divided in two halves, with three defenders, two attacking players, and a goalkeeper in each half. No player may cross the halfway line. The three defenders can play with either a covering player or with a stopper.

**Coaching Points**

• Encourage the marking players to do the following: mark closely on the inside line between the ball and the goal; prevent

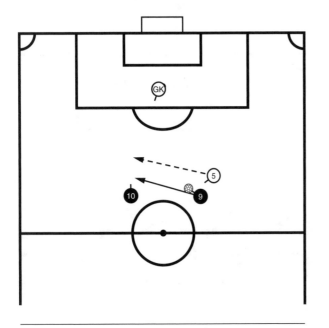

**Figure 8.13**   Delay by forcing the pass.

attackers turning with the ball; challenge aggressively whenever possible; track down any runs made by their immediate opponent; communicate with the stopper.

• Encourage the stopper to anticipate the service; get into the line of flight early; obey the instructions of the defenders behind him; move quickly to challenge any attacking player receiving the ball.

• Encourage the covering player (sweeper) to cut off all through passes; give early cover to the challenging player (i.e., double team); obey the goalkeeper; communicate with fellow defenders.

# TACKLING

A defender must have the ability to mark an opponent far enough away to be first to the through ball and still be in position to intercept or tackle when the short pass is played. The time spent in showing defenders how closely to mark (and where and in what circumstances to tackle for the ball) is often of far greater importance to any defense than instruction in the techniques of tackling. Of course, it is still necessary for defenders to be able to tackle correctly when they decide to do so, but instruction in the techniques of tackling should only be given when weaknesses naturally arise out of game situations.

In a front block tackle, the player's center of gravity should be low. If he is tackling the ball with the right foot, the player should lead with the right shoulder. The player should try to get as much of the foot and leg behind the ball as possible. At the last moment, the player should either push the ball through or lift it over the opponent's foot (see figure 8.15).

Although the slide tackle is usually a last desperate attempt to play the ball, it is nevertheless an important part of a player's skill. If not performed correctly, however, both players risk injury. The leg and foot on top should always tackle the ball. If the

**Figure 8.15**  Block tackle.

lower leg and foot are used, the upper leg may be above the ball—and that could be dangerous.

In the beginning stages of this practice, the defender should be given a definite advantage in reaching the ball first, and no body contact should be allowed. Coaches should take precautions against overdoing this practice, especially on hard, firm surfaces in the summer months when players can suffer severe grass burns. Players should wear long track-suit pants for this practice, and the coach should seek a soft, grassy surface.

As a development, players should strive to keep possession rather than merely kick the ball away or out of play. The defender should raise his foot slightly off the ground and hook it around the ball to form a block. The attacker's momentum might carry him over the blocked ball, allowing the defender time to regain position with the ball under control (see figure 8.16).

**Figure 8.16**   Slide tackle.

## Block Tackle Duel

**Purpose:** To improve the technique of tackling.

**Procedure:** Two players stand facing each other on either side of a line on which a ball is placed. On the signal, they both go for the ball by executing a block tackle. As a variation, ask that each player take one step toward the ball or start three yards away.

**Coaching Point**

• The coach should encourage the players to sink at the hips and knees to form a solid base, as well as push hard through the contact foot.

## Slide Tackle Show

**Purpose:** To improve the technique of slide tackling.

**Procedure:** Two players position in a 10-yard-by-10-yard square with one ball. One player pushes the ball ahead and runs after it. The opponent chases the first player and executes a sliding tackle to knock the ball over the sideline.

**Coaching Point**

• The coach should encourage the defender to go down on his side while breaking the fall with his hand or reach for the ball with his foot and hit it with the instep (or even the toe).

## DEFENSIVE SHAPE AND BALANCE

The defensive shape of the center midfield trio is usually achieved by the nearest player's challenging and the other two's covering. In such a balanced, center-midfield defense we can detect two distinct shapes: first, a triangle, as shown in chapter 7, where the challenging player is covered by two colleagues; second, a dogleg, where one of the midfield defenders is covered by the other two (see figure 8.17).

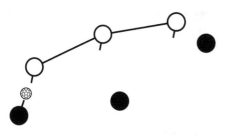

**Figure 8.17**   Dog-leg.

The coach should encourage the midfielders to mark their immediate opponent so that whenever the opponent gets the ball, they can step up the pressure. The coach should also instruct the midfielders to force any opponent in possession of the ball away from goal or across the field. The coach should encourage the sweeper to do the following: decide how far back to retreat or advance; cut off all dangerous avenues for through passes; cover any defender threatened by an opponent with the ball; challenge any opposing midfielder in possession while running at the defense; and communicate with and fine-tune the positional play of his marking backs. The goalkeeper should cover the space behind the defense and communicate with the players in front of her by fine-tuning their marking positions and alerting them to any possible dangers.

In addition to learning defensive plays as a trio, players should also receive plenty of opportunities of practicing one-on-one situations. For instance, in figure 8.18, Black 9 has received the ball with only White 5 between her and the goal. If White 5 is beaten, then Black 9 has an excellent scoring chance.

White 5 should be content to contain Black 9 until one or more of her fellow defenders get back to cover. White 5 should have closed the gap between herself and the forward while the ball is being played to the forward. This situation does not call for White 5 to rush in at the forward because there is no easier defender to beat than the one who comes charging in. If the ball has been played to Black 9 (who has her back to White 5), then White 5 should ensure that

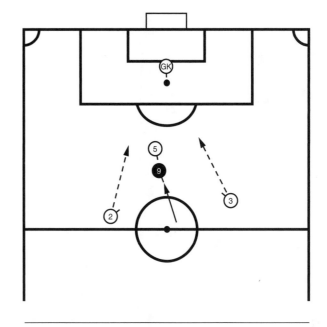

**Figure 8.18**   Contain and delay.

the Black 9 is not allowed to turn and attack the goal.

A forward can often make room, however, to turn and attack the defender. The defender's first thought should now be how to dispossess the forward, but the defender should not attempt to tackle until absolutely certain of winning the ball. If a defender is outside the scoring area, he can fall back in front of the forward. This position inevitably results in the forward slowing down, which not only makes the defender's task of winning the ball much easier but also gives time for other defenders to get back into covering position.

An intelligent defender will "invite" an opponent to dribble past her on one side. If the forward is a right-footed player, the defender should invite her to go past with the ball using the left foot, and vice versa. The stance adopted by the defender is often important, especially if the defender is near the scoring area or one of the touchlines. In figure 8.19, White 2 is facing Black 11 head on, which gives Black 11 the option of beating her on either side. If Black 11 beats White 2 on the inside, it may well lead to a goal being scored.

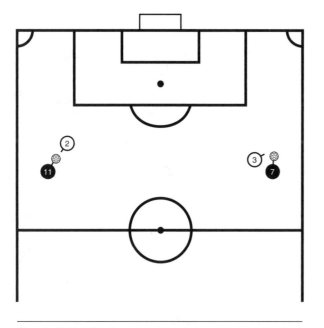

**Figure 8.19**  Forcing the play.

White 3, on the other hand, is inviting Black 7 to go down the line and is cutting off any possibility of Black 7 beating her on the inside. If Black 7 does try to beat her on the outside, the touchline almost becomes an additional defender because it restricts the space in which Black 7 has to play. All White 3 has to do then is kick the ball out of play.

A one-on-one situation within the scoring area poses many problems, the most obvious being that a defender cannot give a forward any space to move into, preventing him from shooting on the goal. The basic problem for a forward who receives the ball in the scoring area is therefore one of creating enough space and the right angle to shoot. Conversely, a defender must aim at denying the immediate opponent the time and space for shots at goal. In and around the scoring area, defenders must therefore mark their immediate opponents tightly.

A team that maintains its shape and provides balance on defense is difficult to penetrate. But, remember, the opposing team will always try to alter the shape and thus upset the balance. So—practice, practice, then practice some more. To help practice such tactics, the games that follow will help players develop an understanding of defensive shape and balance.

# Tactical Superiority

**Purpose:** To prepare teams to play against different formations.

**Procedure:** The Black team should play a 3-5-2 system and should be organized to play against a White team that is playing a 4-4-2 system (see figure 8.20). This organization should be designed for the Black team to dominate three vital areas:

- 2-on-2, in the offensive setup area, immediately in front of the opponent's goal;
- 3-on-2, in the center midfield area; and,
- 3-on-2, in the defensive area, in front of the goal.

This arrangement will leave the Black team with a negative two-on-one situation on each

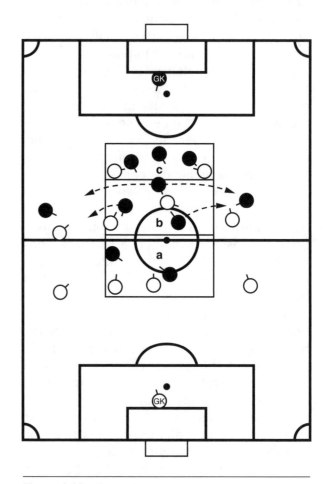

**Figure 8.20**  Tactical superiority.

wing, but a twin stopper can always counter this situation by sliding over. The three situations can be practiced in an appropriate-sized grid if the coach wishes to focus on improving the play of either an individual player or a small group of players.

# ONE-ON-ONE DEFENSE

If we are to base our defensive style of play on a player-to-player system, then our first task is to drill our marking backs into concentrating on their immediate opponent rather than on the ball. The main problem for any coach is to get players to concentrate sufficiently enough to mark their immediate opponent for a continuous length of time (see figure 8.21).

In player-to-player defense, the defender prioritizes his position to intercept the pass, to challenge and win the ball, and to mark tightly to contain an opponent by not letting him turn with the ball. The coach should insist that once a forward receives possession of the ball (while facing away from goal), the forward should not be allowed to turn. The defender should stay close to the forward without any contact. If the forward is foolish enough to turn, then the tackle should be made. Most forwards will mistakenly attempt to turn with the ball, even when a defender is breathing down his neck. This situation puts the forward at a great disadvantage. Whenever the forward turns, he will have a less stable base than the defender, who is in a position to make a strong tackle. In this scenario, some forwards will pass the ball back. This move will buy time for the defenders so that they can get more players back in defense.

If the ball is passed to a forward near the touchline, the defender should maintain a position between that forward and her own goal (see figure 8.22). Even if Black 7 or Black 11 receives the ball before the immediate defender gets a chance to intercept or tackle, the avenue of approach to the goal and into the area of greatest danger will be blocked. Thus, if the ball is passed to Black 11, she will be unable to move the ball to Black 9 or turn in time to take on White 2. Black 11's safest approach is back toward the coach or toward the touchline. Both of these approaches confront the defense with considerably fewer problems than if Black 11 were allowed to turn with the ball or even flick it to Black 9.

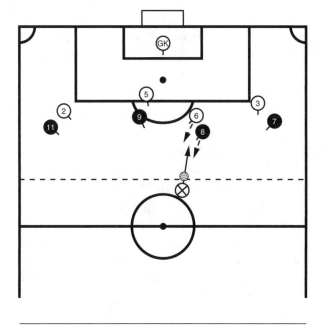

**Figure 8.21**  No-turn.

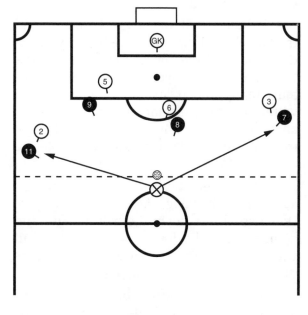

**Figure 8.22**  Take away options by defensive positioning.

The same principle applies to players in the central defensive areas of the field. They should take up a position between their own goal and their immediate opponent. They should also position themselves so that if the immediate opponent goes deep to collect the ball, they are able to force that opponent away from the scoring area. On no account should Black 8 or Black 9 be allowed to turn with the ball to face the White goal; they should be kept moving toward the touchline or back into their own half of the field.

Coaches should spend a great deal of time with their defenders on this particular aspect of play. They should insist that each defender concentrate on marking his opponent out of the game.

## Switch the Play

**Purpose:** To encourage players to change the direction of the attack.

**Procedure:** Four players and a goalkeeper against four players and a goalkeeper in a space of 20 yards by 40 yards, with two goals equally spaced along each 40-yard line. Teams can score on either of the opposite goals. The goalkeeper defends both goals.

### Coaching Points

• Demand that the nearest defender to the ball close down and force the play in one direction. Instruct the players to not allow the challenging players to drop off or take a frontal approach. Instead, each should get within touching distance of the ball player, and with instruction and communication from his covering players, force the play to one side of the field or backward.

• The covering players should encourage the challenging player to press hard. Doing so closes down the ball handler and demands that he force the ball either out wide or into the middle (where the ball goes depends on their covering positions).

• If there is no instruction from the covering players, then the challenging player must decide how to close down and in which direction to force the play. The covering players then take up their marking and covering positions from the cues presented by the challenging player.

• The goalkeeper should be fully involved in every play by assuming a position to cover the goal most likely to be attacked. The goalkeeper should communicate with the challenging defender and encourage her to force the play one way or the other. The goalkeeper should also make sure that the covering players take up solid covering positions on the challenging player.

• The challenging player should avoid following the ball in one-two play. The challenging player should stay with his opposing player and track him down when running into the space behind him.

## Hold It

**Purpose:** To improve players' understanding of "delay" in defense.

**Procedure:** Two attacking players with a ball try to beat two defensive players so that they can take the ball under control over the end line. As soon as the play commences, a third defensive player makes a recovery run to make a defensive unit of three players. The game continues until the Black attackers succeed, the ball goes out of play, or the White defenders win the ball (see figure 8.23).

### Coaching Points

• The coach should encourage the two defensive players: one to challenge, the other to cover. The former should not dive in with a reckless challenge unless she is 100 percent sure of winning the ball.

• After the challenging player (White 1) has closed down the ball handler, she should exercise patience and maintain a challenging position. White 1 should look to either cut off Black 1's pass to Black 2 or force Black 1 to pass to Black 2.

• As the covering player, White 2 should guide White 1 in the "closing down" process.

**End line**

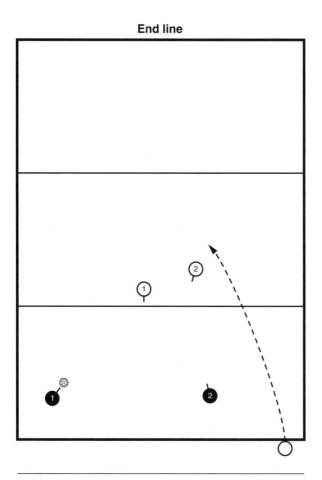

**Figure 8.23**   Hold it.

White 2 should indicate to White 1 which way she wants Black 1 to play the ball so that she can take up an appropriate cover position. The cover position will be dependent on White 1's challenging position and stance.

• Both defenders should be vigilant against a possible one-two play. White 1 should contest any run without the ball into the space behind her made by Black 1. White 2 should be prepared to step inside and prevent Black 2 from giving a return pass into the space behind White 1.

• The recovering defensive player should get back into a covering position by taking the shortest route back, communicate with fellow defenders, and form part of a defensive triangle after retreating into a covering position.

# One Up

**Purpose:** To focus on the advantage of an extra defender.

**Procedure:** Three players and a goalkeeper versus three players and a goalkeeper in an area 40 yards by 30 yards, with miniature goals. An extra player (marked in figure 8.24) always plays with the defending team.

**Coaching Points**

• The coach should demand that the free player recover into a covering position, adopt a solid covering angle and distance, and communicate with co-defenders.

• The challenging player should press the immediate opponent by closing him down and by forcing the play into the covering players. The challenging player should also

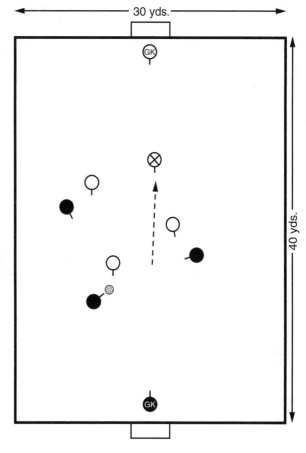

**Figure 8.24**   One up.

listen to instructions and commands from the covering players and goalkeepers.

# SUMMARY

This chapter highlights the following points to help you be a better teacher of defensive skills and techniques.

- Instruct your players regarding their defensive positioning immediately before or as the play develops, and help your players' decision making by identifying the cues in the play as it develops.

- Coach players off the ball. This practice is far more successful than trying to coach the players on the ball.

- Work with midfield players to show them when it is prudent to go forward and when it is safer to remain in a defensive position. This decision is dependent on what is happening on the ball and where the other players are positioned.

- Make it clear that all players must learn to understand and perform the defensive roles and responsibilities of all positions.

# Chapter 9

# TEACHING OFFENSIVE SKILLS AND TECHNIQUES

Coaching defense is concerned with repeated phases of play that constantly occur in the game, in different areas of the field, with two or more players. During the course of a match, the players have to recognize each of the following: danger signals of nonexistent-to-loose marking, inadequate cover, allowing the opposing ball player time and space on the ball, ball watching, failure to track down runners, and numbers-down situations. Coaching offense, however, is the exact opposite. Players should be made aware of the "cues in the display," which signal likely success for the offense. For example, does the opposing defense allow the ball player time and space? Do they have a slow player? Do they play "square" across the back line? Do some of their players "ball watch"? Is their goalkeeper a linekeeper, or does the goalkeeper patrol the area behind the defense? Is their midfield slow to recover into either goalside or ball-side positions? Do their players follow the ball at give-and-goes? Do either of their wide midfield players stay up field after each attack? Where do they defend? Can we exploit a numbers-up situation? And so on . . .

Practices should be designed to illustrate defensive deficiencies and to educate the players how to exploit weaknesses. Players must be physically conditioned and technically adequate to exploit any defensive weaknesses shown by the opposition. Coaches need to spend a lot of time and effort in developing a high level of technical ability in their players, particularly with players in the age group of 8 to 14 years. By the age of 14, a player must have mastery of the ball with all the different controlling surfaces of his body—that is, if he is to succeed at the next level. We too often find players with little technical ability spending their time and energy during a match chasing the ball. In such a situation, the ball becomes their master.

# BALL CONTROL

A player's first technical priority is to control the ball with the initial touch so that it allows him to carry out a chosen offensive technique with the second touch, whether it be to dribble, pass, or shoot. The easiest ball to control is probably the one that comes along the ground, straight at a player. As the ball is on its way, the receiving player should assess the next move by observing the positional play of teammates and opponents, not only in front but also to the side and behind him. The ball handler should disguise intentions by faking to take the ball one way while at the last moment taking it in the opposite direction. The technical speed of control and pass will be greatly increased if the player controls the ball with one foot and then immediately passes it with the other foot to a fellow teammate.

A ball that is arriving in the air at a player's feet is much more difficult to control. The key to successful control in this situation is for the receiving player to get to the ball's landing area early so that he can be poised and balanced at the moment of control. In general, ball handlers have two ways of controlling air passes with their feet. The first is to trap the ball with either the inside or the outside surface of the foot as the ball hits the ground (see figure 9.1). The second is to "catch" the ball on the instep, or the inside of the foot, and lower it gently to the ground (see figure 9.2).

A ball that is arriving in the air just below waist height should be controlled on or with the thigh. If the receiver's intended move includes running with the ball at speed, delivering a quick pass to a teammate, or firing a shot at goal, the receiver should "offer" her thigh to the ball at about a 45-degree angle. Then, a split second before contact, the player should withdraw the thigh so that the ball will drop gently to the ground, immediately in front of him. If the ball arrives in the air at waist height, the receiver might

**Figure 9.1**  Trapping.

**Figure 9.2**  Controlling.

also decide to "pop up" the ball off the thigh, which serves as a platform to lift the ball. This move gives the receiver time to assess offensive possibilities before the ball drops to the ground (see figure 9.3).

**Figure 9.3**  Thigh control.

If the receiver has to receive a ball at chest height, she might decide to angle her chest so that the ball quickly rebounds to the ground. In many cases, this maneuver becomes a heavy and long touch, with the ball running away from the receiver. A different way to control the ball with the chest is to offer it as a platform. A player can do so by leaning backward from the hips and expanding the chest by throwing the arms out sideways on contact. This move will make the ball pop up in the receiving player's immediate vicinity, thus allowing a quick, sometimes decisive, second touch.

The head is probably the most difficult controlling surface to use. Players must learn to use their head to bring the ball down to their feet when it is too high for them to use other controlling surfaces. The key is for the player to get to the ball's landing area early so that he can become balanced, poised, and ready for contact. Just before the ball hits his forehead, the player (while looking up) should bend at the knees to absorb the impact so that the ball drops gently to the ground. It helps if the player has his arms out sideways in a more balanced stance.

# KICKING

Without being able to kick the ball accurately and powerfully, no player can become an accomplished player. The more skilled the player is, the more kicks will reach their intended target. Such accuracy is required, not only when a player can kick the ball unchallenged, but also when a player is on the move; when a player has to receive the ball from an awkward angle; and when a player is challenged by an opponent or has restricted space near the sidelines or goal lines.

Kicks can become passes, shots, crosses, or clearances; their use is determined by the immediate tactical situation. The basic action of kicking is composed of the following parts:

1. The approach
2. The planting of the support foot (the nonkicking foot)
3. The backswing of the kicking foot
4. The contact of the foot and ball
5. The follow-through

## Kicking With the Inside of the Foot

A kick with the inside of the foot is the most frequently used kick in a game. It is the most effective for accurate, safe, and short passing because the largest possible foot surface comes in contact with the ball. The actual kicking surface is the part of the foot bordered by the base of the big toes: the front of the heel bone and the lower side of the inner ankle. During the final approaching stride before a kick, the leg of the kicking foot should be turned outward from the hip. The knee should then be slightly bent so that the sole of the foot is a few inches off the ground (see figure 9.4).

## Kicking With the Instep

The instep is the part of the foot that extends from the base of the toes to the curve of the ankle. In other words, it is the part of the foot that is covered by the laced part of the shoe.

**Figure 9.4**   Inside of the foot pass.

**Figure 9.5**   Instep kick.

To kick with the instep, the player needs to plant the nonkicking foot alongside of the ball so that the ball would travel between her legs (if permitted to do so). The player should point the planting foot toward the intended target. The swing of the kicking foot and the follow-through should be through the ball toward the intended target. The kicking leg should be swung loosely from the hip and bent at the knee as the foot is flung high as a result of the vigorous backswing of the thigh. The foot should be kept pointing slightly downward (see figure 9.5).

## Kicking With the Outside of the Foot

The outside of the foot is the area bordered by the base of the small toe along the outer edge of the instep to almost the outside of the ankle. To kick the ball with the outside of the foot, the player approaches the ball in one of two ways: straight on or with a slight turn. If the aim is to kick the ball in a straight-forward direction without any spin, the approach should be at a slight angle to the intended direction of flight. When the kick is taken with the right foot, the approach should be at a slight angle from the left (and

vice versa). If the objective is to swerve the ball, the approach run can be straight on. This approach makes it virtually impossible to turn the foot inward far enough for the horizontal axis of the foot to be perpendicular to the direction of the kick. The foot then comes into contact with the ball slightly off-center, and the result is a swerved trajectory of ball flight (see figure 9.6).

**Figure 9.6**   Outside of the foot pass.

## VOLLEYING

The technique of kicking the ball when it is in the air is seldom performed as well as kicking a rolling or stationary ball. It should not be neglected, however, because the opportunity for volleying the ball comes frequently in a game. Players can choose from three main types of volleys: the front volley, the half volley, and the side volley.

### Front Volley

In the front volley, the player should arrive at the point where the ball will land and prepare for contact. The player should approach the ball almost straight on, with a small backswing from the hip joint. The knee should be bent with the arms out sideways to keep a balanced position. He should watch the ball as it makes contact with the instep of her foot. The earlier he connects with the ball, the higher the swing of the kicking foot (thus, the higher the volley). The ball will be kept low if the player does the following: First, he lets the ball travel to a point directly in front and almost underneath him; and second, he contacts the ball with the instep, with the toe pointing down to the ground, after a short swing, with little or no follow-through (see figure 9.7). Similarly, a half volley occurs when the foot hits the ball at the exact moment that the ball hits the ground. Many keepers favor the half volley for distribution.

### Side Volley

The side volley is a much more difficult technique to execute. The ball either comes at the player or bounces near him, forcing a volley at waist height. A side volley is usually performed when a player doesn't have the time or space to let the ball come to the ground. The player should plant the supporting foot so that it points in the direction of the intended volley, with the knee slightly bent. The arms should be raised, with the leading arm pointing toward the intended target. He should face the ball or the flight path of the

**Figure 9.7**  A volley shot.

ball, almost chest-on, allowing him to raise the kicking leg as high as possible at the hip joint. The knee should be almost fully bent, with the foot primed for contact. The swing of the leg should begin at the hip, and the leg should be thrown out horizontally so that contact is made between the instep and a point just above the midline of the ball. The knee of the kicking leg should be above the ball at the point of impact (see figure 9.8).

## PASSING

Players will find it difficult to play the game successfully if they continually serve passes that are too soft, too hard, inaccurate, badly timed, or blatantly obvious. If players are to succeed in the modern game, they must become quality passers in confined situations. Remember that a good, solid pass has five distinct qualities: accuracy, speed or weight, controllability, disguise, and timing.

For obvious reasons, the pass must be accurate. To avoid interception, each pass must have the proper speed, often called weight. The receiver should have no difficulty in controlling the pass, and the pass must

**Figure 9.8**   Side volley.

be disguised to gain time for the passing player or receiver. Of course, the pass must always be well timed. The timing depends not only on the passer but also on the timing of the run made by the receiver.

The timing of the pass is probably the most difficult aspect of a quality pass. The timing is largely determined by the receiving player, who moves into position with his head up, just as the ball player is controlling the ball. Any runs made before the ball player has the ball under control are wasted; similarly, runs made too late, after the ball player is ready to pass, are largely wasted. The runs made by the receiving players should dictate the exact spot where they wish to receive the pass. They should try to catch the ball player's eye an instant after he has control of the ball and is in a position to pass it. The timing of the run and the use of body language should be a major part of coaching young players.

Let me share with you some of the small-sided, conditioned games I like to use to develop passing skills with my players.

## Sentry Soccer

**Purpose:** To improve passing skills.

**Procedure**: Four-on-four, in an area 30 yards by 20 yards. One player from each team (the sentry) patrols one of the end lines. The other three players on her team try to pass the ball to her. A goal is awarded for every successful pass to the sentry or for five consecutive passes between the other three players.

### Coaching Points

• Focus on the ball player's first touch. Encourage her to set the ball up so that she can complete the intended second touch.

• Demand that the two players in the attacking team without the ball take up positions where there is a clear line between them and the ball.

• Get their heads up whenever they have the ball.

# Keep Ball

**Purpose:** To improve passing skills.

**Procedure:** In a 30-yard-by-30-yard area, six attacking players (three plus three) play against three defensive players. Award a point for every 10 consecutive passes made by the six players. Whenever one of the three defenders touches the ball or forces it out of the area, all three change places with the three attacking players responsible for losing the ball.

## Coaching Points

• Encourage the six attacking players to spread out.

• Get them to look for opportunities to "switch" the play.

• Ask them to set the ball up on their first touch so that they can complete their second touch quickly and efficiently.

# Four Goals

**Purpose:** To improve passing skills.

**Procedure:** Six-on-six, with four goals, in an area 30 yards square. Each team defends two goals and attacks two goals. Use small goals, three yards wide, with no goalkeepers (see figure 9.9).

## Variations

• Three consecutive passes must be made before a shot.

• Score by scoring a traditional goal or by making six consecutive passes.

• The ball is never out of play, but scoring is only possible from in front of the goal.

## Coaching Points

• Look for the players to receive and turn with the ball.

• Players should make runs to support the ball player. The timing of the runs should

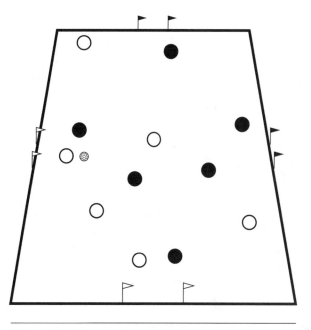

**Figure 9.9**   Four goals.

be just as the ball player receives the ball in the ball player's line of vision.

• Have players pass quickly and avoid running with the ball.

• Encourage the players to do the following: create sharp passing angles by getting a clear line between themselves and the ball; change the direction of the attack; set the ball up on the first touch; be aware of the positions of all other players.

# WALL PASSES

The nearer the player to the opponent's goal, the more accurate, well weighted, and disguised the pass must be. The area immediately in front of the opponent's goal is the land of give-and-goes, and players and teams should practice such techniques in realistic situations.

Wall passes, sometimes known as *one-twos* or *give-and-goes,* can be played in various parts of the field, but players are not encouraged to use them in the defensive third of the field. Profound differences exist between a wall pass played in midfield and a wall pass played in and around the scoring area.

A wall pass in midfield is essentially used in a two-on-two situation. The two attacking players try to get one of them in clear possession in the space behind the two midfield defenders. In figure 9.10, Black 6 has the ball and takes it under control toward White 10. Black 8 realizes that the wall pass is on and moves into a receiving position, thus timing his run to catch Black 6's attention. Black 8's run might well draw White 4 into a tight marking position, so it is important that Black 8 take up a final stance sideways onto White 4 where Black 8 can still see Black 6. If White 4 does not come into a tight marking position, then Black 8 might decide to turn with the ball toward the White goal.

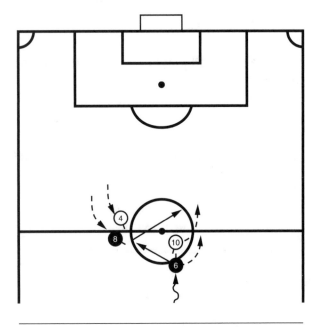

**Figure 9.10**   Give-and-go.

Notice that Black 8's final position allows him to receive the ball on the foot farthest from White 4. This position means that, even with poor control, Black 8 might retain possession of the ball by forming a wide screen between White 4 and the ball. Black 8 can therefore decide on one of several options if he receives the ball sideways onto a tight-marking White 4, where Black 8 can see him. First, Black 8 can play the ball the first time into the space behind White 10 and into Black

6's stride path. Second, Black 8 can hold the ball, wait for Black 6 to get behind White 10, then play the ball into his stride path. Third, Black 8 can take the pass, then spin on White 4 to take the ball into the space behind the midfield defense.

Black 6's role in playing the wall pass is important. Black 6 must approach White 10 at controlled speed to commit him. Then, disguising his intentions, Black 6 should play the ball just before White 10 can make a challenge. The easiest way to achieve this disguise is to play the ball off the front foot. The disguise will be even greater if the ball is flicked off the outside of the front foot, allowing Black 6 to continue running without breaking stride. White 10 will receive advance warning of Black 6's intentions if he tries to play it off his back foot.

Black 6 should concentrate on delivering a firm, accurate pass into Black 8's right foot. As soon as this accurate pass is delivered, Black 6 should accelerate into the space behind White 10. Almost without exception, the direction of this run should be on the blind side of White 10. It is remarkable how often poor midfield defenders will respond to Black 6's pass by following the ball. Even turning their heads can give Black 6 enough time to get into the space behind White 10. At the same time, White 10 should resist the temptation to follow Black 6's pass and thus concentrate on tracking down Black 6 as he runs forward. If need be, White 10 should turn to face Black 6 and run with him, even at the expense of losing sight of the ball. This tracking down action by White 10 forces Black 6 to run wider (and farther) to get into the space behind the midfield defense.

The closer a team gets to the opponents' goal, the shorter, quicker, and more accurate the passes should be. This area of the field is where great attacking teams excel, and players need to practice such situations near their opponents' goal. Likewise, the closer the wall pass is attempted to the opponents' goal, the flatter (or squarer) the ball will travel. A wall pass near the goal is essentially used by two attackers to get behind two or more defenders.

In figure 9.11, Black 9 has the ball, and Black 11, realizing that a wall pass is on, moves toward her. As Black 11 gets across the line of White 4, Black 11 sets up to receive a pass with the foot farthest away from White 4. Black 11's movement, therefore, must be sideways onto White 4 so that Black 11 can recognize many of the available options. Examples of these include the following: performing a first-time pass into the space between White 5 and White 6; holding the ball and looking to play the ball, after a delayed run by Black 9, into the space between White 5 and White 6; shooting at the goal; faking a pass and either spinning or stepping over the ball to attack the space outside White 4.

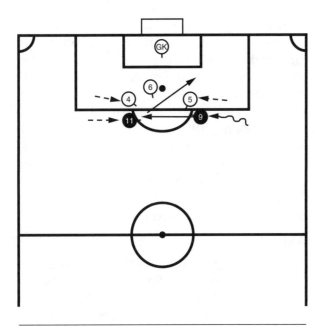

**Figure 9.11**  Initiating the give-and-go.

Although Black 9 might initially play the ball with the foot farthest away from White 5, she is unlikely to be able to play the ball off to Black 11 and get into the space behind White 5. The latter player will be concerned about the space behind her and will have adequate warning of Black 9's intentions to counter the run. On the other hand, Black 9 might well get into the space behind White 5—that is, if she is prepared to risk playing the ball with the foot nearest to the defender. This move might lure White 5 forward

to make a challenge for the ball. At such a point, Black 9 would immediately and accurately flick off the ball to Black 11 and then fall in stride into the space behind White 5 to receive a return pass.

The timing of Black 11's run to set up the wall pass is of critical importance. If it is made too early, then it will give time for White 6 to adjust her covering position and for White 4 to adjust her marking position. If it is made too late, then Black 11 will probably be off balance as she receives the ball; her passing angles will thus be cut off.

Wall passes and give-and-goes require dedicated practice. Practices that will improve your players' execution involve the following exercises.

# Up the Ladder

**Purpose:** To develop wall passing.

**Procedure:** In an area 40 yards by 10 yards (divided into four 10-yard squares), with a defender in square 1 and square 3, two attacking players attempt to take the ball to cross the far end line under control. The defenders are restricted to playing in their own 10-yard square. The defenders attempt to stop the attack by kicking the ball out of play.

### Coaching Points

• Have the ball player attack the defender with the ball so that he might make the defender take a square-on stance.

• Make sure the ball player recognizes when to pass and when to dribble.

• The second attacker should constantly offer a support position, almost square of the ball player, so that a wall pass is always possible.

• Instruct the second attacker to avoid making runs into the second square. Rather, have the ball player pass to the second attacker and immediately accelerate into the second square to receive a return pass.

• Use the front foot to disguise the passes.

# Pin Ball

**Purpose:** To develop the technique of give-and-go.

**Procedure:** Players can work in give-and-go situations as shown in figure 9.12. Black midfielder 1 passes to Black midfielder 2 (solid line 1) and follows the pass (dotted line *a*). Black midfielder 2 lays the ball off to the incoming Black midfielder 1 (solid line 2), who immediately plays a first-time pass to the Black striker (solid line 3). Black midfielder 1 follows the pass (dotted line *b*) and runs onto the Black striker's lay-off pass (solid line 4) for a first-time shot (solid line 5).

### Coaching Points

• The movement of Black midfielder 1 should not be at a constant speed. Instead,

Black midfielder 1 should accelerate immediately after passing the ball and decelerate to receive it.

• Try to get Black midfielder 1, if possible, to strike the pass from a point about 12 to 15 inches in front of her.

• It is much more comfortable and accurate if the player uses the outside of the foot to strike the ball by turning the foot slightly inward.

# Off the Wall

**Purpose:** To develop the techniques and skills of give-and-go short passing.

**Procedure:** Mark an area of 5 by 15 yards. Black attacker 1 has the ball, and the objective is to get the ball to the Black target player from inside the 5 by 15 yards (shaded area). The White defender defends outside the shaded area (see figure 9.13). Black attackers 2 and 3 are available for Black attacker 1 to bounce the ball off them (as in a wall pass). Black attackers 2 and 3 move with the play but can only play on the outside of the shaded space. They are restricted to one touch of the ball, and they are not allowed to pass to the Black target player.

### Variation

• The preceding practice can be developed to include two-on-two inside the longer area (see figure 9.14). Give-and-goes or wall passes

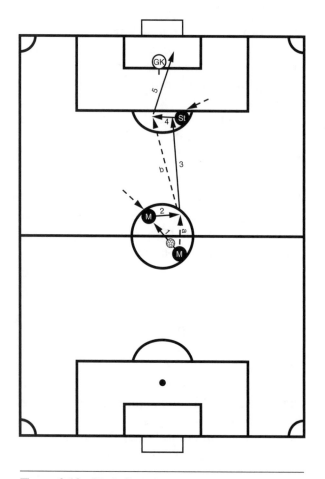

**Figure 9.12**    Pin ball.

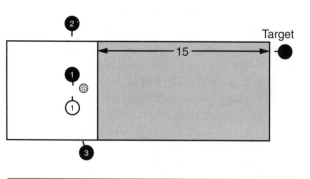

**Figure 9.13**    Off the wall.

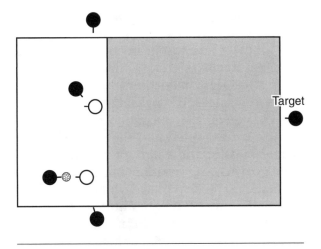

**Figure 9.14**   Off the wall variation.

can be played between the attacking players, either inside or outside the longer area.

**Coaching Points**

• Have the player with the ball attack the defender. The ball should be about 20 to 30 inches in front of the player.

• The side players should move with the play and take up positions alongside the defender while facing the ball player.

• The ball player should strike the pass off the front foot and immediately accelerate on the blind side into the space behind the defender for the return pass.

## Through the Minefield

**Purpose:** To develop passing skills against high-pressure defense.

**Procedure:** A team of three White players plays against four Black defenders in each of two 20-yard squares, which are separated by a 5-yard corridor (see figure 9.15). Position a solitary White player in this 20-by-5-yard corridor. The object of the game is for the White team to first advance the ball to the solitary player, who gets the ball to its other three players. These players ultimately get it to the White target player. Restrict the solitary

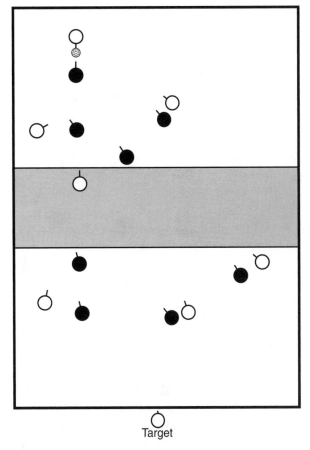

**Figure 9.15**   Through the minefield.

player to three seconds on the ball, but the player can pass the ball both forward and backward into either of the 20-yard squares.

**Coaching Points**

• Encourage the ball player to keep the head up to maintain awareness of the position of teammates and opponents. In particular, the White ball player must be alert to any possibility of getting the ball to the solitary White player in the 20-by-5-yard corridor.

• Get the attacking players off the ball to adopt support positions where the ball can be passed to them without fear of interception by the opposing players.

• Encourage players to pass the ball forward using quick, short, accurate passes.

## Tips for Teaching Passing

- Teach players to move to the ball and into the path of the ball.

- Show that the simple pass is often the most effective pass.

- Instruct players to pass quickly. The player who hangs on to the ball will come under pressure. In addition, the opposing team will close the passing lanes if passes are delayed.

- Make sure players know that the first priority is to pass the ball forward. However, the ball can also be passed square across the field or backward. Square or back passes have a greater element of risk, so accuracy should be a high priority. The passing player should be alerted to the danger of a possible interception by an opponent.

- In most cases, direct players to pass the ball to the feet of the receiving player in the defensive and midfield thirds of the field.

- Emphasize the importance of disguising the pass.

- Discourage long, optimistic, inaccurate passes.

# SHOOTING

I would be a rich man if I received a hundred-dollar bill every time a coach said to me, "We play well and can create chances, but we can't finish." It is frustrating for a team to work hard, playing out of the back, through the midfield, and into the scoring area with a solid opportunity to score, only to then have the player on the ball blow the shot by blasting it over the goal, outside the post, or straight at the keeper. Part of every practice should involve a realistic, small-sided game that emphasizes shooting to help prepare players for game situations.

Shooting on goal is a combination of power and accuracy. Most young players go for too much power and too little control, whereas the great finishers choose the right blend of both. These great finishers have somehow found the knack of "passing" the ball into the goal using the maximum degree of accuracy. We too often find the inexperienced striker blasting the ball high or wide from a solid goal-scoring position. Instead of such a dramatic, explosive image, think of the field as a golf course. The area outside the scoring area is the fairway, from which you can kick powerfully to gain distance. The scoring area is the green, where you delicately blend force and accuracy to put the ball in the cup. That is how shooting should be considered.

Many paragraphs have been written about the mechanics of shooting. They talk about the placement of the nonkicking foot, with the knee bent over the ball, the eye on the ball, the follow-through, and so forth. That's all well and good in ideal situations, but the player in front of the goal seldom receives an ideal ball in an ideal position. True, the player should anticipate the ball and move into its path—that is, if there is time. However, time is not a luxury that the shooter often has. If the shooter takes the time to set up the shot, the scoring opportunity will often be gone by the time the foot meets the ball.

When a player shoots at goal, only one of two results can happen: success or failure. Most players fear failure so much that it stresses them to the point where they can't take an effective shot at goal. With the imagined embarrassment of missing each additional shot, the fear of failure becomes more and more entrenched, making imagination reality. Again, as the coach, you need to address these issues by designing small-sided, conditioned games that allow a high rate of success; by using the benefit of your keen observation and correction to the maximum advantage; and most of all, by including your constant praise for successful attempts. When you give your players opportunities to memorize success rather than rehearse failure, you build their self-confidence so that they can become successful finishers.

## Ultimate Confidence

During the 1995 season, I had the pleasure of coaching Adrian Reyes, a player from Mexico. Adrian was a prolific goal scorer. He could shoot hard and accurately with either foot; he could chip an out-of-position goalkeeper; he could bend balls; and he could head. Simply said, Adrian was good.

During shooting practices, I typically like to observe the shooting player from as close as possible without being clobbered. One day, while Adrian was making a series of fabulous shots, I noticed something. Just before he took each shot, I heard him mutter to himself. I stopped and asked him what he was saying. It turned out that before Adrian takes any shot, he says to himself, "It's in." I found it refreshing to hear such a confident affirmation. Throughout my coaching career, I have had to deal with players whose last thought before shooting was, "Oh, please don't let me miss."

---

Rinus Michels, the famed former Dutch national coach, compared the match to an action movie. The frames move fast, and every frame is different. What was available to the shooter in the first frame may not be there in the next frame. By then, the goalkeeper may be positioned, or a defender may have moved between the ball and the goal. The shooter must therefore take advantage of what is offered in the first frame, being able to shoot any ball received in any position. The accuracy comes not so much from *how* the shooter hits the ball, but from *where* the shooter hits the ball. In the end it comes down to what area of the foot should hit what area of the ball to make the shot accurate. That prerequisite clearly makes shooting an art of instant, instinctive decision making. Such skills are precisely the reason that shooting accurately is difficult and requires endless hours of positive, successful practice. The following are some practices I often use to improve goal scoring.

## Run and Shoot

**Purpose:** To improve shooting technique.

**Procedure:** In groups of three, players combine to shoot at goal (see figure 9.16). Black midfielder 1 passes to Black midfielder 2 (solid line 1), who turns and immediately feeds the ball to the Black striker (solid line 2) to shoot on goal. Black midfielder 2 should concentrate on feeding the pass onto the run that the Black striker makes (dotted line). Limit the Black striker to one or two touches with a minimum of time involved between touches.

### Coaching Points

• The Black striker should begin the run just as Black midfielder 2 has executed the turn. If the Black striker begins the run too early, she will end up too wide or possibly in an offside position. If the Black striker begins the run too late, then the chance is lost.

• When making a run to the right, the Black striker should turn her head to see over her right shoulder. The opposite, of course, will apply on a run to the left.

• The pass from Black midfielder 2 should allow the Black striker to move onto the ball at speed in no more than 4 or 5 strides.

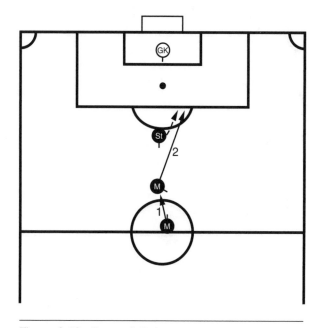

**Figure 9.16**   Run and shoot.

# Cross and Finish

**Purpose:** To improve shooting on goal from crosses.

**Procedure:** The Black winger rounds the cone and crosses for the Black striker to shoot on goal (see figure 9.17). Restrict the Black striker to one touch.

### Coaching Points

• The Black striker should time the run to meet the ball going forward at speed.

• The Black striker should read the cues from the Black winger's approach to the ball. If the ball is rolling quickly as the Black winger approaches it, then it is likely to be a low cross. On the other hand, if the ball is almost stationary as the Black winger approaches it and if he gets the plant foot close up to the ball, then it is likely to be a high cross.

• If in doubt, the striker should attack the space in front of the first post.

• You should encourage the striker to bend the run in a loop toward the ball. This maneuver is much more effective than running in a straight line diagonally toward the ball.

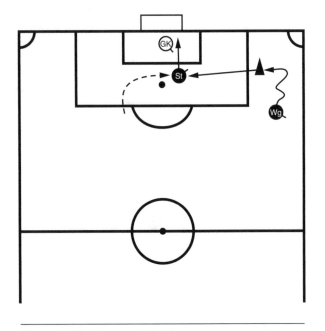

**Figure 9.17**  Cross and finish.

# Spin to Win

**Purpose:** To improve the technique of turning and shooting on goal.

**Procedure:** In pairs, one player passes to a partner, who almost has her back to the goal. The receiving player turns and in no more than two steps, shoots on goal. Allow the shooter only one touch for receiving and turning, and one touch for shooting.

### Coaching Points

• You should encourage the receiving player to get into position to see both the ball and the goal. This objective is easier to achieve if the player turns her back to one of the touchlines.

• The first touch should set up the ball about 2 to 3 yards diagonally behind the player on the side to which he or she turns. If shooting with the right foot, the player should turn over the left shoulder.

• Encourage your players to move to the ball but to ease up just before ball contact. They should use the large surfaces on the outside and inside of the foot to effect the turning touch.

# Platform for Success

**Purpose:** To improve control of high passes leading to shots on goal.

**Procedure:** Standing facing the sideline at a distance of 25 yards from goal and holding a ball, the player punts it about 10 to 20 feet in the air. The player then controls it with either his chest or thigh and immediately shoots on goal. The ball should not bounce more than once after hitting the chest or thigh. The shot can be either a volley or half volley.

### Coaching Points

• Encourage the player to get to the place where the ball will land and be in a ready, balanced position.

• The player should have both feet planted firmly on the ground, about 12 to 15 inches apart.

• The player should use the receiving surface—the chest or thigh—to lift the ball upward and slightly forward.

# CROSSES

Dealing with crosses is probably the greatest difficulty for most goalkeepers, who are particularly vulnerable at the near-post and far-post areas (see figure 9.18). Attacking players should practice serving the ball into these areas at speed and at a height that the forward can reach. The receiving players should recognize the cues from the crossing player's final stride to the ball and decide whether it will be a near-post or far-post delivery, or a high or low cross. If the ball is kicked (crossed) when it is out in front of the plant foot, it is likely to be a near-post service; if the ball is kicked (crossed) when it is level or slightly behind the plant foot, it will probably go to the far post.

Receiving players should anticipate the service and make runs into the near-post or far-post areas as the ball arrives in the area. They only need to redirect the ball with their foot, body, or head at the near-post area to create a scoring chance. At the far post, however, the ball will likely have to pass over the heads of several players to reach the attacking player, who in most instances will have to use heading ability to create a scoring chance. The attacking player should hold her run until she analyzes the posture of the crossing player. If she calculates that it will be a high cross into the far-post area, she should time her run and takeoff to reach maximum height as the ball arrives in that area. The following are some practices I use to develop crossing and finishing.

## Across the Goal

**Purpose:** To improve quality of crosses into the near-post and far-post areas.

**Procedure:** A wide player has a supply of balls and dribbles at speed along a corridor marked between cones and the sideline. As soon as he passes the end cone, he crosses the ball across the face of the goal for two attackers to try to score goals. Each attacker is permitted only one touch on the ball, with the foot, thigh, chest, or head.

### Coaching Points

• Get the wide player to cross the ball while running at speed.

• The wide player should hit his crosses across the face of the goal to threaten the near- and far-post areas. The player should avoid hitting crosses at catchable height immediately in front of the goal.

• The wide player should cross the ball at a place that is dependent on his touch and the plant of his nonkicking foot. The player's concern should be to hit the near- or far-post areas. It is up to the two attackers to calculate where the cross will arrive.

## Down the Channel

**Purpose:** To improve understanding between wide players and attackers when dealing with crosses.

**Procedure:** A field is marked out from one 18-yard line to the opposite 18-yard line with a goal at each end defended by a goalkeeper. A line of cones is placed 10 yards infield from

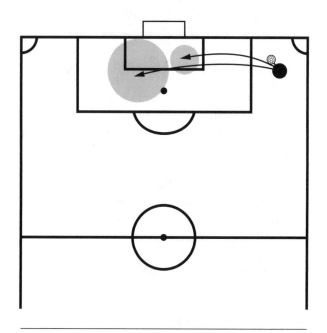

**Figure 9.18** High, low, near, and far crosses.

each sideline. A right and left wide player for each team play uncontested in each half of this corridor. Two attacking players, one defending player, and a goalkeeper play at each end in front of the goal. The wide midfielder in possession of the ball delivers a variety of crosses into the goal area. Each attacker is only permitted one touch on the ball (see figure 9.19).

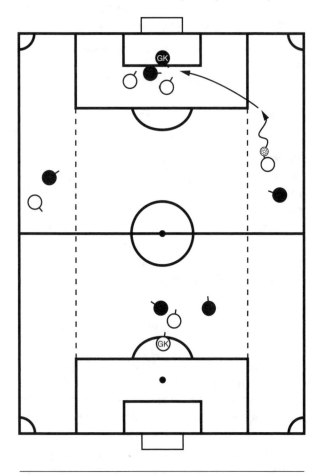

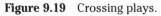

**Figure 9.19**   Crossing plays.

### Variations

- Have two defenders and three attackers at each end.
- Have an extra player in the center of the field. If required, the goalkeeper can play the ball to the extra player so that he can deliver a quick pass to either wide midfielder.

### Coaching Points

- Have the wide midfield player who is receiving the ball turn his back to the sideline so that he can view the whole field.

- Have the wide midfield player control and turn with the ball in the intended direction as quickly as possible.

- The wide midfielder is allowed to cross the ball at any time, but he should not be allowed to dawdle and take forever to complete a cross. If the wide midfielder takes too long in delivering a cross, then restrict the time allowed on the ball to five seconds.

- Demand the wide midfielder to hit the ball across the face of the goal but away from the goalkeeper. If the goalkeeper comes out too far, the wide midfielder can shoot (cross) directly into the goal.

- Get the two attackers to read the wide midfielder's intended cross from his final approach to the ball via the plant of his nonkicking foot in relation to the ball and his angle of approach to the ball.

- Ask the attackers to hold their runs until the last possible moment so that they can have momentum in their last 2 or 3 strides to the ball.

- Look for the attackers to stay behind the ball to avoid offside calls.

- Tell the attackers to make bent runs rather than run straight into the near-post or far-post areas.

- Require the attackers to redirect the ball with any part of the body, except arms and hands, in the near-post area.

## SHIELDING (SCREENING)

In most situations, when the player with the ball is pressured heavily by an opponent, she will need to shield the ball. A player does so by turning sideways onto the opponent and by playing the ball with the foot farthest away from that opponent. If the opponent tries to challenge for the ball across the face of the ball player, the latter should hold off the challenge by making a solid base by sinking at the knees and hips while using arms to widen the screen (see figure 9.20). In no way, however, should a player use her arms to push away the opponent. If the opponent tries to go behind the ball player to

**Figure 9.20**   The sideways-on screen.

challenge for the ball, then the ball player should pivot quickly to play the ball with the other foot, still keeping a sideways-on position in relation to the opponent.

When coaches introduce shielding to young players, they should instruct players to do it in a small space without physical contact from the defender. As the screening player improves her skill and increases her confidence, the coach should allow the defender to become more aggressive in winning the ball. But under no circumstances should the defender be allowed to push or pull the ball player.

As soon as the ball player is able to pivot and protect the ball, she should learn how to run with the ball while still protecting it against an opponent. One skill I look for when first viewing a player is her ability to maintain possession of the ball while she is under pressure from one or two opponents. She must be able to screen the ball, play out of trouble, or delay until help arrives. Alas, too many of our players lose the ball one on one, try the impossible shot, make a hopeless pass, or lose the ball over the touchline or goal line. The ability to maintain possession while under pressure takes

the confidence and determination that can only come as a result of numerous successful practices.

When players screen the ball, the most common mistake they tend to make is that they turn their backs to their opponent. Doing so puts them at a great disadvantage. They form a narrow screen so that a defender can easily get at the ball. Moreover, if screeners and defenders have no body contact at all, then the screening players in this position have difficulty in predicting the movement of the defender. Instead, they should screen sideways on and play the ball with the foot farthest from their opponent. This maneuver not only gives them a wider screen, but it also allows them to see the movements of the defender.

> ### Tips for Teaching Screening
>
> - Teach all players to screen effectively. Even defenders in possession may have their passing lanes blocked momentarily.
> - Work on weight distribution. Most players would benefit if they were to bring their center of gravity down a bit, especially when screening the ball.
> - Coach players to turn around the opponent if they are screening and to attempt to beat the opponent. Turning in to the opponent and showing the ball often result in loss of the ball.
> - Emphasize that before turning around the opponent, the player with the ball should fake the opponent. The player with the ball should get the opponent thinking that she is going to do something and then do something else.
> - Point out that when a player with the ball screens well, the defender may for an instant lose sight of the ball and panic. This lapse of concentration may cause the defender to do something foolish, which your player can then capitalize on.

I like using the following small-sided, conditioned games to practice screening.

## Keep It Safe

**Purpose:** To improve ball protection.

**Procedure:** A group of players, each with a ball, plays in an area about 30 yards by 30 yards. Three players without a ball individually attempt to get possession of any ball. Players with a ball can run away with the ball or screen the ball from an opponent. An opponent who wins the ball now becomes the possessor and either dribbles or screens. A player who has lost a ball is not allowed to attempt to win back the same ball.

**Coaching Points**

• Ask your ball players to be aware of all the players in the area, particularly the ones without a ball.

• Insist that they turn away from defenders rather than try to dribble past them.

• Your better players will have the ball on the side farthest away from the defender, and they will take a sideways-on screening position.

• Your weaker players will probably screen the ball with their backs to the defender. This screen is too small; the defender can easily steal the ball.

## Keep to Shoot

**Purpose:** To improve ball protection.

**Procedure:** Divide two teams into several one-on-one groups. All the players on the White team have possession of a ball, and each player's immediate opponent tries to take the ball and force it out of the 30-by-30-yard area. The player who keeps possession for 15 seconds is allowed a free setup pass (of no more than five yards) and a shot on goal.

**Coaching Points**

• Ask the White players to get sideways-on to their opponent and to control the ball with the foot farthest from the opponent.

• If they wish to change direction, they should immediately pivot to get the oppo-site shoulder against the opponent in the sideways-on position and control the ball with the opposite foot.

• Insist that they turn away from rather than into their opponent.

## Noah's Arc

**Purpose:** To create goal-scoring opportunities when heavily marked.

**Procedure:** A defender marks an attacker inside the arc (top of penalty area). A second attacker passes the ball into the arc, and the first attacker has five seconds to get off a shot on goal. The ball should remain inside the arc in possession of the attacker until he makes the shot. If the ball goes outside the arc, then the defender has won the game.

**Coaching Points**

• Get your attacker to take up a position where he can see both the defender and the second attacker just before receiving the ball.

• Encourage the attacker to develop a repertoire of turns, fakes, and touches to set up a shooting opportunity.

• Have the attacker shoot on goal whenever he has a chance to do so.

## Last Man In

**Purpose:** To improve ball protection.

**Procedure:** In a space of 40 yards square, two groups of players (one group with a ball) play one-on-one "keep ball." The first group, with the ball possession, is team A, while all the players without a ball form team B. A player is only allowed to challenge her immediate opponent. The players in team A try to keep the ball for as long as possible, and the players in team B try to force it out of the area. The last three players in team A to keep their ball each receive a point. Players on team B take the ball, and the roles are reversed. The first player to accumulate three points wins the game.

**Variation**

- Have one extra defender who might challenge any ball player, thus creating a double-team situation.

**Coaching Points**

- Encourage the players with the ball to avoid being trapped in the corners.

- Have them spin away from their opponent and run with the ball on the foot farthest from their opponent.

- Demand that the ball players avoid bumping into other players.

## RECEIVING AND TURNING

Receiving the ball, whether under pressure or not, is another technique at which U.S. players do not excel. Receiving the ball and turning with it is an essential tool for every player, especially for attacking players, who often receive the ball with their backs to the goal. Under screening, I mentioned that the first question we ask when looking at a player is, "How well does the player maintain possession under pressure?" The second question we ask is, "How is the player's first touch on the ball, and is it in preparation for the second touch?"

The speed of the game has increased so much over the last few decades that players who are receiving a ball are almost immediately pressured by an opponent. The era of comfortably trapping the ball and then deciding what to do with it is long gone. In fact, the term *trapping* is antiquated. Today's players must know what is going on around them before they ever receive the ball. And even before receiving the ball, players must be able to fake the opponent. Players receiving the ball must control it, change its direction, and turn with it all in one motion.

Players have two methods of receiving the ball and turning with it. In the first, players come to the ball in a slightly sideways-on position and take the ball with the inside of the back foot. As the ball makes contact with the foot, players drag it back so that the ball ends up 2 or 3 yards diagonally in front of them after they have turned. Play-

ers rotate on the supporting foot (see figure 9.21).

The second method involves a preliminary fake. Players look as if they are going to receive the ball with the inside of the back foot, but instead they take it on the outside of the front foot. Again, the touch should set up the ball 2 or 3 yards diagonally in front of them after they have turned (see figure 9.22).

**Figure 9.21** Receiving and turning in the sideways-on position.

**Figure 9.22** Faking and turning with the ball.

### Tips for Teaching Receiving and Turning

- Allow players to practice without pressure at first. Thereafter, slowly increase pressure until you are practicing under match conditions.

- Watch to see that players are well balanced when receiving the ball.

- Make sure that the players' first touch on the ball has an unpredictable result. For instance, they can fake to cause the defender to believe that they are moving the ball to their left and instead move the ball to their right. At first, most players will control the ball directly in front of themselves, which is a very predictable situation. Skilled opponents will read their intentions and play off the player who is receiving the ball.

- Observe to see that players who are receiving the ball are aware of the players around them, both teammates and opponents.

Use the following small-sided, conditioned games to practice receiving and turning.

---

## Relay Turns

**Purpose:** To improve the techniques of receiving and turning at speed.

**Procedure:** Several teams in groups of four or five players line up about 15 yards apart (see figure 9.23). Teams race against each other to move the ball through the middle players to the end player and back to the starting player five times. End players can have only one touch, whereas the middle players have one touch for the turn and one for the pass.

### Coaching Points

- Get your players to understand that if they pass the ball quickly and accurately to the next player, then it will be easier for that player to make a quick turn on the ball.

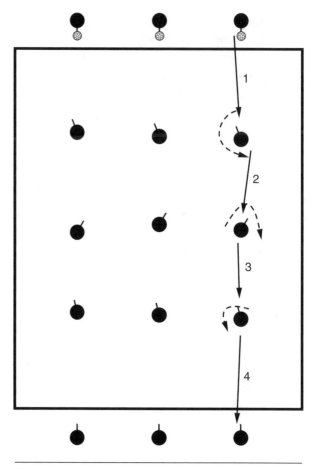

**Figure 9.23**   Relay turns.

- The inside receiving players should move to the ball. But just before the point of contact, they should ease into a relaxed, balanced position. Their feet should be about 20 inches apart, one foot in front of the other, with the chest at about a 45-degree angle to the passing player.

- The simplest turn is to take the ball on the inside surface of the rear foot while pivoting over the rear shoulder. Players should drag the ball back to a point about a yard or two immediately behind them. From this position, players can immediately get off the next pass.

---

## Pass, Turn, Shoot

**Purpose:** To improve direction and timing of runs into scoring positions.

**Procedure:** As illustrated in figure 9.24, in groups of three players, the player with the ball

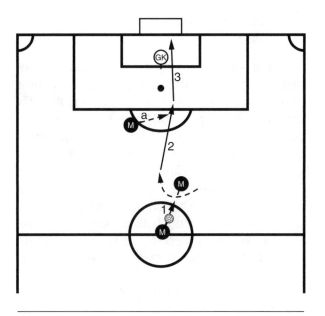

**Figure 9.24**  Pass, turn, shoot.

passes to the second player in front of the center circle (solid line 1). The third player makes a run to receive the ball in a scoring position (dotted line *a*). The second player must receive and turn with the ball in one touch, then immediately play the pass to the third player (solid line 2), who has one touch to shoot (solid line 3).

### Coaching Points

• Try to get the third player to understand when, where, and how the second player can pass the ball to her.

• If the third player runs for a pass before the second player has controlled it, the third player is likely to make too long a run or be in an offside position.

• Get the second player to turn with one touch and deliver the pass with the second touch. This maneuver will make it easier for the third player to time the run.

• Have your third player make a looped, diagonal run. Remind the second player that the challenge is to deliver the pass into the stride path of the third player's run.

# Switch the Play

**Purpose:** To develop the technique of turning with the ball.

**Procedure:** Two areas, 40 yards by 20 yards, are divided by a narrow corridor, 20 yards by 2 yards. A goal is placed midway on each of the 20-yard end lines. Three White players and a goalkeeper play against three Black players and a goalkeeper in both of the 40-by-20-yard areas. A solitary player plays in the narrow corridor (see figure 9.25).

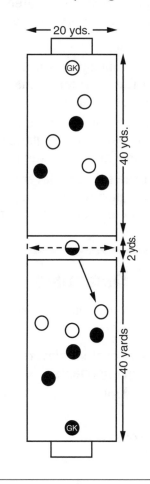

**Figure 9.25**  Switch the play.

Whenever a team wins ball possession, it must pass the ball to the solitary player in the middle area. The solitary player must immediately pivot and pass to one of the other three players in the same color jersey in the other 40-by-20-yard area. The game continues until the opponents win the ball or it goes out of play. They now try to get the ball to the solitary player who will control, pivot, and pass, using a maximum of two touches, to any of their players in the opposite 40-by-20-yard area.

## Variations

- Have two attacking players in the narrow corridor.
- Have an extra attacking player in each end to make four-on-three situations.
- Have the goalkeeper distribute the ball quickly and accurately to the player in the narrow corridor.

## Coaching Points

- Have the solitary player move up and down within the corridor to make the best angle to receive the ball.
- The solitary player should ideally be half-turned to get a quick glance over his shoulder before (or as) the ball is coming.
- Instruct the solitary player to maximize the use of the narrow corridor by "staying away" at the far side so that he can come to the ball.

# DRIBBLING

The key factors in proficient dribbling techniques are as follows:

- Awareness of other players—both teammates and opponents
- Close control
- Balance
- Change of speed
- Change of direction and the use of fakes

When coaches design practices to develop players' dribbling, they should include one or more of the key factors in this list. If a practice develops habits in a player that are contrary to the aforementioned techniques, then that practice should be eliminated from the training program. An age-old favorite (supposedly designed to develop dribbling skills) is called Dribbling Through Cones. I cannot recommend this practice because it encourages players to dribble with their heads down, which is contrary to the aim of developing awareness.

An important consideration for young players is to know when and where to dribble—as well as where and when not to dribble. The guidelines set in figure 9.26 should apply for where to dribble.

Dribbling is not a dying art: It is the technique players need to use to play out of trouble, to create space for themselves or teammates, and to create scoring opportunities. Unfortunately, most of the offensive emphasis in the modern game is placed on passing. As a coach, emphasize to your players that dribbling skills are not only important, but essential.

Dribbling is a skill that excites players, coaches, and fans. It is about the unexpected and the inventive; and when used in the opponent's half of the field, it can destroy that

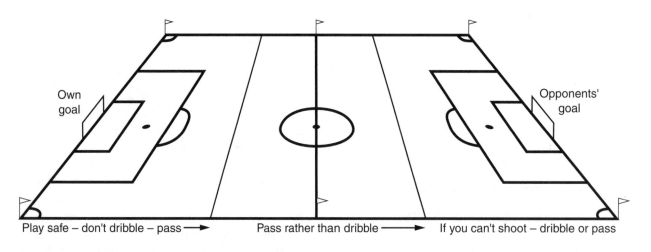

**Figure 9.26**   Risk and safety areas.

team's defensive shape and balance. When dribbling is mentioned, most people think of intricate moves and turns with the ball. Although ball manipulation should certainly be part of every player's arsenal, it is not the only skill that contributes to effective dribbling. In our haste to teach the intricate details of the game, we sometimes overlook the simpler, yet equally effective, means to an end.

## Supersub

During the NASL years, Elson Seale played for the Portland Timbers. After the demise of the NASL, I coached him for a little while. Elson was an exciting dribbler and loved to take on players one on one. The Timbers used him as a substitute. The fans would frequently yell for the Timbers coach to bring on Elson, and they cheered when he came into the match. They wouldn't be disappointed. As soon as Elson got the ball, he looked for an opponent to take on. After finding one, he quickly proceeded to beat him. At that point, you would have expected him to continue toward the goal, pass, cross, or shoot. Not Elson; he loved the one-on-one so much that he patiently waited for the beaten opponent to catch up with him so that he could beat him again.

Dribbling means running with the ball, away from an opponent or at an opponent. If the run is away from the opponent, especially if the dribbler is going toward the goal, then speed and control are everything. But if the run is at an opponent, nothing unsettles that opponent more than sudden changes of pace. It's a simple skill, but an often-overlooked one. Some players have explosive speed. When they come at an opponent slowly but then suddenly explode with the ball into the space behind the opponent, they may leave the opponent standing. Another change of pace is for a player to come at an opponent at speed, slow down, then speed up again, which may cause the

opponent to stumble or at least be caught on the wrong foot. Another tactic that can leave defenders in an awkward position is for a player to take on an opponent at speed and suddenly change direction. This move can be particularly effective if the player can change direction several times.

All players should practice the more intricate tools of dribbling and faking. The tricks can be as simple as pretending to go to the left and instead going to the right (and vice versa); faking to kick but kicking over the ball; faking to pass the ball one way but instead stepping over the ball and turning the other direction; or faking to heel-kick the ball but instead stepping over the ball and playing it with the other foot to the side.

### Tips for Teaching Dribbling

- Encourage dribbling in the attacking third.
- Discourage dribbling in the defending third, especially when under pressure.
- Have players show their favorite move with the ball. If you approve of the move, ask all players to duplicate it and practice it.
- Practice various moves designed to beat an opponent in one-on-one situations. If the move is successful, the player may finish with a shot at a goal, which is protected by one of the goalkeepers.
- Teach players that when a dribble has successfully beaten an opponent, they should explode into the space opened up by the dribble. Players too often create an opening then continue at the same pace, allowing the defender to recover. They shouldn't have to beat a defender twice.

As I have mentioned, dribbling is an art getting lost in the glamour of passing and shooting. The following are a few of the small-sided, conditioned games I use for dribbling practices to keep players' habits sharp.

## To and Fro

**Purpose:** To improve quickness in turning with the ball.

**Procedure:** Mark two parallel lines three yards apart. Players line up with one foot on the ball on the first line. They race to find which player can move the ball over the second line then back over the first line five times, finishing with the foot on the ball on the first line. Restrict players to two touches: one touch to turn and the second touch to move the ball.

### Coaching Points

• Explain to the players that they must develop a forward touch on the ball so that they get to it just as it crosses the line.

• Encourage them to use both the inside and the outside of the foot in making the turns.

• Show them that the best turns are made not when the ball is stopped but when it is dragged back in the opposite direction.

## Run the Gauntlet

**Purpose:** To develop fakes, feints, and tricks in dribbling.

**Procedure:** Mark three 10-yard-by-10-yard squares, and place a defender in each square. A line of attacking players, one at a time, attempts to get through the space and shoot into the unguarded goal.

### Coaching Points

• Get your attackers to go at the defenders with the ball at controlled speed.

• Encourage the attackers to develop feints and fakes on the ball.

• Remind the attackers that they can develop a larger repertoire of fakes, feints, and tricks on the ball if they dribble with the ball directly in front of them. When confronted by a defender the ball should never be more than one yard from the front foot.

## HEADING

Few players have difficulty with a defensive, clearing header that plays the ball high and far. Such a statement is probably true because the ball is hit below its center and feels more natural. But heading in attack is one of the most poorly executed skills in American youth soccer. Few players can outjump the defense at the far post and come over the ball to head it powerfully down into the goal. Even fewer can get to an air ball at the near post first and redirect it, with outstretched neck, past the goalkeeper. As a coach, you can do much to improve on this weakness in your players with realistic practices that teach heading to clear, control, score, and pass.

Even those who can get up and over the ball may fail when opponents challenge them. It takes a courageous player with a love for body contact to get up high in a crowded penalty area to meet a hard-driven ball, get over it, and head it down powerfully without consciously thinking of an incoming challenger. Players who can do so are worth their weight in gold.

The mechanics of a powerful header are not that difficult because the entire body from the feet to the head is what contributes to the power. Have your players try the following exercise so that they can get a feel for the body involvement in the header: Ask them to place their right foot sideways, about 24 inches behind a forward-pointing left foot. Now have them rock back, then forward, as if heading a ball without leaving their feet. All the muscles used for that rocking motion are used in a powerful header.

Another way your team can learn the mechanics of heading is by viewing videos in slow motion of players capable of heading with power to score. One of my favorites is former Dutch national team player Ruud Gullit.

### Tips for Teaching Heading

- Ask the players to judge the path of the ball early. They should move to meet the ball, even if it means first taking a step back.
- Instruct players to jump off one foot.
- Players should not lose sight of the ball.
- Teach players to bend the body backward to form a bow and to release the bow just before contact.
- The feet and lower legs come forward; the lower body moves back; and the upper body, neck, and head snap forward.
- Use plyometrics to increase the vertical jumps of your players.

For the following small-sided, conditioned games, observe whether the players are using the proper mechanics.

## Use Your Head

**Purpose:** To improve heading on goal.

**Procedure:** Groups of three players play together. One player has the ball in a wide position and, from the second touch, must cross the ball in the air to the area in front of goal. The other two players each have one touch on the ball to score. One of these touches must be a header, and the header must go directly into the goal or be used as a pass to the partner.

**Coaching Points**

• Inform the player delivering the crosses that she can get a high, accurate cross more often by kicking the ball just before it stops after the first touch. This maneuver allows the player more time to place the plant foot adjacent to the line of the ball, thus allowing a full swing of the kicking leg.

• Have the players in front of the goal make looped runs to the ball, one covering the front post and the other the back post.

• Allow the receiving players to make decisions on whether to head for goal or make a headed pass. The decision depends on the amount of power and accuracy they can get on the ball as well as the positioning of the goalkeeper and the teammate. Players should head for goal if they think they can score.

## Heading in the Right Direction

**Purpose:** To improve heading on goal.

**Procedure:** Groups of players line up facing each other at a distance of about 30 yards on a line drawn diagonally through the middle of the goal (see figure 9.27). The players behind the goal each have a ball, and each serves (in turn) the ball in the air, over the crossbar, to the immediately opposite player. Goals can

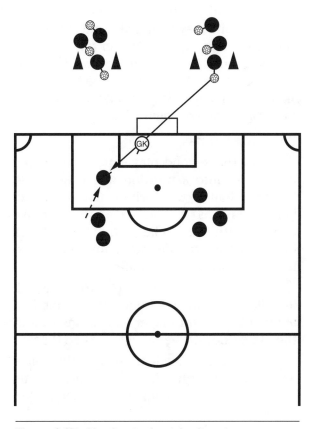

**Figure 9.27** Heading in the right direction.

only be scored off a header with both feet off the ground.

### Coaching Points

• Ask your serving players to kick the ball so that it lands in the space some 5 to 10 yards in front of the heading players.

• Get your heading players to attack the ball and hit it hard with their heads.

• Players should look at the ball at the moment of impact.

## Flick-Ons

**Purpose:** To improve the technique of flick-on heading.

**Procedure:** In groups of three, one player with a ball stands at the top of the arc, the second player stands on the six-yard line, and the third player stands behind the goal. The third player takes a throw-in toward the second player, who must flick-on the ball with the head for the first player to catch.

The second player should come to the ball, and just before the ball hits her forehead, the player should lift the chin so that the forehead forms a backward angle. The ball should skip off this angled surface into the hands of the first player (see figure 9.28).

### Coaching Points

• Ask the second player to move to the ball to get into a position where he could head the ball forward while standing at full height. Just as the ball is about to make contact with the forehead, the player takes the head back to offer an almost horizontal forehead surface to the ball.

• Ask the third player to throw the ball in a flat trajectory, straight at a point just above the second player's head. Insist that the player not deliver a high, lobbed throw.

• Always use hand-stitched leather balls when practicing heading. You can let some air out of them when introducing heading to beginners.

**Figure 9.28**   A flick-on header.

## In the Ring

**Purpose:** To develop a variety of offensive headers.

**Procedure:** A ring of six players forms around a "target man" with one ball. The ball is played in the air to the target man, who executes a variety of headed passes, including the angled knock-down, the back header, the basic lay-off, and the header on goal.

### Coaching Points

• Ask the heading player to back off so that she can come to the ball.

• Instruct your players to decide which header to execute as the ball leaves the kicker's foot.

## Round the Cone

**Purpose:** To improve offensive heading.

**Procedure:** A server on the goal line throws the ball or kicks the ball out of his hand to a heading player, who has just rounded a cone placed on the penalty line. The running player attempts to head the ball past the goalkeeper.

### Coaching Points

• Encourage the heading player to aggressively attack the ball.

• Instruct the heading player to "hit" the ball with the forehead.

• Teach the heading player to head the ball powerfully downward and toward the goal line.

## Clear Your Lines

**Purpose:** To develop defensive heading techniques.

**Procedure:** Three players stand on the goal line, under the crossbar of a full-sized goal. From outside the penalty area, several other players, each with a ball, try to score with a shot that will enter the goal above four feet high (as marked on each upright). The defenders on the goal line try to head the ball out of the penalty area without it bouncing. If one of them succeeds or if the kicking player kicks the ball over the crossbar, then the players change positions.

### Coaching Point

• Ask the defending players to attack the ball aggressively with their head so that it goes high and far. The defending player should look at the ball as it comes toward her, then hit the ball off the forehead, using the legs, trunk, neck, and arms to generate power through the ball.

# RUNS

The timing of runs is probably the most difficult skill for any attacking player to learn. Players should always make their runs in the ball handler's line of vision. For players to make a run for the ball when the ball handler can't see them simply does not make sense.

Badly timed runs can take two forms. The first is when the player makes the run too early and thus too far; the second is when the player makes the run too late. A well-timed run usually covers no more than 5 to 15 yards. The player initiates the run just as the ball handler makes her controlling touch. The ball handler and runner cannot wait until they establish eye contact. By then, it is too late. It is the movement of the running player (his body language) that informs the ball handler where and when he wants the ball.

## Off the Ball

After we beat Brazil 1-0 in the 1989 FIFA Under-17 World Cup finals in Scotland, the Brazilian coach paid the American players the ultimate compliment during the postmatch press conference. He said that his team found it extremely difficult to regain possession of the ball after they had lost it. The skill level shown by the American players had been high, and their movement off the ball outstanding.

It was no coincidence that the Brazilian coach should mention some of the topics that we had concentrated on during our training camps leading up to the World Cup finals. Skill on the ball was not the only skill that made the likes of Claudio Reyna, Imad Baba, Nidal Baba, Joel Russell, and Jorge Salcedo so proficient; it was also their movement off the ball.

## Tips for Teaching Runs

- Determine whether the runner and the passer established eye contact before the passer received the ball.
- Teach players to bend their runs so that when they receive the ball, they are already facing the goal.
- Be ready to point out the effectiveness of the run to the player who made it but didn't get the ball. The player may be frustrated. Many goals are scored because the player making the run took defenders into poor positions, thereby creating space and time for a teammate.

Players can improve timing their runs only by lots and lots of practice. Here are some small-sided, conditioned games to help players improve their off-the-ball runs.

# Big Ben

**Purpose:** To improve timing of runs.

**Procedure:** Groups of four players with one ball play pass-and-move with no opposition. Players must play the ball with one or two touches within two seconds. The players off the ball may sprint or walk only—no jogging. Players are not allowed to talk; they can communicate only through body movements. The ball can be passed only to a running player.

**Coaching Points**

- Get your players to initiate their runs just as a player receives the ball.
- The moving players' runs should be in the receiving player's line of vision.
- The receiving player should deliver the pass to the space or spot at a speed dictated by the shape and direction of the moving player's run.

# Five-on-Two

**Purpose:** To improve movement off the ball.

**Procedure:** Five play against two in the penalty area. A point is scored each time one of the five players can place a foot on top of the ball on one of the shorter (18-yard) lines of the penalty box. They must alternately attack one line, then the other. The five offensive players are restricted to two touches on the ball in each possession.

**Coaching Points**

- Demonstrate to your players that the ball player should always have at least two teammates in positions where the ball can be played to them, without interception by opponents.
- The ball player should deliver the pass before being closed down by an opponent.
- The two nearest supporting attackers should take up positions almost in a straight line, one on either side of the ball.
- Insist on high-quality, quick, accurate ball movements.

# Stop and Go

**Purpose:** To improve understanding of when and where to make a run.

**Procedure:** A group of 8 to 10 players form a circle with a diameter of 20 yards, with two-on-two plus one inside the circle. The outside players are restricted to two touches in two seconds. The three attacking players make runs to receive passes off the outside players; they then turn and pass to the other side of the circle or pass the ball to another inside attacker. If the two defenders win the ball, they now become the attacking pair to play with the third attacker.

**Coaching Points**

- Time the run to coincide with the readiness of the outside player.

• Angle the run so that at some point the player can see both the ball player and the intended target.

• The players should deliver quick accurate passes.

• Encourage the outside passers to offer advice, as appropriate, such as "turn" or "man on."

• If one of the three players inside the circle is not intending to make a run, that player should stand still—no jogging allowed.

# TAKEOVERS

Takeovers can be played in various parts of the field. But keep in mind that takeovers played in the midfield are different than those in and around the opponent's goal. The reason is that defenders are more likely to mark tightly the closer they get to their own goal.

Before any takeover can be played, the ball player must attempt to outrun the immediate opponent with the ball and threaten the space diagonally behind her. The first

priority for the ball carrier is to be able to run at speed with the ball outside the line of her body on the side farthest away from the defender. As soon as the second attacking player recognizes that a takeover is on, she attempts to move toward the ball player along the line of the latter player's run.

At the point of takeover, the player carrying the ball on the right foot leaves it for her teammate, who then takes it with her right foot and immediately transfers it to the left foot. If the takeover is well executed, the new carrier will then be able to take the ball into the danger zone with the second touch (see figure 9.29). The takeover is often unsuccessful when the carrier tries to pass the ball to his or her teammate. This move leaves too much space between the two defenders for the takeover to be executed and for the new carrier to get into the space behind the two defenders.

When properly executed, the ball should be left by the ball carrier for the receiver to takeover. Players should never exchange verbal communication; rather, they should develop a mutual understanding through frequent practice and thorough knowledge of each other's movements.

**Figure 9.29**   The takeover.

# The Merger

**Purpose:** To develop understanding of how two players perform a takeover.

**Procedure:** Two players face each other at each end of the arc, just outside the penalty area. One player has a ball. This player runs with the ball on the foot farthest from the goal toward his teammate. A takeover is completed inside the arc for the second player to take an immediate shot on the goal, which is defended by a goalkeeper.

### Variations

- Have a defender shadow the first ball player.
- Have a defender shadow the second player.

### Coaching Points

- Make sure the first ball player protects the ball while moving toward his teammate.

- Demand that there is little or no space between the two attacking players when they pass each other.

- The first ball player should leave the ball on the takeover. Don't allow the player to pass it or stop it.

- Look for a delicate, controlling touch from the second attacker to set up the ball for a shot on goal.

# OVERLAPPING

Overlapping is a term recently introduced to soccer to describe a player's coming through from behind to give support to another player. This type of move is often seen in the midfield where a defender or midfield player moves into the space alongside a teammate. Thus, in figure 9.30, Black 4's passing possibilities are restricted, and she is prevented from taking the ball forward by White 10. Black 2 moves forward into this space alongside Black 4 so that she can take the ball forward or pass unchallenged to a forward player. It is a wise plan to encourage

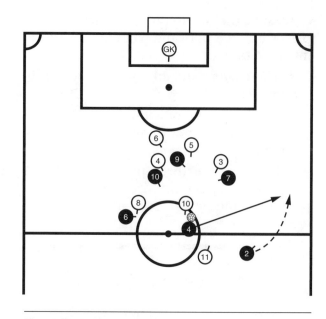

**Figure 9.30**   Overlapping.

defenders to support in this way, because it puts a player in clear possession of the ball in the setup area. Admittedly, this player is a long way out, but she has plenty of time to pick a spot for a pass into the scoring area. Again, having players supporting from behind makes it much easier for the defense to play the ball out safely, and it cuts down the risk of losing possession in the midfield.

The player with the ball and the one supporting from behind absolutely need to know what they are doing. As soon as the decision is made to move forward, the player running from behind should let the player with the ball know that she is overlapping. The supporting player's run should be well wide of the player in possession so that the risk of interception is eliminated. To reduce this risk even further, the pass to the supporting player should be made early, before the opposing player can move close enough to tackle. This pass must be of the highest quality so that Black 2 can take the ball forward in stride. If it is too strong, it could go out of play; if it is too weak, the supporting player could be caught in possession.

As soon as the supporting player has made the overlap and moves forward with the ball, she needs to display the same level of skill as a player normally found in that position. If Black 2 moves forward with the ball, it is essential that Black 2 be competent at crossing the ball accurately from the right. We too often find defenders, having made the overlaps, cross the ball over the goal line or straight to a defender.

In figure 9.31, Black 4 has played the ball to Black 7. The timing of Black 2's run is important. If Black 2 goes too soon, she may get caught offside. If Black 2 goes too late, she may find that White 3 has already closed in to tackle Black 7. Black 2 should therefore tell Black 7 to release the ball as she runs into the shaded area. This call is of vital importance because Black 7 is often unaware that Black 2 is going to overlap.

The direction of Black 2's run is also important. If Black 2 runs through on a line that passes close to White 3, then Black 4's pass will have to pass close to White 3. This makes White 3's task of interception considerably easier. It is unlikely that Black 4 would attempt to make such a pass, however, because the likelihood is that Black 4 would push the ball through wide of White 3. But this makes Black 2's task more difficult because Black 2 will now take the ball on the outside. This position gives White 3

the opportunity to fall back and keep Black 2 close to the touchline. But again, if the line of Black 2's run is well wide of White 3, it will enable White 3 to fall back to a position between Black 2 and the goal. In many ways, this position is worse than when Black 4 had the ball, namely because Black 2 has less space to work in. Ideally, Black 2 should run through on a line not too wide from White 3. The direction of this run should enable Black 4 to make an easy pass—that is, one that White 3 cannot intercept to the overlapping Black 2.

Overlapping as a skill doesn't come naturally; it requires constant drilling. Here are some practices to improve it in your players.

## Go Outside

**Purpose:** To recognize overlapping opportunities.

**Procedure:** Six attacking players position against four defenders and a goalkeeper in a half-field, with the width reduced to the size of the penalty area (44 yards). Only one attacking player at a time is allowed in the outside space.

### Coaching Points

• Have the overlapping player communicate with the ball player, especially if the overlap is started from a position behind the ball player.

• Get the overlapping player to bend his run behind and around the ball player.

• If an overlapping run is made, under no circumstances should the ball player lose the ball through risky play.

• Ask the ball player to release the ball as the overlapping player enters his line of vision. Get the ball player to recognize when the overlapping player can be used as a decoy. This scenario usually happens when the challenging defender has been drawn out of position to cover the run of the overlapping player, thus allowing the ball player a decisive forward pass.

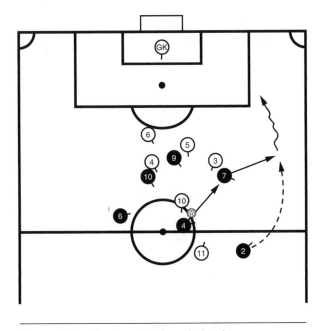

**Figure 9.31** Overlapping from behind.

# Side-Door Entry

**Purpose:** To develop overlapping play.

**Procedure:** Five defenders and a goalkeeper play against five attackers in a half-field. Two additional attackers are stationed wide on each side of the field on the halfway line. The five attackers create attacking opportunities to bring either of the two additional attackers into the game through overlapping runs.

**Coaching Points**

• The ball player must escape from the immediate heavy pressure of the nearest defender to allow the time and the space necessary to deliver a pass into the area wide of the defense.

• The overlapping player should "stay at home" if the ball player is under severe pressure and should instead support from behind in anticipation of receiving a back pass.

• Attacking players should avoid making runs into the wide areas, because doing so will bring in defenders who will clog the overlapping lanes.

# SUMMARY

To watch a team play attacking soccer with confidence and flair is a big thrill. Before a team can do so, however, you must give attention to the development of the offensive techniques needed to mount effective attacks. The reminders that follow will help you develop those techniques.

• Coach players to move the ball quickly, not only down the length of the field but oftentimes across the field before actually moving downfield.

• Work hard with the players so that they become quality passers of the ball in confined situations.

• Emphasize that shooting on goal is a combination of power and accuracy. Solid finishers find the knack of "passing" the ball into the goal using maximum accuracy.

• Practice heading a lot; it is one of the most poorly executed skills in American youth soccer.

• Teach the players to screen by turning sideways-on to the opponent and playing the ball with the foot farthest from the opponent.

• Spend time on developing players' ability to simultaneously receive the ball and turn with it.

• Be patient when working on timing of runs. This skill is probably the most difficult offensive skill for any player to learn.

• Make sure that players make their runs in the ball handler's line of vision.

# Part IV

# COACHING TACTICS

# Chapter 10

# REVIEWING KEY TACTICAL SYSTEMS

Before going into the teaching of defensive and offensive tactics, we think that it may be of benefit to first look at the development of key tactical systems during the history of soccer. Doing so will serve to better understand the need and reason for the tactics we use today.

## EARLY SYSTEMS

Soccer has changed dramatically from its chaotic origins in medieval times to today's sophisticated formations and styles of play. Its origins were found in street battles between rival communities, where no holds were barred as opposing mobs tried by whatever means to force a ball into an area marked as a goal.

The game became more organized and more civilized in the early 1800s in the public schools of England (those schools would be considered private schools in the United States). Before the 1860s, an offside law came into effect that dictated the style of play. Any player ahead or in front of the ball was considered to be offside, which is similar to the law of modern-day rugby football. The game therefore became a contest of dribbling skills that featured a series of individual breaks. Little consideration was paid to defending, and at least seven players on each team would chase the ball all over the field, looking to attack through dribbling the ball.

In the 1860s, the offside law was changed, and an attacker was deemed to be onside if three or more opponents were positioned between him and the opponents' goal. It was Queen's Park, the great Scottish amateur club of the era, that first recognized the rather obvious value of being able to pass the ball over a distance so that it traveled quicker than any one player's dribbling it down the field. Thus, the passing game that we now see today had its origins in Scotland. Queen's Park also developed a formation that included two fullbacks, two halfbacks, and six forwards. Positional play was born. No longer was the ball played forward by dribbling through crowds; it was now passed from one player to another. Players realized that a passed ball simply travels faster than players can move. Thus, the players of Queen's Park constantly unbalanced clustered opponents. Their tactics gradually spread south to England and were adopted by many teams in the new professional league—the Football League—that was formed in 1888.

The first championship, as well as the FA Cup, was won by Preston North End, which featured a strong Scottish contingent in their lineup. Preston had slightly modified the Queen's Park formation to the following: a goalkeeper, who had a right fullback and a left fullback standing in front of the goal; a right-half, center-half, and left-half; and a five-player forward line (outside right, inside right, center forward, inside left, and outside left; see figure 10.1). The new center half provided a new balance between offense and defense by serving as a link between the two.

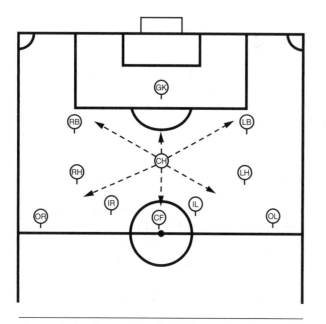

**Figure 10.1**   Preston North End formation.

The Preston formation was widely adopted by most teams throughout the world. The key player in this formation was the center-half, who was expected to control the play in the center of the field, much like a central midfielder does today. The center-half in the late 1800s and early 1900s was also expected to attack as much as defend.

In the early 1920s, Newcastle United refined an *offside trap* that continually frustrated their opponents. Bill McCracken, an Irish international fullback well ahead of his time in tactical understanding, together with his fellow fullback, cleverly timed a forward move that regularly caught opposing forwards in an offside position. More and more, Football League teams copied this method of defending, which resulted in fewer goals being scored and thus dwindling attendances. As a result, the offside law was changed again in 1925 to the one still in use today. The number of defenders needed to allow an attacker onside was reduced from three to two.

Naturally, the change in the offside law initiated a tactical rethink. As teams increased their numbers in the "goals for" column (mostly scored by the center forward), the response was to restrict the role of the center-half mainly to defense. It was Arsenal, under the leadership of Herbert Chapman, who developed this strategy. The midfield creativity was now thrust on the shoulders of the wing-halves and the inside forwards, and the WM formation was born (see figure 10.2). This system was used extensively from the 1930s well into the 1950s and 1960s.

Teams from Europe, however, were the first to expose the rigidity and the weaknesses of the WM formation. For instance, the Italians developed defensive tactics that became the basis of Italian play and the play of many other countries throughout the world, including Brazil, Argentina, and Uruguay. Although conventional styles of play required defenders to mark zonally, the Italian method was a rigid one-on-one style, with a "libero" (or sweeper) behind them to plug any gaps that might open up. It was stiflingly effective and led to Italian success in World Cup finals in the 1930s, as well as European Cup success for their club teams in the 1950s and 1960s.

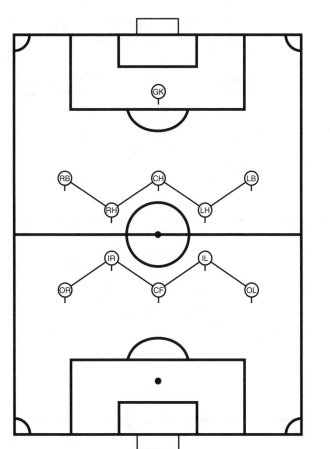

**Figure 10.2**   The WM Formation.

In 1953, Hungary arrived as Olympic champions to play against England at Wembley Stadium. At this time, England still played a WM formation with the center-half detailed to mark the opposing center forward. The Hungarians pulled their two wingers and their center forward, Nandor Hidegkuti, deep into midfield. Harry Johnston, England's center-half, did not know whether to follow him or stay back and cover. The two players who were expected to perform as traditional deep-lying inside forwards in a WM formation were thus sent upfield to torment the "stopper" center-half. This system of covering fullbacks meant that neither Puskas nor Koscis, the Hungarian inside forwards, were in danger of being caught offside. England was eventually demolished by a score of 6-3. They were further humiliated on the return trip to Budapest, where they lost 7-1. They also suffered a 5-0 loss to Yugoslavia in their travel to Hungary.

## MODERN SYSTEMS

The evolution of tactics and team formations had begun in earnest, but English teams were slow to learn the lesson. In South America, the Brazilians, hurt by their failure in the 1954 World Cup, were experimenting with new tactics. They were quick to copy the Italian method by deploying four defenders in a line across the width of the field. Their fullbacks took up positions alongside the opposing wingers, which denied the wingers the opportunity of receiving the ball in space. Their two central defenders then provided cover for each other in the middle of the defense.

Throughout the history of the game, coaches have experimented with team formations and styles of play. This constant experimentation reminds me of the old saying that "soccer is a simple game made difficult by coaches." Even so, it was Brazil who eventually found a system that suited their exquisite ball skills. They decided to play the libero (sweeper), who usually wears the number-five shirt in Brazil, in front of the defense rather than behind it (see figure 10.3).

The number-five player in the Brazilian system was called a "stopper" (or a defensive midfield player), but in Brazil such a player

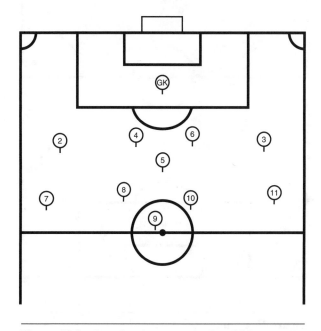

**Figure 10.3**   Brazilian lineup in the late 20th century.

was also often referred to as the "windscreen wiper" player. His role was to confront opposing dribblers, cut off the supply line of passes to the opposing forwards, or sandwich them if they received the ball at their feet.

An analysis of the game of soccer at any level, from local recreation to World Cup games, indicates that an overwhelming number of goals are scored from shots taken from a position near the goal. What must be clearly understood is that the team that dominates or commands the setup area will usually create the most goal-scoring chances. The younger the players, the closer to the scoring area they will need to be to create a goal-scoring chance. Figure 10.4 illustrates roughly the extent of a setup area at the professional level.

A team with ball possession has three main ways of advancing the ball from the setup area to the scoring area so that one of its players can shoot or head the ball into the goal.

- Players can go around opposing defenses to cross the ball into the scoring area (see figure 10.5).
- Players can play the ball over or behind defenders for an attacking player to run on to (see figure 10.6).
- Players can interpass, dribble, or shoot the ball through opposing defense (see figure 10.7).

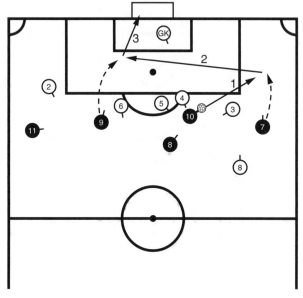

**Figure 10.5**   Going around the defense.

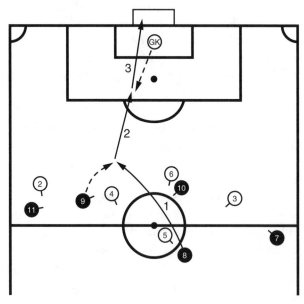

**Figure 10.6**   Going over or behind the defense.

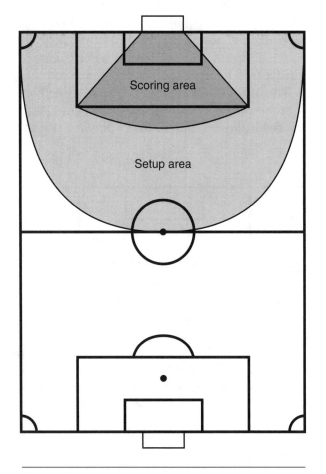

**Figure 10.4**   Important areas.

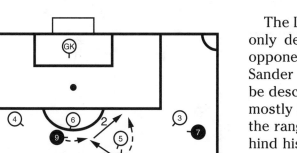

**Figure 10.7**   Going through the defense.

Opposing coaches will, of course, work out tactical plans to deny opposing teams their preferred methods of attack. The Liverpool F.C. team that achieved an historic "treble" of championships in 2000-2001 denied their opponents the opportunity of going around them or getting in behind them by playing the formation as indicated in figure 10.8. What was implicit in the Liverpool F.C. tactical plan was that the favored offensive play of most British teams was to either *(a)* advance the ball down the flanks to cross it in front of the goal or *(b)* play the ball in behind the defense for an attacking player to run to.

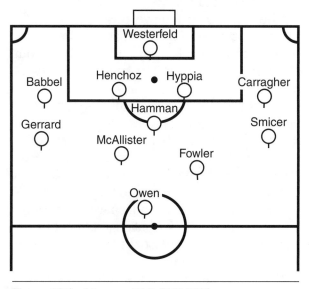

**Figure 10.8**   Liverpool F.C. 2000-2001.

The Liverpool F.C. defensive play was not only designed to deny and frustrate their opponents, but it also suited their players. Sander Westerfeld, the goalkeeper, could be described as a "shot stopper." He played mostly in his six-yard box but did not have the range to play as a "sweeper keeper" behind his defense. The defensive line of Babbel, Hyypia, Henchoz, and Carragher was therefore forced to play deep so that there was no space behind them. The partnerships of Babbel–Gerrard and Carragher–Smicer formed formidable defensive blocks that prevented opponents' penetration down the flanks. Opposing play was therefore forced down the middle where Hamman and McAllister would contest every pass or dribble. Not only was this a defensive style and formation that suited Liverpool, but it also brought out the opposing team so that Michael Owen in particular, with his breakaway speed, could find space behind the opposing defense.

Liverpool F.C. was therefore described as a counterattacking team, and they received severe criticism from the pundits for their defensive approach. Stung by such criticism, Liverpool F.C. signed a new goalkeeper, Dudek, who had a much greater range than Westerfeld and thus allowed the Liverpool F.C. defense to draw up their defensive line farther upfield. The dilemma for the coaching staff was the choice of a partner for Hamman in center midfield. Hamman was decidedly the defensive midfielder (stopper) for Liverpool F.C. The problem was that the second center midfielder not only had to assist Hamman in his defensive duties, but he also had to link up with his forwards (see figure 10.9). Several players were tried—McAllister, Gerrard, Berger, Murphy, and Littmanen—but all found the excessive workload of defending in deep positions and linking up with their forwards to be beyond their physical abilities.

So what can we learn from the experiences of Liverpool F.C.? As coaches, we must be fully aware, not only of the technical demands that certain formations or styles of play impose on players, but also the physical demands required of all players in a team.

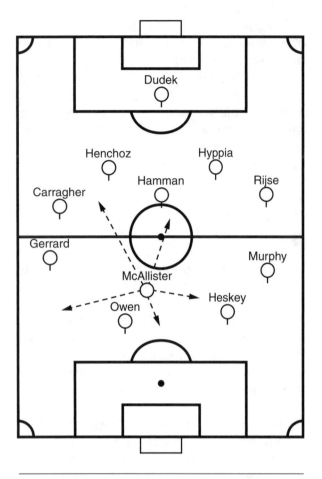

**Figure 10.9**   Liverpool F.C. 2001-2002.

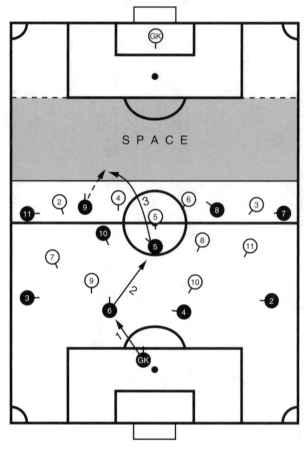

**Figure 10.10**   Space to attack.

I used the example of the Liverpool F.C. team of 2000-2001 for a reason. I wanted to describe a common occurrence that coaches confront whenever they try to devise a team formation or a system of play to suit their team. The team with a line keeper or shot stopper (commonly referred to as a "hockey goaltender") is forced to have its defensive line play deep. If there is a big gap between the last defender and the goalkeeper, then it spells big trouble for the team (see figure 10.10), particularly if the opponents have a fast forward player.

Two goalkeepers who stand out in my memory as "sweeper keepers," with the ability to command the area behind their defensive line, were Higuita of Colombia and Campos of Mexico. I am sure that both of these goalkeepers gave their coaches some anxious moments. They were both prone to eccentricities,

and they would both often indulge in risky play through faking and dribbling. They did, however, command a large area, which allowed their defensive line to play farther upfield.

The topic of defensive positioning brings us to a critical decision. We, as coaches, have to decide not only how our team defends, but also where it defends. The farther our players are from each other, the more space the opponents have to exploit. Conversely, the less space between our players, the more difficult it is for the opponents to attack successfully.

Top-level, quality players, such as those representing Argentina, have the ability and the tactical understanding to force opponents to play without time and space (see figure 10.11). Black 2, who is challenged by White 11, has two options: either pass the ball to Black 7, who is closely marked by White 3 and who, in turn, is covered by White 4; or pass it back

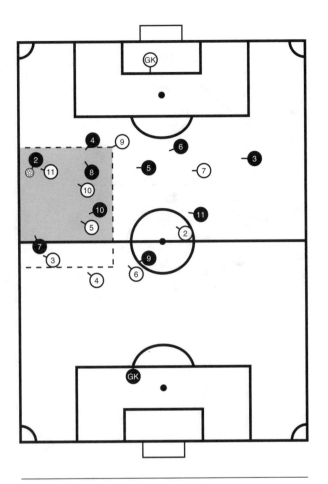

**Figure 10.11**    Denying time and space.

it. It should be the other way around. Coaches should first evaluate their players, then devise a system or team formation that suits them.

The first and most critical decision the coach has to make is to evaluate the goalkeeper's range. Doing so will determine, to a certain extent, the distance required between the last defender and the goalkeeper. Afterward, the coach needs to evaluate the central defenders:

- Are they fast?
- Are they tall?
- Do they communicate well?
- Are they aggressive?
- Do they combine well defensively with others?

The answers to such questions decide where a team will defend. For instance, assume that a particular team has a goalkeeper with a large range of command and a set of defenders who are tall, fast, and aggressive. For such a team, one defensive scheme would be to press in the other team's half of the field (see figure 10.12). The team's chances of success would be increased if their forwards were fast, aggressive, relentless pursuers of the ball, supported by hard-working midfielders who contested every pass and every dribble made by the opposition. Of course, this is a rather untidy, if not ugly, form of soccer, but it suited the players who represented Wimbledon in the 1980s and early 1990s, as well as the highly successful Norwegian national team of the early 1990s.

Most teams, however, do not have the players to press in the other team's half of the field. Their goalkeeper usually does not have a large range of command, and their defenders are neither tall, fast, nor aggressive. In such situations, we often find teams who line up to defend the middle third of the field. This setup is a compromise between a deep-lying defense and an all-out press in the other team's half of the field. In fact, most of the top teams in the world now draw up their defensive line to contest the middle third of the field (or less).

to Black 4, who will be immediately challenged by White 9. This arrangement gives the White team time to regroup for the next attack.

To a large extent, ball possession determines tactics. Coaches naturally expect that all 11 players on the team without the ball will defend. Formations are therefore labeled primarily to describe defensive lineups. For example, we have 4-4-2, 3-5-2, 4-3-3, 3-6-1, and so forth. The first number in each formation denotes the number of defenders; the second number, the number of midfielders; and the third number, the number of forwards.

## CHOOSING YOUR SYSTEM

A common mistake made by many beginning or novice coaches is that they first choose a system, then try to make their players fit into

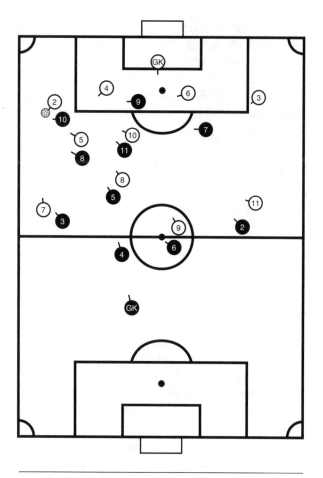

**Figure 10.12**   Full press.

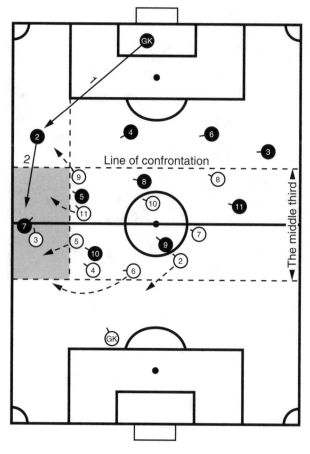

**Figure 10.13**   Forcing play down the wings.

All players in the team fall back into this area in the following situations:

- The opposing goalkeeper has the ball in hand.
- A free kick is awarded to the opposing team deep in its own half of the field.
- A goal kick is awarded to the opposing team.

This defensive lineup often entices the opposition to play a short pass to one of its defenders. Whenever the ball is advanced to the "line of confrontation," the nearest forward forces the play through certain channels, either down the wings (see figure 10.13) or through the middle of the field (see figure 10.14). This strategy allows the remaining members of the team—midfielders, defenders and goalkeeper—to take up appropriate marking and covering positions. Of course, if the forward player, when channeling the play,

can win the ball, he should do so and immediately set up a counterattack.

If the opposing team advances the ball—either by dribbling, passing, or kicking it past the forwards—then one of the forwards should immediately move up onto the line of the opponents' last defender (see figure 10.15). Here, White 10 can push up unnoticed by Black 4, unless the latter is alerted by Black 6. The diagonal run behind Black 4 will often catch the Black defense unaware. White 3 and White 5, who have double teamed Black 7, must be aware of this passing opportunity, and they must deliver a telling, accurate pass into the stride path of White 10 without hesitation. Failure to react results in a great number of missed opportunities to create quick goal-scoring chances when the ball is turned over in midfield.

Teams that line up as a defensive unit across the middle third of the field are complying with one of the most important defensive principles: compactness. Defending

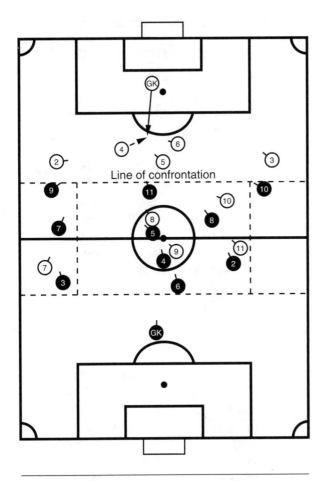

**Figure 10.14**   Forcing play down the center channel.

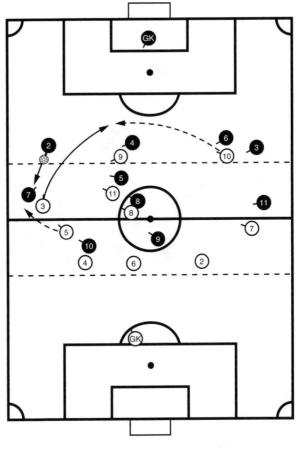

**Figure 10.15**   Pushing up to the line of the last defender.

one-third of the field is obviously easier than defending the whole field. Some astute coaches have not only recognized that their teams can achieve compactness down the field, but they can do so across the field. South American teams in particular have the ability to prevent teams from switching the play from one side of the field to the other. The covering players read the approach of their challenging teammates so that they can deny forward passes or dribbles, or across-the-field passes. The ball handler is often forced to pass the ball back to a supporting player.

The decision of where the team defends is of critical importance to any coach and team. If carefully worked out, the team can put the opposing team in situations where the ball has been turned over in great counterattacking situations. The likely event of the opposing defense's being in disarray is probable, and the team should be prepared for such eventualities (see figure 10.16). Here, Black 4

has tried to pass the ball to Black 5, but it has been intercepted by White 10, who dribbles past Black 4 to score a goal. Black 2 and Black 6 do not offer any cover because they did not expect Black 4 to lose the ball in this way.

# YOUR SYSTEM AND YOUR PLAYERS

Just as in a boxing match, where fans enjoy an all-action bout, many people in many countries enjoy a soccer match where both teams go at each other for the duration. However, such "blood and thunder" events often turn into "thud and blunder" events. The objective of each team is to force the other team to make mistakes, rather than create great scoring chances. Thus, our beautiful game of soccer is turned into an ugly affair, with neither team keeping possession for very long. Naturally, some coaches are forced to

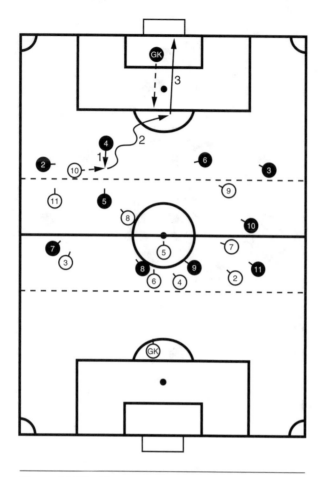

**Figure 10.16** Disarray.

prepare their teams to play an all-action game because all of their players are warriors; that is, they have no artists on the team. Highly successful teams are, of course, made up of a combination of both warriors and artists.

The truly great teams of the last half-century have all had in common at least one artistic legend on their team who created many of their goal-scoring chances and scored many of their goals. Puskas of Hungary; di Stefano of Real Madrid; Cruyff of Holland; Pele of Brazil; Maradonna of Argentina; Platini of France; Rivaldo of Barcelona; Zidane of France; and Figo of Portugal all come to mind. The secret for every successful coach is to find the player who can be truly described as an artist at the level in which he plays. Unfortunately, many coaches squash the artistic development of some of their players by insisting on work rate, speed, stamina, endurance, attitude, and so forth to the detriment of skill.

## Experiencing Scotland

In 1988, the U.S.A. Under-17 National team visited Scotland in preparation for the FIFA Under-17 World Cup. "Friendly" games were arranged against Greenock Morton, Glasgow Celtic, Scotland U.17, and Glasgow Rangers. After the first three games, the U.S. team was undefeated. They entered the Rangers game full of confidence, only to be told that the Rangers were fielding a team made up entirely of full-time professional players. The U.S. team's tactics that day were designed to prevent their two wing-backs from receiving the ball. This strategy would force their two center backs, the least technically efficient members of their team, to have significant ball possession and thus become their playmakers. The Rangers' center backs astonished the Americans by the tirade of abuse they gave their teammates for not moving into spaces. This abuse reached a crescendo when an intended pass from one of their center backs was intercepted, and the U.S. team went up field and scored. The United States managed to score a second goal to record a comfortable but unexpected 2-0 victory. After the game, Andy Roxburgh, the Scotland World Cup team coach, congratulated us with the parting remark of "What a great experience for a U.S. team to play against the Rangers." I have often wondered what he meant by that.

Again, just as in boxing—where two fighters can be wary of each other and rarely throw a punch—we find coaches in soccer who are overcautious. If both teams are ultradefensive, the game can be a bore (especially if at the slightest sign of danger, the team withdraws deep into its defensive half of the field). I find this scenario often to be the case in Brazilian club soccer, where teams are allowed to advance the ball to the halfway line unchallenged as the defending team withdraws into its own territory. They then attack with 4 or 5 field players against the opposing 10 players and seldom succeed (see figure 10.17). The ball is turned over, and the sequence is repeated in the opposite direction. The flip side of the coin is that when the attack succeeds, it is usually the result of some exquisitely performed piece of attacking—either through a mazy dribble, a display of intricate interpassing, or a thunderous, long-range shot.

The scenario illustrated in figure 10.17 suggests that top-level offensive skills are developed through playing against a top-level, intensive, aggressive, numbers-up defense. I believe that it is impossible to develop offensive skills to a high level without encountering stern defense. In practices with younger teams or teams with less experienced players, I advocate the adoption of player-to-player defense. This strategy virtually ensures that every time a forward receives a pass, she will be challenged by at least one defender.

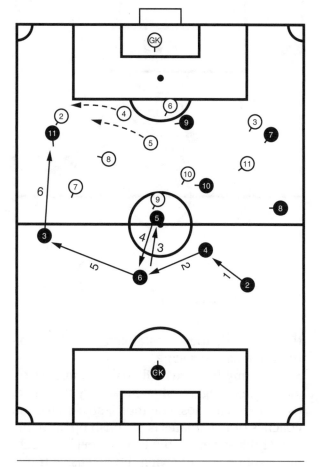

**Figure 10.17**   Outnumbered.

This arrangement also makes the thinking far easier for the defenders because the concept of passing on players is a difficult one for young and inexperienced players to absorb. If the offensive player is to improve her skills and achieve any sort of success, she will have to play against intensive player-to-player defense.

Post-World War II soccer has seen coaches and teams experiment with defensive lineups of 3, 4, or even 5 players. Such teams are mostly concerned with getting a numerical advantage over the opposing team's forward line. If the opposition plays with two forwards, then they will confront them with three defenders; if the opposition plays with three forwards, then they will confront them with four defenders. On the rare occasion that opposing teams play with four forwards, then a defensive line of five players will be used.

In 1966, when England overcame West Germany in overtime to win the World Cup, they used a formation as shown in figure 10.18. The key to their success was the defensive triangle of Bobby Moore, Jack Charlton, and Nobby Stiles. Moore and Charlton marked the two German forwards while Stiles "swept" in front of them by cutting off the passing lanes and thus contesting any German possession in the pocket in front of the defense. Nobby Stiles' contribution to the English success was enormous. He almost single-handedly won the battle for control of the setup area for the English team. Sadly, he was no longer a starting player in the English national team in the 1970 World Cup Finals. He was replaced by Alan Mullery, who although technically superior to Stiles, did not relish the defensive midfield role. Arguably, England had a much better group of players in 1970 than they did in 1966. But as a result of failing to control the setup area, they did not achieve the same success.

An essential element of the attacking mode of the England 1966 World Cup team was the role played by the fullbacks. Before Alf Ramsey's appointment as coach, fullbacks had performed a mainly defensive role in the team. Afterward, Ramsey wanted his fullbacks to exploit the space that wingers

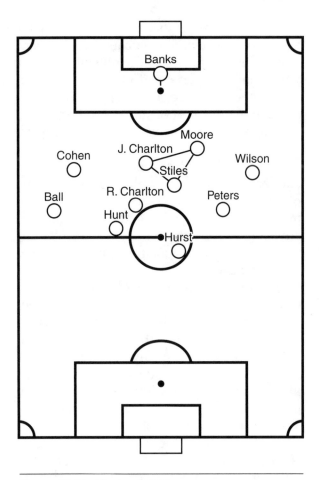

**Figure 10.18**   England, 1966.

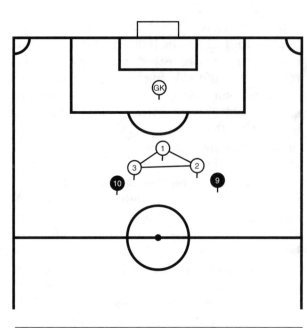

**Figure 10.19**   Back sweeper.

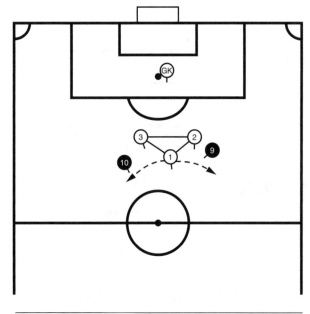

**Figure 10.20**   Front sweeper.

had previously occupied. It was the Brazilians who had first recognized the offensive importance of their fullbacks. In fact, Brazil has been renowned for producing fullbacks with great attacking flair. Their teams have included players such as Carlos Alberto, Junior, Cafu, and Roberto Carlos.

Whenever an opposing team plays with two forwards, they will likely be confronted by three defenders who form a triangular shape. The triangle will sometimes be lined up as illustrated in figure 10.19, with White 1 as a covering player behind his colleagues. At other times, the triangle will be lined up as in figure 10.20, with White 1 sweeping in front of his two central defensive colleagues. And at other times, the trio of players in the triangle will play flat across the field so that they can push up when their team has the ball far up-field (see figure 10.21). As soon as possession is likely to be lost, such as immediately before

the turnover, they reestablish the shape of their defensive triangle.

Opposing forwards will do their utmost to upset the triangular shape taken by the three defenders. The most common instruction from coaches or teammates is to "push up onto the line of the sweeper [the last player]." A much more subtle way of giving the defensive trio a

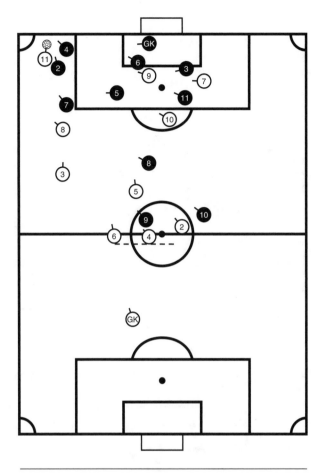

**Figure 10.21**    Flat across the back.

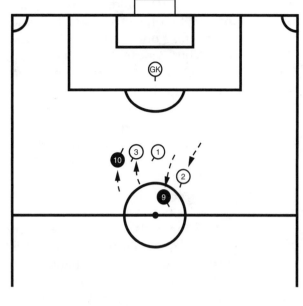

**Figure 10.22**    Upsetting the triangle.

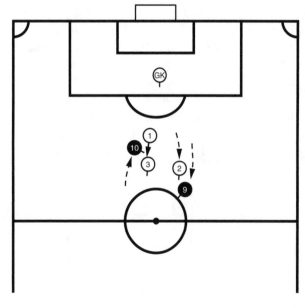

**Figure 10.23**    Reorganization.

problem in maintaining their triangular shape is for one attacker to play up and the other to drop off. Thus, we could get a defensive shape, as seen in figure 10.22, with opportunities for passes to be played into the area behind White 1 and White 3. A well-organized trio of players should not have any difficulty in dealing with this problem. White 1 would simply communicate with White 3 that he will mark Black 10, while commanding White 3 to sweep in front to cut off the passes to Black 10 and give cover to White 2 (see figure 10.23).

Of course, simple readjustments, as just described, require a lot of understanding between the trio of defensive players. Those players need to be aware of their own defensive strengths and weaknesses, but they should also know the strengths and weaknesses of their two opponents. They should calculate whether White 1, White 2, or White 3, when exposed to different situations, is able to

defend such a situation successfully. Do they have the patience to maintain a solid defensive posture? Do they have the speed to defend the space behind them? Are they vulnerable against give-and-goes? Can they stop a clever dribbler? If the answer to any such question is "no," then their organization should be such that the player with the weakness is not exposed. On the other hand, if the strength of the opposing two forwards, Black 9 and Black 8, is in running onto passes behind the defense, then White 2 and White 1 must drop off an extra yard or so to give them a better chance to get to the ball first (see figure 10.24). Conversely, if the strength of the two forwards is in their ability to come to the ball and turn on it, then White 2 and White 1 must play them tightly while White 1 sandwiches them from the front.

A different problem which usually confronts the trio of defenders is what happens when one of the two forwards retreats deep into the midfield area. A simple rearrangement is for White 1 to instruct White 3 to shadow him while White 1 moves to play in front of Black 9. Clever opponents will recognize this readjustment and push up a different player, Black 8, into the space vacated by White 3 (see figure 10.25).

Even if spotted by White 1, who will mark Black 8, we now have a situation as the one shown in figure 10.26. This is a solid attacking position for Black 9 and Black 8. If one of them comes to the ball, he will break up the partnership of White 2 and White 1. It is clearly up to White 1 to prevent this situation from arising. As the last defenders, he and the goalkeeper must alert White 3 to pick up Black 8,

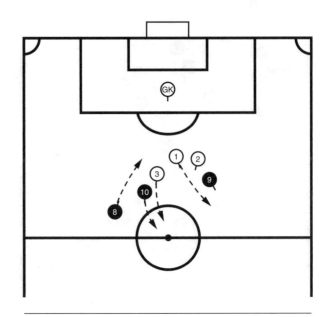

**Figure 10.25**  Readjustment.

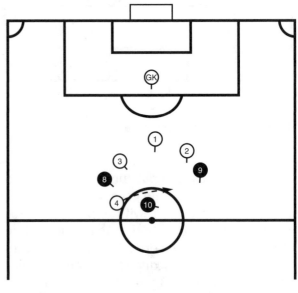

**Figure 10.26**  Maintaining shape.

and they must also alert a midfielder to pick up Black 10.

The aforementioned examples are but a few of the many problems that can confront a team's central defense. Players should be confronted with such problems on the training field and should be helped by the coach to find successful solutions. The coach needs to set up plays where such problems are encountered. Doing so helps players identify the relevant cues in the display so that they

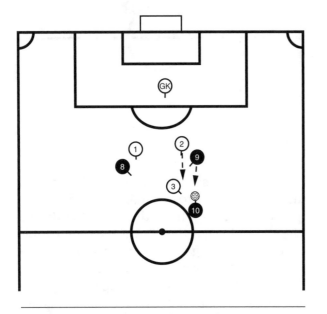

**Figure 10.24**  Breaking up the triangle.

can take appropriate corrective action. The key is to get the players to do two things: first, recognize and understand the problem posed by the opponents, and second, adjust their defensive structure and positioning to eliminate the threat.

Coaches, players, and fans sometimes get confused when talking about team formations of 3-5-2, 4-4-2, 4-3-3, and so on. The reason is that the defensive triangle is often composed of two defenders and one midfielder. However, little difference exists between the roles of the players in a 3-5-2 system and a 4-4-2 system. What is more important is that each player understands defensive responsibilities and offensive opportunities. Much time and energy has to be spent on the practice field to ensure that all players in the team fully understand their responsibilities and opportunities. For example, they should be prepared at any time during the game to adjust their lineup if the opponents decide to play with three forwards. One midfielder should be immediately assigned to drop back into the defensive line while an adjustment is made in the midfield. If Black 8 joins Black 9 and Black 10 as a third forward, White 5 could then be detailed to go with her and mark up while White 8 goes to the stopper (defensive midfield) position (see figure 10.27).

Players that fill wide positions on a team have had different expectations and require-

ments throughout the history of tactical development. As long ago as the 1950s, when the WM formation was still in vogue, the "wingers" hugged the touchline and the full-backs were expected to mark them. Wingers such as Sir Stanley Matthews were expected to be the "wizards of dribble," whereas full-backs were primarily defenders who stifled the wing play. Modern soccer demands that most wide players fulfill both requirements. Today's players must cover the length of the field while being prepared to attack when their team has ball possession or while filling a defensive role when their opponents have ball possession.

Once again, it was the Brazilians who were at the forefront of tactical change in the play of their fullbacks. If one of their fullbacks in their four-player defensive line went forward on an attacking run, then the other three defenders made adjustments, as shown in figure 10.28. White 2, White 4, and White 6

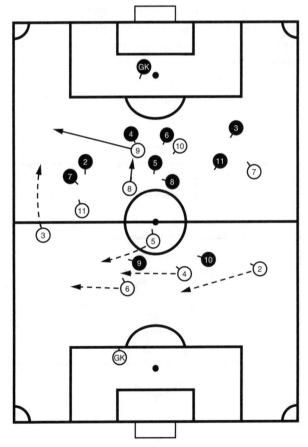

**Figure 10.28**   Sliding over.

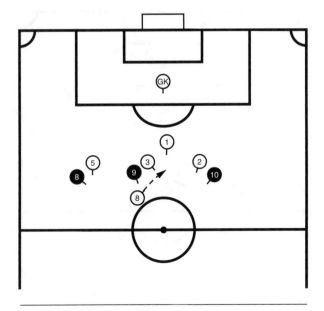

**Figure 10.27**   Marking three forwards.

would slide over so that White 2 and White 4 were the markers while White 6 covered the space vacated by White 3. If ball possession were lost, then the most likely channel for opponents to attack would be down their right-hand side (that is, the space now covered by White 6). The Black team would therefore need time to switch the field and attack down the left wing.

Teams playing a 3-5-2 system usually have only one wide player on each side of the field. When opposing a team playing a 4-4-2 system with two wide midfielders, the single midfielder can often be in situations where she is caught in a two-on-one (see figure 10.29). Here, Black 2 makes an overlapping run on the outside of Black 7. Black 8 runs diagonally across the line of the White defense, taking White 4 with her and out of a covering position. Most teams playing a 3-5-2 system have avoided this problem by playing with two stoppers, each with a responsibility to cover the nearest wide midfielder (see figure 10.30). If the ball is played down the opponents' right wing, then White 6 will cover White 11. If the ball is played down the opponents' left wing, then White 5 will cover White 7. Developing a pair of "twin stoppers" in a 3-5-2 system relieves White 10 of many of the defensive bur-

dens required in the modern game and allows her to become the playmaker (the artist) in a team. White 10 can therefore float, or find space, before ball possession is regained. She can also assess the likely weaknesses in the opponents' defensive positioning.

Developing the necessary understanding in the play of twin stoppers is not an easy task. They must forge a partnership whereby one covers the other. If one goes forward to support the attack, then the other must stay "at home" (see figure 10.31). If one supports her wide midfield player, the other must slide across to cover the central area in front of her defense (see figure 10.32). At all times, though, both players should follow the instructions of their three defensive players, particularly their sweeper and their goalkeeper, who each have a better view of the field.

What is important to understand is that each and every player on your team knows his responsibilities as an individual player and his role as a team player. Then heed the following motto: *Systems do not win games; players win games.*

The coach's function is to choose the right players and make them clearly understand their roles and responsibilities in each game. If the coach has not adequately prepared a

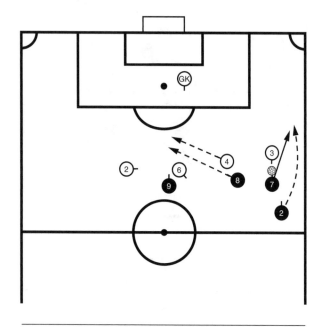

**Figure 10.29**  Overlapping run.

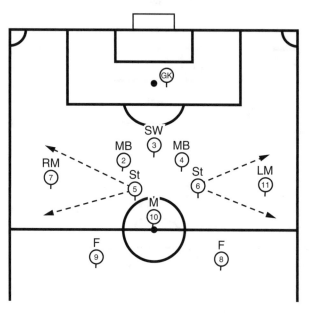

**Figure 10.30**  Twin stoppers.

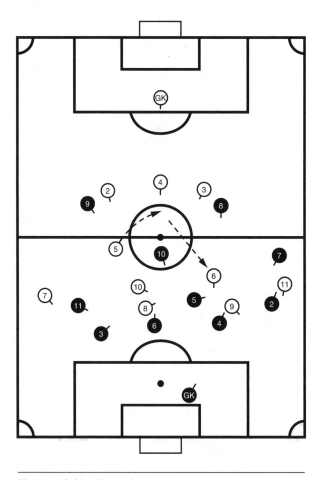

**Figure 10.31** Pivotal play.

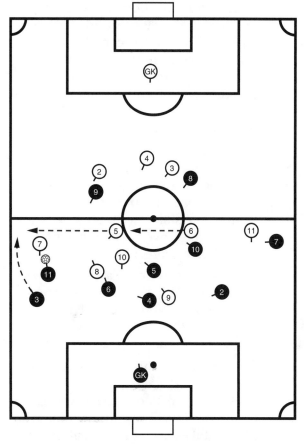

**Figure 10.32** Slide across.

team and fully briefed the players, then the coach has *speculated* the result of the game rather than *calculated* the result of the game. The Roman motto of *E Pluribus Unum* ("Out of many, one") should be adopted by all teams. Coaches should have objectives for devising a game plan that prevent the opposition from achieving success through the following tactical decisions:

- Attacking down the flanks to get around the defense

- Getting the ball over or behind the last defender

- Interpassing or dribbling through the heart of the defense

- Set pieces—corner kicks, free kicks, and throw-ins

At the same time, the coach may have a large concern of whether one or more oppo-

nents should be marked on a strict one-on-one basis. Conversely, the coach should prepare the team's offense to expose any weakness in the opposition's defense through exploitation of one of the four methods of offense previously mentioned. The coach should observe the opposing team and understand not only *how* they defend but also *where* they defend, as well as *who* commands their defense. Here are examples of how to find this information:

1. Do the opponents have a sweeper who drops deep to cut off passes or dribbles behind the defense? Is this sweeper one who commands her team from this deep-lying position? If so, can the coach push up one of her forwards onto the line of this sweeper so that the sweeper has to become occupied with this threat and thus lose some connection and command of the midfield? (See figure 10.33.)

2. Does the opposition get stretched out from their defensive line to their forward line? If so, can the coach organize the team to exploit a three-on-two situation in center midfield (in the setup area)? (See figure 10.34.)

3. Does the opposition play a 3-5-2 system? If so, do their stoppers or defensive midfielders give support to their wide midfielders? If they don't, can the coach prepare the team to exploit possible two-on-one situations through overlapping down the wings? (See figure 10.35.)

4. Does the opposition play with three forwards? If so, how are the defensive responsibilities reassigned to cope with the third forward? (See figure 10.36.)

5. Does the opposition only play with one forward? If so, how does the back line and midfield reorganize? (See figure 10.37.) In this situation, Black 6 takes a covering position on White 9 while Black 5 "sandwiches" from the front. This maneuver allows Black 4 to push up into the midfield, but with strict instructions to track down any runner out of the midfield.

6. Does the opposition play a player-to-player defensive marking system? If so, can forward players take defenders away from the attacking lanes to create space for midfield players to run into? (See figure 10.38.)

7. Does the opposition have a weak player in their defensive line who is slow? If so, how can we either isolate or press that player? (See figure 10.39.) Here, the offense has managed to isolate Black 3 versus White 7 by overloading the left side of the attack. Black 3 is not a fast player, and White 7 can beat Black 3 in one-on-one situations.

8. Does the opposition have a player in their defensive line who is techni-

cally poor? If so, situations should be created whereby she can get the ball so that the team can then press her. (See figure 10.40.)

These examples are only a few of the hundreds of questions a coach may ask when devising different tactical plans. But remember, these tactics will only be successful if you do the following:

- Evaluate your opponent's strengths and weaknesses correctly, and identify their preferred methods of offense and defense.
- Know your team's strengths and weaknesses.
- Devise a tactical plan that negates the opposition's strengths and exploits its weaknesses.
- Choose the right players on your team to carry out your tactical plan.

The key role of team tactics is to make the best use of the talent at your disposal. Do not copy the team formations used by the top clubs; rather, look at the different types of players your team has, then design your team formation and style of play.

Critics often blame "discipline and organization" for stifling individuality in the game. The contrary is probably more accurate. The Brazilians and Argentinians play to a rigid, structured, and organized game plan that creates situations where the individual player flourishes.

## CHOOSING A STRATEGY

As a general rule, the field of play can be divided into three areas (see figure 10.41). The defensive area is the one area in which defenders should take no risks of losing ball possession because lost possession could well result in the opposition scoring a goal. Safety is the first essential rule of sound defending, and the player who takes risks in the defensive area may pay dearly for any mistake that he makes. "If in doubt, put it out" has become the clarion call of all top-class defenders.

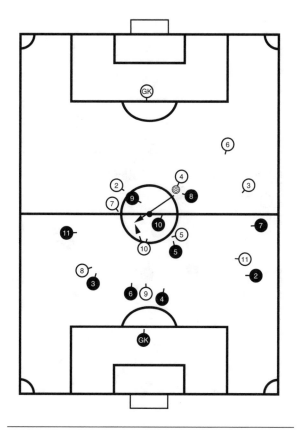

**Figure 10.33** Occupy the sweeper.

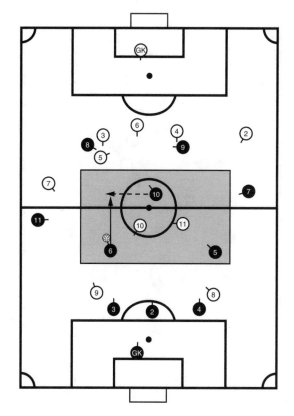

**Figure 10.34** Stretched out.

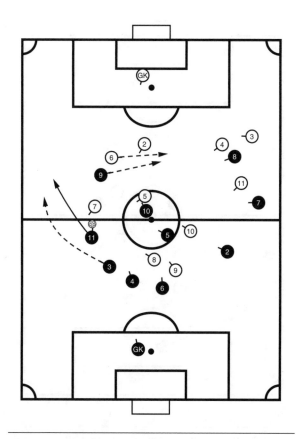

**Figure 10.35** Using the wings.

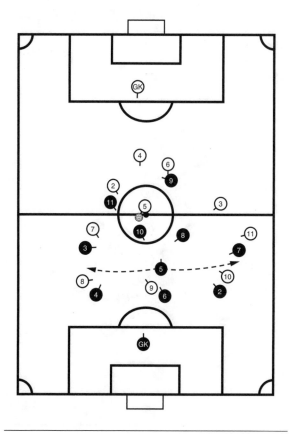

**Figure 10.36** Playing against three forwards.

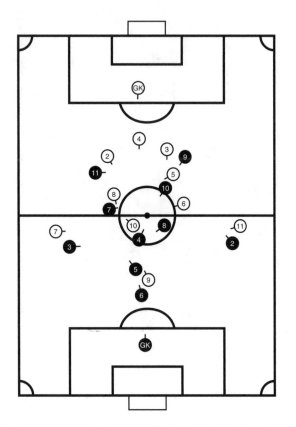

**Figure 10.37** Playing against one forward.

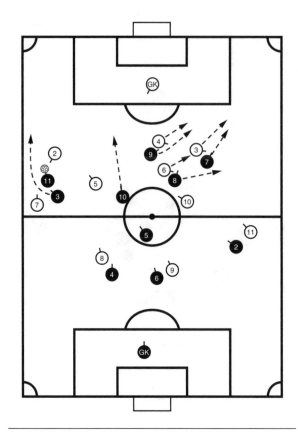

**Figure 10.38** Taking the marking players away.

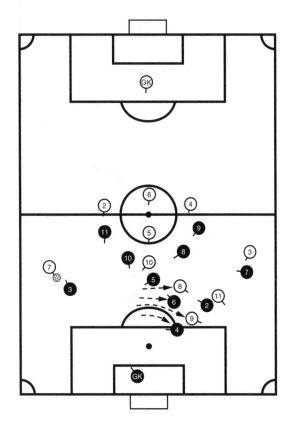

**Figure 10.39** Isolating weakness.

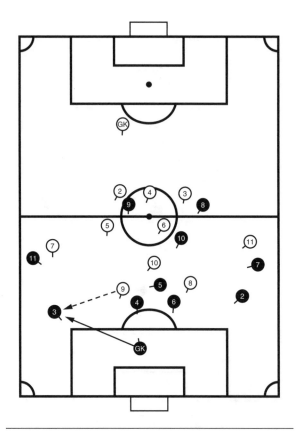

**Figure 10.40** Giving a weak player the ball.

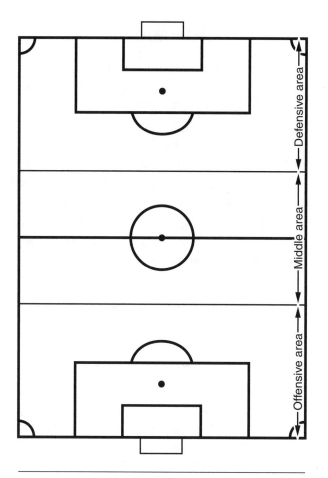

**Figure 10.41** The three areas of the field.

The offensive area is the one area in which attacking players can feel justified in taking risks. In this area, the player who can take on one or two defenders will be most effective. A player with this ability will create havoc against any defensive system, and such an ability will be most useful in this area of the field. Likewise, very little will be achieved if she uses dribbling skills in the defensive area of the field. A team could also be justified in taking risks with long, penetrative passes into the offensive area, especially if the opposing defense has been drawn into square positions and if there is space behind them for forwards to run into.

The question of space behind a defense leads us to consider the area that offers attacking players the greatest opportunity to score. Without being too rigid, a reasonable guide for young players is that all shots from fewer than 20 yards present a scoring threat to the defending team; however, the narrower

the angle of the shot, the less likely it is to score. We might then agree that an attacking player in possession of the ball in the scoring area close to the goal presents a real threat to the defending team. Experience has shown that the majority of goals are scored from strikes on goal taken from within this area.

Soccer coaches should therefore base their strategies and tactics on the following, as shown in figure 10.4 on page 134:

- *Defending*—how to prevent the opposition from getting the ball to one of their players inside the shaded scoring area.

- *Attacking*—how to get the ball to an attacking player inside the shaded scoring area near to the opponents' goal so that she can shoot, head, or redirect the ball into the goal.

The team that is the most successful in achieving both objectives is likely to win the match. Virtually all tactics, strategies, team formations, and systems of play in soccer are based on the simple principle of either getting the ball into the scoring area or preventing the opponents from doing the same. However, players also have a second major consideration when dealing with this subject. As we already know, the area immediately outside the scoring area can be regarded as the setup area. A pass or dribble could be made from anywhere inside the setup area to get the ball into the scoring area.

As a coach, if you have the opportunity to analyze why a goal was scored—either through watching film or videotape, or through observation during a match—you will notice that in virtually all instances, a player will have been allowed to pass or dribble the ball from the setup area into the scoring area. This pass from the setup area into the scoring area could take one of many forms. Some examples could be a throw-in, a corner kick, a free kick, an overlap followed by a cross, a give-and-go in the setup area, or simply a long, hopeful kick deep into the scoring area. It could also be a combination of a pass and dribble or simply a run onto a pass over or through a square-lying defense. The issue at stake is that any team that allows its opponent unchallenged possession in the setup area nearest its goal is in deep trouble. Conversely, a team that can secure solid possession in the setup area nearest to the opponent's goal is in a commanding position to win the match. Command of the setup area therefore becomes the key component of defensive or attacking tactics. How to achieve this command remains the most difficult, but most stimulating, tactical challenge for any soccer coach. A team is most likely to achieve this command if it adheres to the principles of play.

## Summary

- Players have three ways to advance the ball—by playing around, over, or through the opponent.
- The team that dominates the setup area will most likely win.
- Choose a system that fits your players.
- The key role of team tactics is to make best use of the talent at your disposal.
- Make sure that no matter what system you use, all your players understand their individual responsibilities.

# Chapter

# 11

# TEACHING DEFENSIVE TACTICS

A player's performance involves three basic factors: individual skill and technique; understanding the intricacies of the game and finding solutions to the problems that arise during a match; and physical and psychological fitness. These factors are interdependent, and no player should miss an opportunity to improve in each aspect of the game.

Although coaches in the past largely concentrated on improving players' technique, they now recognize and accept the following realization: However technically efficient players may be, their failure to apply technique in the right situation at the correct time will render them ineffective. I am sure that we are all familiar with the player who can juggle the ball with ease yet never has an impact on the game.

## THE PRINCIPLES OF PLAY

The greatest challenge for any soccer coach is to teach the players to have an understanding in combination and team play. The coach must be able to present the 11-player game in such a way that all young players, at all levels of ability, understand the problems and solutions inherent in the game. The basis for this learning is called the *principles of the game*. Whatever system of play or tactical consideration you use, the players on a successful team must obey these principles. Keep in mind that these principles of the game are not new; they have applied since 1925, when the present offside law was introduced. And unless the laws of the game undergo radical change sometime in the future, coaches and players have no reason to suspect that these principles will ever change. The principles of the game are as follows:

| Attacking Principles | Defensive Principles |
| --- | --- |
| Support | Cover |
| Penetration | Delay |
| Width | Compactness |
| Mobility | Balance |
| Creativity | Patience |

Every coach and every player should understand that when players and teams adhere to these principles of play, they are much more likely to achieve command of the setup areas and consequently win the match. If you were to analyze a team's failures, you would probably find that a player (or players) on a team did not observe one or more of these principles. On the other hand, you would see that a successful team's players would consistently adhere to the principles of play.

Both the offensive and defensive principles of play are a combination of tactical and technical skills. For instance, when a player on defense is trying to delay the attacking player, the challenging player's stance, distance, and angle are of primary importance. The distance and angle of support then provided by the covering defender, or second defender, are also crucial to success. That the third defenders provide balance is also of a tactical and technical nature. Simply put, the entire team's skill and tactical awareness in maintaining compactness requires technically well-developed players.

## COVER

Defenders have two primary concerns: first, restricting possibilities for attacking players to collect the ball in front of them; and second, playing the ball into the space behind them. Defenders therefore attempt to restrict the gaps through which the opponents can make penetrative passes.

Players who challenge the ball handler need to have support, which means that teams cannot play in straight lines on defense. In figure 11.1, the three White defenders (2, 3, and 5) are positioned in a line across the field. A through pass that beats one of them beats all of them. They are neither covering one another nor the space behind them. In figure 11.2, on the other hand,

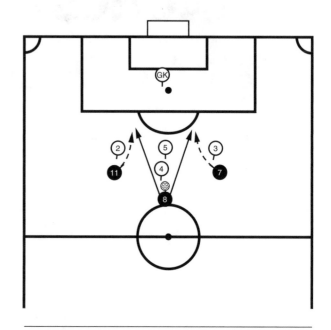

**Figure 11.1**   Straight-line defense.

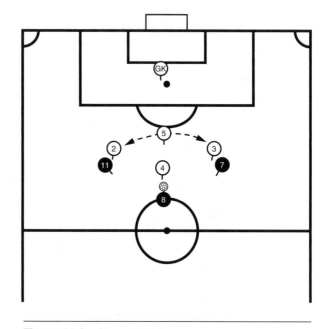

**Figure 11.2**   Covering defense.

White 5 has dropped back to cover the space into which Black 8 might wish to pass the ball. The defenders' positions allow Black 8 to pass to Black 11 or Black 7 (although the defenders are not beaten by this particular pass).

When the sweeper gets put in a position of commitment, his teammates will need cover. This scenario leaves the attackers with an equal or greater number of players than the defenders. In other words, if two players attack two defenders, one of the defenders must challenge for the ball. The other defender, although possibly a marking defender, must support the challenging defender. If the challenging defender gets no support, then the attacking player has a one-on-one opportunity. In addition, the attacking player with the ball could play the ball into the space behind the second defender for the second attacker to run on to. The second defender must therefore provide cover or support in case the first defender is beaten by a dribble, and he must also guard against a through pass or wall pass. The second defender must do so from a position that allows him to close down the second attacker, should the first attacker play the ball to the second attacker.

Coaches and players should also be aware of when defenses can push up. Defenses can push up and play flat across the back only in the following instances: when their attackers are in possession of the ball; when the opposing player in possession of the ball is facing away from her goal; or when the defense can put immediate and intense pressure on the opponent in possession of the ball, thus forcing that player to look down at the ball. When a team loses possession, a well-organized defense will not push up and become flat across the back unless there is immediate and intense pressure on the ball. If the opponent in possession of the ball is unchallenged and can play the ball behind the defense, the situation is too dangerous for the defense to push up. The opposing forwards or midfielders need only to time their runs into the space behind the defense to receive a pass and have a clear run on goal. Defenses that play flat across the field are easily beaten by such a pass, or even by a dribble.

The number of players required to provide cover or support in defense depends on the number of forwards the opponent is using. Teams usually find it necessary to have a numbers-up situation on defense. Although not as glamorous as an offensive drill, the following is a small-sided game that promotes a player's understanding of cover.

## Quick-Cover Game

**Purpose:** To practice the second defender's covering position.

**Procedure:** The game starts with two attacking players just outside the penalty area and two defenders in the penalty area. The player with the ball enters the penalty area and is challenged by a defending player. The second defender provides cover so that she can pick up the player with the ball in case that player beats the first defender. The second defender's angle and distance of cover must be such that she can close down the second attacker in case the first attacker passes to the second attacker. Should that happen, the player who was the first defender must provide cover for the defender, who is then putting pressure on the ball.

So that the defending players can get accustomed to providing cover at the proper angle and distance, have the players play the game without allowing the attacking players a shot at goal. Once the defenders become more proficient, the attackers may shoot at goal at any opportunity after entering the penalty area.

### Coaching Points

• The defender, without overcommitting, should put immediate pressure on the player with the ball.

• The angle and distance of support (cover) provided by the second defender must be such that (1) she can pick up the opponent with the ball should that player get by the first defender, but not so deep that (2) the second defender can't get to the second attacker, should the second attacker get the ball (see figure 11.3).

• If the first defender's body position takes away the attacking player's passing option, the second defender may shorten the angle and distance from the first defender.

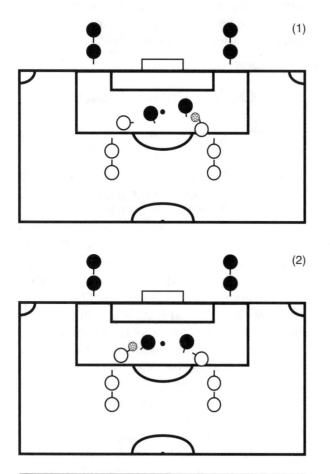

**Figure 11.3**  Quick cover game.

___

# DELAY

A major objective in attack is penetration; therefore, an obvious principle of defense must be delay. Once a team has lost possession, its first task (if it cannot immediately regain possession) is to get its defense organized so that it is not vulnerable to a quick counterattack by the opponents. The forwards and the midfield players should ensure that the opposition take a long time in building up their attacks so that the defense can be reorganized.

Delay in defense should begin the moment that ball possession is likely to be lost. The opponent who has gained ball possession must be put under pressure as quickly as possible by the nearest player so that his teammates can make their recovery runs into their defensive positions. The challenging player must make a quick recovery from an attacking position and get between his opponent and the goal. This swift recovery takes extra effort, especially if the challenging player is a forward (see figure 11.4). Here, the White team has lost the ball, and players 9, 10, and 11 (the forwards) have to make long recovery runs.

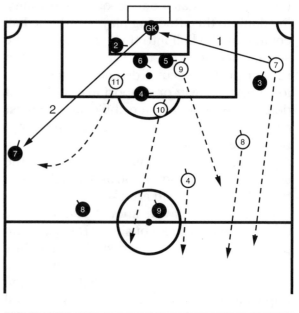

**Figure 11.4**  Recovery runs.

The deeper inside the opponents' half of the field these delaying tactics are used, the longer the defense will have to get reorganized. All forwards must therefore realize the importance of "tackling back." Whenever ball possession is lost, the forward nearest the defender must become the "delay" player by challenging the opposing defender in possession. Such a player must, if possible, dispossess the opponent. But he should also remember that a wild challenge, which allows him to be beat by the opponent, is enough to expose other members of his team to a quick counterattack.

Not only must forwards be instructed to get goalside of their opponents when they have lost possession, but midfield players and defenders must also realize the value of slowing down the opponents' attacks. A team that falls back in front of an opposing attack invariably slows it down. The attack is then delayed, and valuable time is gained for defensive reorganization.

In figure 11.5, White 8 and White 10 have lost possession deep in the opponent's half of the field, and the ball has been played quickly to the Black 10. The White defense is outnumbered six to five, and it is the task of White 4 to delay the Black attack until White 7, 8, and 10 can recover into goalside defensive positions. White 4 has taken up a position between Black 10 and Black 4, and she is "inviting" Black 10 to pass either to Black 11 or Black 4. In either case, White 4 is achieving the aim of gaining time. As in the first case, a pass made to Black 11 will be a

pass made away from the scoring area, and an early square pass to Black 4 will achieve little in penetration because White 4 has time to move to the left to block Black 4's approach to goal.

While the attackers still retain a numerical advantage, they will want to achieve penetration as quickly as possible. Black 10 must commit White 4 so that Black 10 can push the ball to Black 4, who can then attack the defense. Basically, Black 10 and Black 4 against White 4 is a two-on-one situation, and the attackers must exploit this as quickly as possible. The defender would then aim to delay the attackers so that her teammates have time to get back to reduce the numerical disadvantage. As soon as White 4 sees that Black 10 is bringing the ball at her, she must try to slow down Black 10 by falling back. How such a simple tactic results in the dribbler's slowing down is truly remarkable, especially at the youth level.

When the dribbler has slowed down, White 4 can then decide to tackle—but on no account should White 4 lose the ball. If White 4 attempts to tackle and then fails to win the ball before White 7, 8, and 10 have gotten back, then White 4's defense will be outnumbered to the extent of 6 to 4. Any defender who is placed in a similar situation to White 4 should therefore never attempt to tackle unless she is absolutely sure of winning the ball. That defender will be far better off falling back to just outside shooting distance, where opposing forwards (despite holding numerical advantage) will have less space to work in. Players should also notice that defenders should not fall back into their own penalty area to delay the opposing forwards. When the opposing forwards arrive with the ball just outside shooting distance of their goal, they must then make a stand. If they have managed to slow down the opposing forwards just outside shooting distance, then their task of making a solid tackle will be made much easier.

The great Hungarian team of the early 1950s had an unwritten but clearly understood rule in their tactical plan: If a player gave ball possession away, then that player had to give immediate chase after the ball

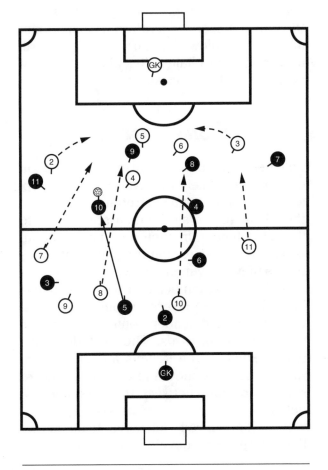

**Figure 11.5**  Restoring the balance.

and keep running until ball possession had been regained. Although the message is clear, it should be emphasized that quick recovery alone is not enough. Many players confront their opponent, but fail to pressure him. Standing in front of an opponent is not going to deter his making a pass or trying to run through with the ball. Defenders must get close enough to the opponent so that they can touch him with an outstretched hand. This pressure should ensure that the opponent drops his head to keep his eyes on the ball, which would thus prevent any quick, forward passes.

When challenging, a player needs to remember that stance is important as well. If the challenging player stands "chest-on" to the opponent with ball possession, such a player is exposed to fakes and feints. The ball player has momentum and can thus dictate the outcome of the confrontation. The challenging player should adopt a stance not unlike that of a boxer—with a shoulder facing the opponent—so that the challenger is better positioned and better balanced to turn quickly and move either forward or backward. The angle of approach at which a challenging player confronts an opponent is also critical. The angle should be such that it denies the possibility of playing the ball forward; therefore, it forces the opponent away from possible passing angles upfield or even crossfield.

Having developed a solid stance—one that allows the player to easily go forward or backward—the challenging player then needs to adopt an aggressive attitude. When opponents realize that they will come under pressure the moment they receive the ball, they will be keen to play the ball hurriedly. Controlled pressure is vastly different from the hasty, lunging efforts that concede free kicks. Having recovered, closed down, and confronted an opponent by applying controlled pressure, the challenger watches closely for the moment when the opponent drops his head to look at the ball. This position now means that the opponent cannot see other available passing options. At this

point, the challenging player should use body feints and fakes on the player with the ball. It is too often accepted that attackers make feints and fakes on defenders—so why not get the upper hand by posing the opponent with problems that include a few faked lunges? The opponent will often lose control of the ball, allowing the challenging player to win the ball, either with a firm tackle or, preferably, with a steal.

If we assume that the opponent in possession retains the ball, the challenger's next priority is to force the opponent to turn away from his intended path. If the opponent is forced to turn sideways, he can either risk a back pass or opt for a square, crossfield pass. Either pass gives the recovering team the chance to consolidate their defensive positions; it also draws the sting out of the attack. Forcing opponents to turn back toward their own goal is even better. Now they are not only facing the wrong way, but their teammates have probably raced into attacking positions and left open gaps. It is then the time to become relentless. The opponent must not be allowed to turn. To win the ball now gives the challenging player the best possible kind of possession.

## COMPACTNESS

Coaches generally recognize that any team on defense is likely to have defensive problems when that team is stretched out longer than 35 to 40 yards from its first defender to its last defender. In such a scenario, the attacking team can exploit the abundant space that is inevitably made between each player on defense. Remember that when the ball is lost, all of your players become defenders; thus, the first defender could very well be one of your forwards. The best defensive teams, such as the Italians and the Argentinians, seldom allow more than a 35-yard space to develop between their first and last defender.

A well-organized defensive team allows limited space to develop between and behind players so that the player challenging for the ball will be closely supported. This coaching point is easily demonstrated in figure 11.6, where White 1 and White 2 have to get past Black 1 and into the shaded area behind Black 2. (Black 1 and Black 2 are restricted to playing in their own squares.) If we change this practice to allow Black 2 to move forward to cover Black 1, then White 1 and White 2's task becomes much more difficult. This task becomes even more difficult still if we have three defenders spaced out over 35 to 40 yards.

To merely place defenders within their squares in a grid area is not enough. They must learn to play, not as 3 individuals, but as units of 2 or 3 players. An example of this unity is illustrated in figure 11.7, where Black 1 and Black 2 are playing as a pair. Black 1 has maneuvered White 1 into a tight position

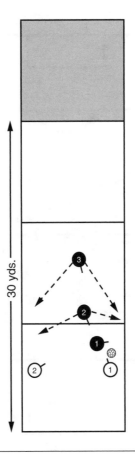

**Figure 11.7** Basics of compactness.

near the sideline. Black 2 then covers Black 1 in such a way that Black 2 can tackle White 1 if she beats Black 1. Or, Black 2 can engage White 2 if White 1 decides to pass to White 2. Notice that Black 1 has closed down on White 1 and is facing her in the boxer's stance, sideways on. Once Black 1 has engaged White 1 in this way, Black 1 must become relentless and continue to apply pressure on White 1. Black 3 must weigh the options available to White 1 and be prepared for the most likely outcome. Black 3 should read the stance and challenging position of Black 1 to determine the most likely option taken by White 1. At the same time, Black 3 should communicate with both Black 1 and Black 2 to ensure that if the ball is not won by a tackle, then it will be channeled into her covering position.

How the compactness in defense practice is observed in a game is illustrated in figure 11.8. White 2 is challenged by Black 10 in

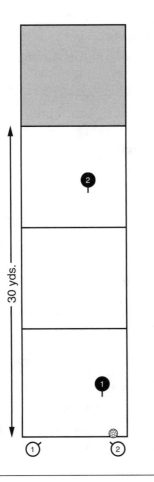

**Figure 11.6** No or minimal compactness.

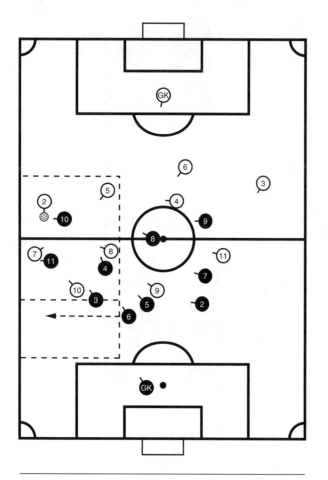

**Figure 11.8**   Compactness.

through which passes can be made, and they aim to prevent an attacker from running with the ball. Defenders cover not only each other, but they also cover the spaces for which the whole defense is responsible.

# Strategic Withdrawal

**Purpose:** To improve the team's understanding of where, when, and how to defend.

**Procedure:** Two teams of seven-on-seven play on an 80-by-50-yard field. They play a regular game with all the rules, but with the following condition: When the goalkeeper has the ball, the entire team without the ball must withdraw into its own half of the field. As the play develops (or immediately before), the coach should find opportunities to make the following points through the coaching-in-the-game method.

### Coaching Points

• All players on the team without the ball are defenders.

• The activity of the defending player nearest the ball determines the defensive positioning (marking and covering) of the other defenders.

• Players who must make recovery runs into defensive positions must do so immediately and at speed to limit the opposing team's counterattack opportunities.

• Players on the defensive team must communicate.

• When a team has possession of the ball, some of its players must still think defensively and take up positions to prevent a quick counterattack.

• The other players on the team take up their marking and covering positions using the cues given by the defender nearest the ball and by the movement of opponents.

• The defender nearest the ball forces the play to either side and does not allow the ball to be played across the field (figure 11.9).

such a way that White 2 is forced to advance the ball through a pass or dribble down the wing. Black 3, 4, and 11 mark up tightly on their immediate White opponents while Black 6 covers the space behind his teammates.

Top defensive teams not only compact the distance from the first to the last defender to about 35 to 40 yards, but they also do so with the spaces between players across the field. When teams learn to execute these maneuvers as part of their game, they deny the opposing team the opportunity to switch the play from one side of the field to the other.

In general, the defensive team is involved in restricting space through which and into which attacking players can move unchallenged. Defenders aim to restrict the spaces

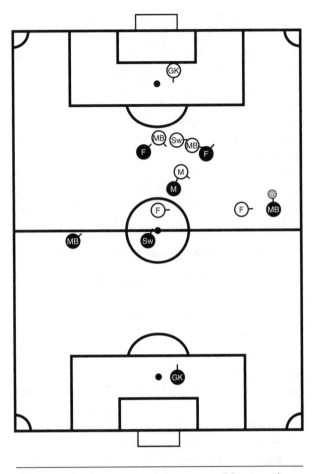

**Figure 11.9**   Strategic withdrawing and forcing play down the channels.

# BALANCE

Defensive players must be concerned with the maintenance of cover at all times. Attacking players will make runs specifically to draw defenders out of position to create space for themselves and other attackers. The defense must be balanced against these threats. Two factors are important in the maintenance of balance in defense: first, identifying the role of a free defender; and second, tracking down players.

When most teams defend, they hope to outnumber the opposition by at least one player. The role of this additional player is usually to provide cover for the other defenders and to shore up any gaps in the defense. This additional player will some-

times be employed to meet the opposition's attacks during the buildup in the setup area so that the opposition is denied the opportunity of getting the ball into the scoring area. The player in this role would commonly be known as a front sweeper. In most cases, the sweeper (or libero) will be employed to cover the space behind his defense. This player's responsibility is to ensure coverage for any co-defenders threatened by an opponent. Thus, the sweeper in figure 11.10 (White 4) covers White 2, who is threatened by Black 11, while the other defenders (White 5 and 3) mark their immediate opponents.

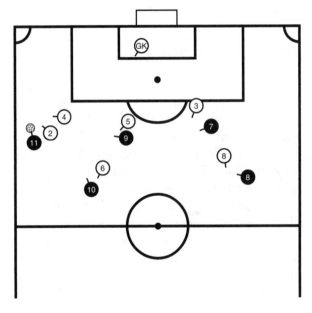

**Figure 11.10**   A well-balanced defense.

The midfield defenders, White 6 and 8, have the responsibility to close down their immediate opponents if the ball is played to them by Black 11. They also have the responsibility to track down their immediate opponent should that player threaten to run into spaces between and behind the defense. In figure 11.11, White 8 is particularly vulnerable if the ball is played back to Black 10 because White 8 might be caught ball watching and thus allow Black 8 to run into the space behind her. In such circumstances, we might expect the sweeper to pick up any midfield opponent who has not been tracked down.

**Figure 11.11**   Ball watching.

An experienced sweeper might demand that White 3 cover the space threatened by Black 8 while she picked up Black 7, who is White 3's immediate opponent. Once the danger has passed, White 4 would ask White 3 to pick up Black 7 again so that White 4 could revert to the role of sweeper.

If an opposing player receives the ball unchallenged in the setup area and attacks the defense, the sweeper has the responsibility to come out to challenge. The marking players can then concentrate on marking their immediate opponents (see figure 11.12).

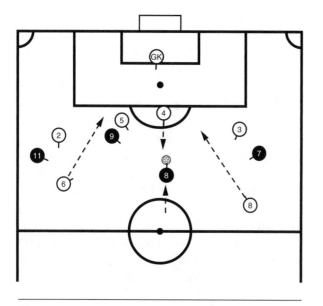

**Figure 11.12**   Coming out to challenge.

Here, we find Black 8 in clear possession while the sweeper, White 4, comes out to challenge. On no account should White 4 risk being beaten by lunging into the tackle. Rather, White 4 should concentrate on delaying the attack until White 6 and 8 have recovered into a defensive position, goalside of the ball, so that the defense can reestablish its balance.

Every team needs to practice the art of balancing their defensive cover. The following game will help players better understand well-balanced defense.

# Three Zones

**Purpose:** To develop understanding of defensive tactics.

**Procedure:** This conditioned game can be played with any number of players, from 5 on 5 to 11 on 11, and it uses a field divided into three zones (figure 11.13). A field 90 by 50 yards is divided into two end zones of 35 by 50 yards and a middle zone of 20 by 50 yards. With nine players on a team, for example, each team would have one goalkeeper, three defenders, three midfielders, and two forwards. Each player is restricted to a zone. The object is for the goalkeeper, defenders, and midfielders to get the ball to their forwards so that they can score.

## Variations

- A defender may move forward into the middle zone if a defender on the same team passes the ball to one of its midfield players. When the team loses the ball, the defender must recover immediately into the team's end zone.

- Similarly, a midfield player may move forward into the attacking zone on the same conditions.

- Further variations that use both conditions might see four defenders, four midfielders, and two forwards in each zone; or four defenders, three midfielders, and three forwards in each zone.

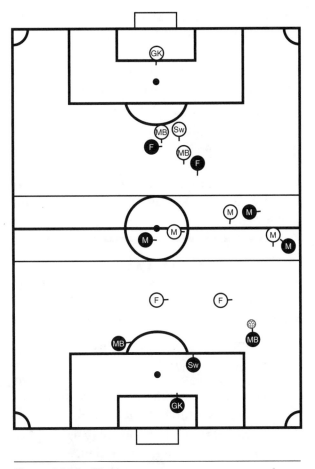

**Figure 11.13**   Three zones.

# PATIENCE

Defenders too often give up sound defensive positions because they become impatient and go for balls that cannot be won. Every player should recognize that a defender's three priorities are as follows:

- To intercept
- To challenge and tackle
- To delay and contain

In figure 11.14, the ball has been played forward to Black 9 to a position where it is difficult for White 5 to attempt an interception. In this situation, it would be foolish for White 5 to commit to a challenge because this position might give Black 9 the opportunity to pivot and beat him. White 5 should instead restrain his actions and be content to maintain the numbers-up situation that he and White 6 have achieved.

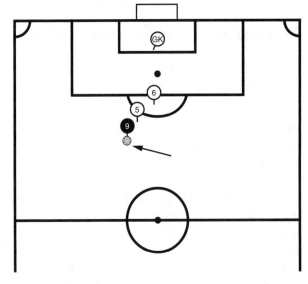

**Figure 11.14**   Restraint.

In figure 11.15, White 2 should again be content to keep Black 11 facing the touch-line to prevent her from turning to face the danger area. This arrangement allows White 4 time to recover into a covering position. Only when commanded to do so by White 4 should White 2 attempt to challenge and win the ball. In this situation, defensive players too often allow the attacking player to collect the ball and turn to face the danger area. No attacking player should be given the freedom to turn if it is at all possible to keep her facing away from the scoring area.

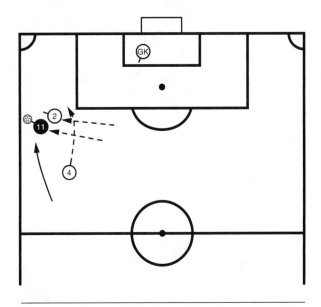

**Figure 11.15**   Hold your position.

# Patience: Five-Second Delay

**Purpose:** To develop patience and delaying tactics when challenging.

**Procedure:** Create an area 40 yards by 20 yards, with a small goal on each end. Several players station themselves beside each goal. From the halfway line, a ball is played in to one of the goals. One player, the attacker, receives the ball. The attacker's job is to try to score on the other goal. The moment the ball is played, a player from the other goal (the defender) goes out to meet the attacker. The defender's job is to delay the attacking player. After three seconds, a second defender leaves the same goal as the first defender did. The second defender's job is to provide cover, to communicate, and to encourage the first defender to tackle the ball away. After gaining cover, the first defender should make a serious effort at tackling the ball away. After the tackle, the two defending players should ideally be in possession of the ball. They should then attack the other goal, whereas the lone attacking player should try to prevent it from happening. When the game goes well, you can add a second attacking player, who leaves the line when the second defender leaves.

### Coaching Points

• The first defender must close down the attacker quickly. The defender should give the attacker as little distance into the field as possible.

• The defender, when approaching the attacker, should be under restraint and should be balanced to avoid overrunning the attacker or being caught flat-footed.

• The defender, particularly in the last few strides, should approach sideways, preferably facing the closest touchline.

• By jockeying and through body position, the defender should be able to slow down the attacker, force the attacker outside, and then contain him.

• Once covered, the defender should force the attacker to make an error and tackle the ball away.

# SUMMARY

As you work on teaching defensive tactics to your team, consider the following points:

• Command of the setup area is the key component of any tactical plan. Helping your players achieve this objective is your most difficult, but most stimulating, coaching challenge.

• Demand that all of your players be part of the defensive tactical plan.

• Decide on your tactical plan before working out systems of play and team formations.

• Make sure all players understand their roles in a defensive tactical plan, whether they play sweeper, marking back, stopper, any of the midfield positions, or forward.

• The key defensive principles are compactness, depth (cover), delay, balance, and patience.

# Chapter

## 12

# TEACHING OFFENSIVE TACTICS

Every defensive principle has an attacking principle to counter it. The attacking players use support to overcome tight cover; they use penetrating runs and combination play to upset balance on defense; and they attack wide to defeat the defense's attempt to compact them. Simply stated, the offense uses mobility and creativity to offset the defensive principles of delay, balance, and patience. Let's take a close look at each principle of offense:

- Support
- Penetration
- Width
- Mobility
- Creativity

## SUPPORT

A player in possession of the ball should always have one or more opportunities to pass the ball to other members of the team. This rule means that players on the team in possession who are "off the ball" should therefore move into positions that allow the ball to come to them. By just waiting for the ball to come to them, these players allow defenders to get between them and the ball. In other words, if the supporting player finds a defending player between herself and the ball carrier, then the supporting player is in the wrong position. She should move to a position where the ball carrier can easily pass the ball. But remember that the ball carrier, if under pressure from an opponent, needs help as well. Players should never run away from a person who needs help. As long as the player with the ball needs help, the supporting players should come to the player in need and provide the help. Once the ball carrier is out of trouble, the supporting player can then start looking for runs ahead of the ball.

When players stand in lines, either down or across the field, they will find it much more difficult to pass the ball. In figure 12.1, the Black forwards have taken up flat positions and have thus considerably reduced Black 10's passing possibilities. In these flat positions, the forwards are not making themselves available for an easy pass from Black 10. To increase their attacking possibilities, the forwards (Black 7, 8, 9, and 11) should aim at giving support to Black 10, allowing an easy, uncontested passage of the ball from ball handler to ball receiver.

In figure 12.2, both Black 11 and Black 8 have moved toward Black 10. By doing so, they have increased Black 10's passing possibilities because Black 10 can now pass quite

**Figure 12.2**   Excellent passing options.

easily to either of these players. The movement of Black 11 and Black 8 also poses serious problems for White 2 and White 6. They must now decide one of two things: whether to track down their immediate opponents and leave a space unguarded behind them, or allow Black 11 or Black 8 to collect the ball unchallenged in the setup area in front of the defense. If they decide to follow Black 11 or Black 8, then Black 9 and Black 7 can move into the space left unguarded to receive a through pass from Black 10.

The example in figure 12.2 indicates that if some players move toward the ball player, whereas others move away, then the passing possibilities for the attacking team and the problems confronting the defending team will be increased enormously. Most young players tend to run away from the ball player. To accurately pass to a player who is running away is extremely difficult. Even if the pass is accurate, considerable demands will be made on the ball control of the player receiving the ball, especially if he is being marked. Nothing is more frustrating for a player than to find every teammate running away when he is looking to pass the ball.

The player in possession should ideally have the option of passing the ball forward, sideways (across the field), or backward to

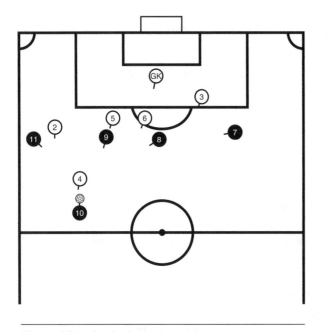

**Figure 12.1**   Lack of passing options.

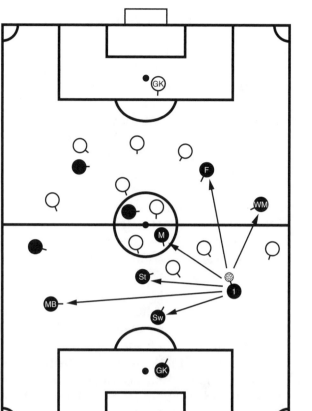

**Figure 12.3**   Passing options galore.

other players on the team. In figure 12.3, for example, the Black marking back can pass to the wide midfielder, the sweeper, the stopper, the midfielder, or even to one of the forwards.

As a coach, instruct your players not to abandon the ball handler. The following game will help your players understand the concept of support in play.

## Confined to Base

**Purpose:** To develop forward play using two forwards.

**Procedure:** Two forwards play against three defenders and a goalkeeper in each half of a 40-by-20-yard field with goals. Players are not allowed to cross the halfway line, although they are allowed to pass the ball over it (backward and forward). Only the

forwards can score. Observe all laws of the game, except the corner-kick law.

**Coaching Points**

• Observe that most forwards want to come toward the ball. In the beginning stages, they will tend to kill their space and position themselves near the halfway line. Notice the position of the Black forwards in figure 12.4.

• They will be much more successful in receiving the ball if they push up on the line of the sweeper. This scenario makes it much easier for them to get the ball. First, they have more space to come to the ball, and second, they have an opportunity of running onto the ball in the space behind the defense.

• The two forwards should work harmoniously. If the first forward goes to the ball, then the second forward should normally hold on the line of the opposing sweeper.

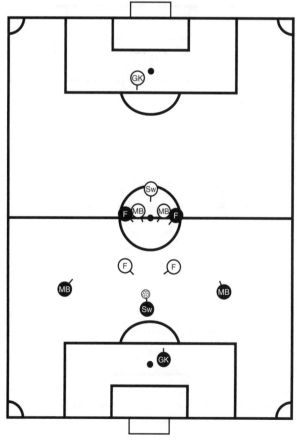

**Figure 12.4**   Black forwards have killed their receiving space.

• If the first forward is able to turn on the ball, then the second forward has three main options: make a diagonal run behind the defense; move away from the first forward, allowing the latter to have a better one-on-one dribbling opportunity; or offer himself as a target for a wall pass.

• If the first forward receives the ball facing away from the second forward (and is heavily pressured by an opponent), then the second forward should be alert to the first forward's possibly passing backward as a prelude to a penetrating pass. This move might be described as a one-three (figure 12.5).

• The first forward will often move to the ball too early, but that first forward will also take a defender with her. This opportunity allows the second forward to make a run into the space created by the first forward's movement.

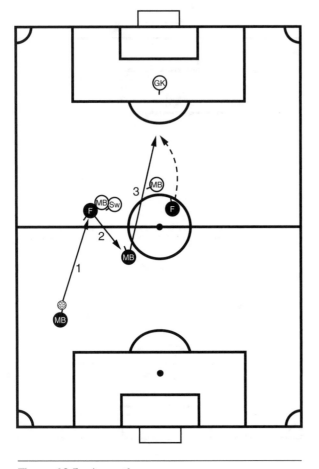

**Figure 12.5**   A one-three pass.

## PENETRATION

Any team wishing to achieve penetration in attack must have players in front positions as far forward as the laws of the game will allow them to go. The ball can then be played forward to these front players so that they can either shoot at goal, dribble past defenders, or lay off for supporting players. Teams are too often forced to play square because they haven't got a forward who is willing to take the responsibility of playing on the line of the opponent's last defender.

Another situation we see too much is when we find forwards who almost invariably come to the ball instead of making runs in behind defenses. This movement is perfectly understandable because defenders are bound to mark tightly near their own penalty box. Perhaps one of the chief qualities of a forward who is playing in these front positions is that he displays great courage. He must be prepared to withstand keen tackling in this area, often with a back to the opponent's goal. Once he starts to look for the ball out on the wings or come back into midfield for it, his team will be forced to play square because there will be nobody to play the ball forward to.

The player in possession should pass the ball in a forward direction whenever possible. The objective of the game is, of course, to score goals, so the ball must ultimately get into the scoring area if a team is to score a goal. Experience has shown that the quicker a team plays the ball forward, the more likely the opposing defense will be disorganized. A successful team can play the ball quickly and accurately to its front players. This objective means that the runs of the front players allow the team the opportunity of playing over, around, or through the opposing defense.

In figure 12.6, Black 11 has the ball and is confronted by White 2. Black 11 has the option of beating White 2 (who is covered by White 4) or passing to Black 10. In either case, little will have been achieved in terms of penetration because the attack is still a long way from getting the ball into the scor-

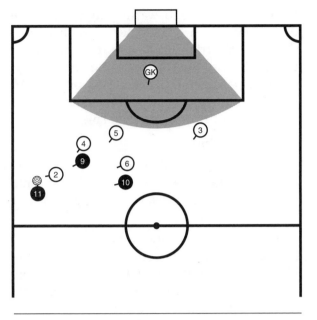

**Figure 12.6**    Killing space.

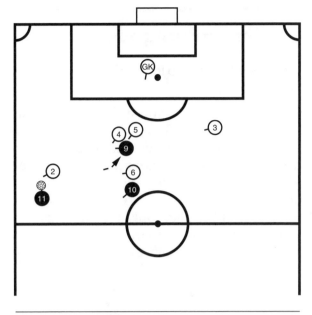

**Figure 12.7**    Creating space.

ing area. A speculative cross will also be covered by White 5 and 3, who are restricting the space into which the attacking players may move.

In this situation, the attacking team should not allow the defense the luxury of covering defenders. Black 9 should therefore move toward the sweeper and stay as far upfield as the laws of the game will allow. This situation immediately poses problems for the defense, especially if White 4 has been detailed to mark Black 9. Does White 4 go with Black 9, or does White 4 take up another role? If White 4 does go with Black 9, as in figure 12.7, then it means that Black 9 is now committing two defenders, which reduces the problem for the other forwards to that of one on one or two on two.

If White 4 chooses not to go with Black 9 and stays to cover White 2 and White 6, then it might be possible for Black 11 or Black 10 to play a quick one-two (give-and-go) with Black 9 (see figure 12.8). Here, Black 11 passes to Black 10, who pushes the ball through to Black 9, who lays it off for Black 10, who is following up. It is essential here that Black 9 show himself as a target for Black 10's pass and that Black 10 follow up after making the pass.

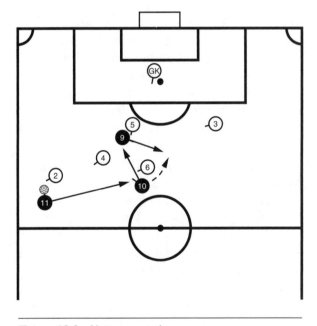

**Figure 12.8**    Using created space.

Too often, the ball is played toward the danger area, and attackers do not follow up to receive layoff passes. Alternatively, if Black 9 has solid ball control and can turn quickly, Black 9 could turn with the ball and take on White 5. Or, if White 5 lays off, he could then take a shot on the goal.

The concept of penetration is not an easy one to grasp. The following are games that put into practice this complicated skill.

## Three-Pronged Attack

**Purpose:** To develop forward play using three forwards.

**Procedure:** The simplest way of preparing three forwards to combine is to play a realistic, small-sided, conditioned game. In this game, three forwards play against four defenders and a goalkeeper in each half of a 40-by-30-yard field. Restrict all players to their half of the field. Only the forwards can score. Players can pass the ball backward or forward over the halfway line. Observe all laws of the game.

### Coaching Points

• You should make certain that the forwards understand the coaching points made when only two forwards play against three defenders. With the addition of another forward and another defender in each half of the field, the number of opportunities for combination play greatly increases. You can now focus on having one of the three forwards get in behind the defense. The offense will usually be unsuccessful if all three forwards persist in making runs toward the ball.

• If you wish to play with three forwards, you may find it best to play with one advanced striker (primary) and two withdrawn strikers (secondary). The primary striker's responsibility is to push up on the line of the sweeper while the two secondary strikers look for the ball in the space in front of the defense.

• If a secondary striker or the primary striker receives the ball and is preparing to drop it to a supporting midfielder, then the other secondary striker should look to make a diagonal run into the space behind the defense.

## Penetrating With Three Against Five

**Purpose:** To further develop forward play using three forwards.

**Procedure:** Three forwards play against five defenders and a goalkeeper in each half of the field. Restrict all players to their half of the field. Only the forwards can score. Players can pass the ball backward or forward over the halfway line. Observe all laws of the game, except the corner-kick law.

### Coaching Points

• The coach should make certain that the forwards understand the coaching points made when three forwards play against four defenders.

• The addition of another defender in each half of the field makes opportunities for combination play more difficult to capitalize on. You should focus on getting one of the three forwards in behind the defense. The offense will usually be unsuccessful if all three forwards persist in making runs toward the ball.

# WIDTH

Coaches and players should remember that the principles of play are based on the considerations of defensive players who are guarding the spaces behind and in front of the defense to a position in which an attacking player may shoot at goal. If the attacking player collects the ball unchallenged in the space in front of the defense, that player's chances of making a quality pass into the shooting area are increased enormously. Players and coaches should also realize that the space on the wings of centrally concentrated defenses can be utilized and exploited by attacking players.

In figure 12.9, Black 7 has the ball and is confronted by a centrally concentrated defense. Black 2, realizing that there is space outside Black 7, moves down the wing to take a pass. When this happens, one of the defenders must immediately move out to challenge Black 2; otherwise, Black 2 has time to steady herself and make a solid pass into the area in front of goal. From this scenario, we can deduce that the setup area in front of the defense can now be enlarged to include the spaces down the wings.

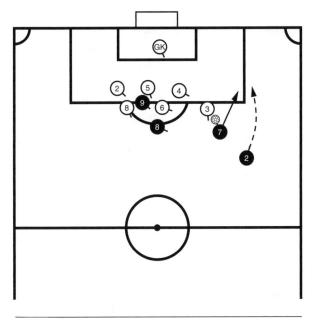

**Figure 12.9**  Creating space through wide play.

The following are small-sided games that help develop a player's understanding of width.

# Three and One

**Purpose:** To practice width on offense and to develop forward play using three forwards and one midfielder.

**Procedure:** Set up as you did in the previous game, with three forwards playing against five defenders and a goalkeeper in each half of the field. Next, add another player to each team. These additional players play without any conditions and can cover the whole field. Restrict all other players to their half of the field. Only the forwards can score. Players can pass the ball backward or forward over the halfway line. Observe all laws of the game except the corner-kick law.

**Coaching Point**

• The addition of an extra, unrestricted player on each team creates the opportunity of developing the concept of creating space for others. Players must now begin to think of taking defenders out of covering positions, rather than taking them into covering positions.

# Attack in Numbers

**Purpose:** To develop attacking play.

**Procedure:** You can develop the previous small-sided, conditioned game to include two or three unrestricted players on each team. Opportunities become available for creating space for others, overlapping, running at defenses, and interpassing.

**Coaching Points**

• When the ball is passed to a wide player, teammates always have the opportunity of making a looped run to the outside of that player. This type of run usually allows the offense to penetrate on the outside of the defense. Or, when the defense tracks down the overlapping player, it allows the wide player to cut inside.

• One of the unrestricted players will probably manage to get possession of the ball in the space behind the opposing unrestricted players. This move allows the player to run at the opposing defense.

• Players also have numerous opportunities of combination play through interpassing. The key to success is to get quick, simple, but accurate ball movement. If the ball sticks with one player for longer than a couple of seconds, then it is likely that the defense will have sufficient time to reorganize.

# MOBILITY

Probably the least understood offensive principle is mobility in attack. In America, we are far too "position conscious." In many teams, we see players who confine their activities to certain areas of the field. The biggest culprits are probably the wide players: the wing fullbacks and the wide midfield players. The reality is that a player who plays in a fixed position and remains in a certain area of the field for the whole game is easily marked. Likewise, a player who plays with a degree of freedom and mobility is much more difficult to mark.

Most soccer coaches have found it extremely difficult to operate "set" attacking plays in the match situation. To predict the movement of opposing players is impossible. Even the simplest and best-rehearsed move may fail because of the problems created by the opposing defense. To allow attacking players the opportunities and assistance necessary in solving these problems is therefore much better. They should be encouraged to react naturally and intelligently to outwit the defense. In attacking play, too much regimentation kills imagination, and too much organization can be restrictive. When players are faced with the problems posed by a defense, they must be allowed to experiment with solutions.

One of the simplest ways of upsetting a defense is for the forwards to switch positions. A fullback who is marking a winger on the same side of the field for the entire game has a comparatively easy task, especially if that player has had the better of the early exchanges. If, however, the winger is continually switching positions with the other forwards, the fullback's problems will be increased. He will then have to contend with 3 to 5 different players during the game.

A player who plays with a degree of freedom and mobility is much more difficult to mark. In figure 12.10, Black 7 (the wide midfielder) makes a run inside while Black 8 (the midfielder) moves to the outside. In essence, Black 7 and Black 8 have exchanged positions. What is more important is that the exchange of positions has created problems for the defensive players White 3 and White 6. They now have to decide whether they'll be more successful by staying in their positions or by tracking down their immediate opponents.

An attacking team should make full use of diagonal and overlapping runs when dealing with an organized and compact defense. In figure 12.11, Black 11 has the ball and is challenged by White 2, who is covered by White 4. Black 10, who is marked by White 8, makes a wide, overlapping run outside of Black 11. At the same time, Black 7 makes a diagonal run to threaten the space just behind White 5, who might have been moved out of position by Black 9's run out of the central position. Black 8 will make an overlapping run into the space vacated by Black 7. Black 8 will then be likely to get free into this area because her immediate opponent, White 5, will in all probability be watching the ball.

By executing the maneuver illustrated in figure 12.11, the Black team has effectively destroyed the White team's defensive balance and cover by the use of diagonal and overlapping runs. Black 11 now has two solid opportunities to create a scoring chance.

**Figure 12.10**   Exchanging positions.

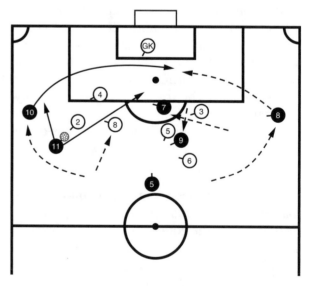

**Figure 12.11**   Destroying defensive balance.

Black 11 can either play the ball to Black 7 or Black 10, who can then cross the ball into the scoring area for either Black 8 or Black 7 to have a strike at goal.

All players, of course, face a great risk that the ball will be lost in the confusion of all these runs and opportunities. A misplaced pass would catch the Black team in a poor defensive position. Black 5 needs to fill the space behind her fellow attackers, and she needs to be prepared to challenge any White player who brings the ball out of defense. Doing so will allow her teammates time to recover goalside of the ball.

All movements of attacking players near the scoring area have to be watched closely and judged quickly by defenders. Defenders are never quite certain whether an attacking player is moving to receive a pass or moving to tempt a defender away from a position to create space for others. Diagonal runs should be made precisely for this purpose. Attacking players should run into positions in which they are an immediate threat (should they receive the ball) and in which they open up the possibility of a pass to a teammate who is just as dangerously positioned.

The more direct the run that the attacker makes toward the opponent's goal, the more immediate the reaction of the defender must be in response. A direct run toward the goal by an attacker must be covered by a defender, but this type of run has three major drawbacks. First, it is often difficult to pass the ball to a player who is running directly toward the goal. Second, it is difficult for the player to make this run and keep an eye on the ball. Third, the choice of action is solved for the defender: She has to go with the runner, unless she suspects that the attacker is running into an offside position. Much greater success can be expected if attackers make diagonal runs to threaten the space behind the defense.

In figure 12.12, Black 9 runs diagonally forward into the space behind White 5. In this type of run, Black 9 should maintain eye contact with Black 8. I remember that when I was coached in the professional ranks, I was

**Figure 12.12**   Effective diagonal run.

told when practicing diagonal runs to "keep your left eye on the defender and your right eye on the ball." Exactly how one can achieve such an objective is questionable, but the instruction made clear what was expected of me. On no account should Black 9 turn her back on the ball. Black 8's task will now be to bend the ball around into the stride path of Black 9's run by using either the inside of the right foot or the outside of the left foot. Black 9 could also threaten the space to the right of White 5, in which case Black 8 would have the responsibility of bending the ball with the inside of the left foot or outside of the right foot into Black 9's stride path.

Black 8 and Black 9, of course, have to forge a partnership through mutual understanding of each other's play. Black 8 should be aware of Black 9's preferred run. Black 8 should also control the ball with the first touch to set it up for striking a pass with the appropriate part of her foot on the second touch.

Not all diagonal runs should be made away from the ball player. A great deal will be added to the attacking possibilities of a team when players in advanced positions near their opponent's goal make diagonal runs to the ball.

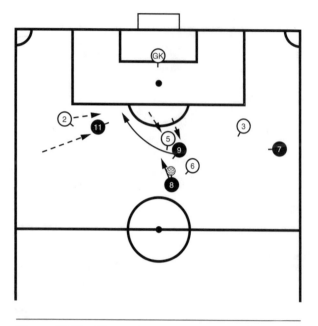

**Figure 12.13**   Diagonal run to create space for a third player.

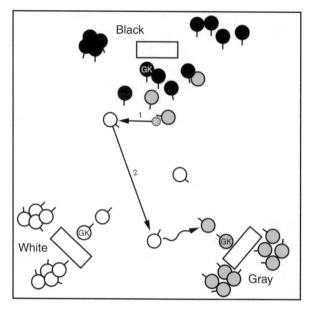

**Figure 12.14**   Three-goal game.

In figure 12.13, Black 9 has made a short diagonal run toward Black 8. As a result, Black 9 has drawn White 5 away from the central defensive area. Black 9 has thus enabled Black 8 to play a short pass to him so that he can immediately feed Black 11, who is running into the space behind the defense. Note that Black 9 is half-turned toward White 5 so that not only does Black 9 see the movement of the defender, but he also is in a position to receive the ball with the foot farthest from the defender while observing Black 11's run. It is much more difficult for Black 9 if he cannot see White 5.

# Three-Goal Game

**Purpose:** To develop the players' offensive understanding of the balance between risk and safety.

**Procedure:** This small-sided, conditioned game uses three goals set out in a 50-yard equilateral triangle. Three teams of four players line up against each other (figure 12.14). Each team defends one designated goal while trying to score on either of the other two goals. A team may gang up with

another team, but they should beware of being double-crossed.

## Coaching Points

• Teams often neglect the defense of their goal during the initial stages. Too many players go forward, leaving only one or two players to defend their goal.

• The smarter players soon learn that to win they must get all their players goalside of the ball. When on the offensive and in possession of the ball, the players must calculate the balance between safety and risk. If one or more players go forward on the offensive, then the remaining players must organize themselves so that they are least vulnerable to a counterattack.

• The player in possession should also realize that an attack in one direction is easy to stop. Players usually find it better to suddenly switch the point of attack and go to another goal. The player in possession must also calculate whether it is prudent to pass the ball to one of the players on another team. How likely is a double cross?

• When a team has possession, the players without the ball have many difficult decisions. "Do I stay in a defensive position?" "Do I move forward on the attack? If so, where do

I go?" "Do I move into a supporting position behind the ball? Do I advance in front of the ball? Or, do I take a wide support position?"

# CREATIVITY

To unlock modern defenses, we need players with skill, flair, and imagination. The player who is prepared to do the unexpected and the unorthodox is much more likely to succeed against well-organized defenses than the players who are drilled and predictable.

All players should be encouraged to develop awareness and imagination during their formative years in soccer. Each player, particularly those in forward positions who are likely to be tightly marked, should develop a range of tricks with the ball that are likely to deceive their immediate opponents.

## Dave Sexton

I am reminded of the story about Dave Sexton, the former Chelsea and Manchester United coach, during a time when I was at a coaching course at Lilleshall in England. When asked by Walter Winterbottom (then the director of coaching for the FA, as well as England's coach) to give an example of creativity in attack, Dave Sexton performed a "bicycle kick" from just outside the penalty box to the astonishment of all present.

Without doubt, the key to the development of creativity is total awareness of immediate opponents. Players should make full use of their visual, auditory, and tactile senses to determine the exact position and intention of every immediate opponent. If they know where their immediate opponents are positioned and what their likely intentions will be, then they can call on their repertoire of tricks and skills to deceive this opponent.

For most forward players, it is sound planning to allow themselves to be tightly marked just before the ball is ready to be played forward. When doing so, they establish the starting position of the defender

by using sight and touch. To execute this maneuver successfully, they will need to be slightly sideways-on to their opponent. They will need to lean against the defender and establish the starting position, which they can do by reaching out with an arm.

In figure 12.15, Black 2 has received the ball from Black 6, but she is not yet ready to play it forward. Black 9 advances as far as possible toward the White goal, making White 5 mark her closely while forcing White 6 (the sweeper) to play square. In this position, Black 9 can dictate the line of the White defense and create a space (bounded by White players 4, 5, 6, and 10) in which she will eventually receive the ball from Black 2.

Black 2 has the ball under control and is ready to play it forward. Black 9 makes a move to receive the ball. As Black 9 comes off White 5, the pressure on Black 9's arms and side will indicate how closely White 5 will follow. At the

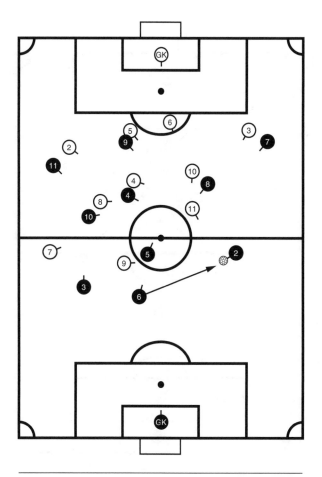

**Figure 12.15**   Creating space to receive the ball.

same time, Black 9 should face the touchline to receive the ball, with White 5 in view out of the corner of her left eye. Some players will also pick up cues of White 5's movements by listening to the sound of the foot beats.

We might now expect a situation to have developed as illustrated in figure 12.16. Black 9 comes off White 5 and receives the ball from Black 2 facing the touchline. From visual and tactile cues, Black 9 knows that White 5 has tracked down her run and is marking her tightly. Black 9 also sees that Black 7 and 8 have initiated penetrative runs to get into the space between White 3 and 6. Black 9 is therefore faced with three major options:

1. Flick a pass to Black 7 or Black 8.
2. Hold the ball and lay it off to Black 4.
3. Step over the ball and pivot to beat White 5.

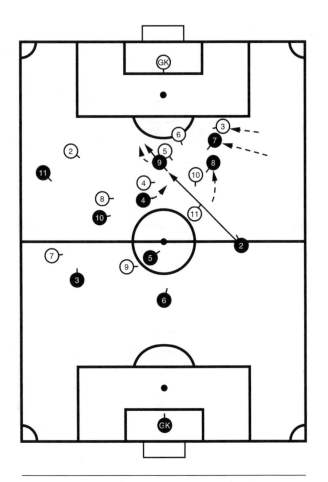

**Figure 12.16**   Options after receiving the ball.

Inventive, creative players will recognize all three options. These players will not only have the technique to carry each option out, but they will also have the skill to recognize which will be most effective. Players should frequently be challenged and encouraged to do the unorthodox, particularly when they are outnumbered by defenders.

Some may argue that you cannot teach creativity. Perhaps this is true in a sense, but with a little practice, players can certainly improve their creative thinking. The following games, will help develop a player's understanding of creativity, and they will also help the player recognize opportunities to express creativity. A player who has been trained in this way may become better at creative thinking on the field than another who is more naturally creative but has not specifically thought about how they can use that creativity in a game.

## Three-Cone Game

**Purpose:** To develop the offensive play of a pair of attacking players.

**Procedure:** Place three upright cones 20 yards apart in an equilateral triangle in one half of the field. Two play against two in a game to see who can knock down any cone with the ball. Mark out a boundary line, usually about one half of a soccer field.

**Coaching Points**

• The player in possession of the ball often must screen the ball from a defender. The player in possession should take a sideways-on position so that she can see the opponent, the teammate, the second defender, the ball, and the cones.

• The player in possession will also have to run with the ball and protect it at the same time. This will often mean dribbling the ball with the foot farthest away from the challenging defender.

• The dribbling player will have to effect sudden changes of speed and direction.

• In changing speed, the player will usually perform a fake turn before sudden acceleration.

# SUMMARY

The hardest offensive component to coach is improvisation. Players must be willing to play with flair, and they must dare to take risks. You must create an atmosphere and environment in which players aren't afraid to do so. The following points will help you in making your team more effective and efficient in offense.

- Stress that forwards should time their runs to coincide with what is happening on the ball.

- Coach two (or more) forwards to work harmoniously. If one goes to the ball, then the second should hold on the line of the opposing sweeper.

- Make the second forward understand that if the first forward is able to turn with the ball, the second forward must provide one of three options—a diagonal run behind the defense, a move away to create space for the first forward to dribble, or a target for the pass.

- Show attacking players how to create space for others by taking defenders out of covering positions.

- Remember that if you're playing with three forwards, it may be best to play with one advanced (primary) striker and two withdrawn (secondary) strikers.

- Remember the key offensive principles: support, penetration, width, mobility, and improvisation.

# Part V

# COACHING MATCHES

# Chapter
## 13

# PREPARING FOR MATCHES

During the regular season, you not only have opportunities to watch your next opponent play, but you also have one or two practice sessions to prepare your team for that particular match. If you are in a tournament or play-off situation, however, you will have neither luxury, but it is important to analyse your opponent and prepare your players for specific matches whenever possible.

When you can watch your next opponent and then schedule one or two practice sessions to prepare for the match, your true worth as a coach is established. Each regular season match becomes an opportunity to ask yourself the following questions: Have I identified the key strengths and weaknesses of the opposing team and players? How do they relate to my team's strengths and weaknesses? Have I designed practice sessions that will clearly show my players how they can combat the strengths and weaknesses of the opponent?

## SCOUTING THE OPPOSITION

Preparing teams for matches divides coaches into two extreme schools of thought. The first school tends to ignore all information about the upcoming opposition and concentrates all energies on perfecting the team's own game. The second makes detailed reports of the upcoming opposition, relays this information to the players, and makes whatever adjustments are needed to counter any major strengths in the opposing team.

Both approaches hold dangers. The first might ignore some major tactical strategy, the influence of a key player, or a match-deciding set play the opposition frequently uses. The second might create "paralysis by analysis," whereby the strengths of the opposition are overexaggerated. The team may then make too many changes in its tactical plan in an attempt to nullify those strengths. The most sensible and reasonable approach is to compromise, whereby a report on the opposition might include information on the following areas:

- Team formation
- Defensive strategy
- Midfield shape
- Forwards
- Key players
- Set plays
- General conditions

Figure 13.1 is a sample scouting report form that includes each of the areas listed. It properly balances the two approaches and will provide invaluable information.

## Team Formation

When looking at an opposing team's formations, coaches need to discover what I consider the biggest factor in scouting: How many forwards does the opposition use? Do they use 1, 2, 3, or even 4 forwards? If so, who marks each opponent?

The number of forwards used in the opposing team's offense indicates the likely number of players they employ in the midfield. If they use four midfield players, their formation will usually be two wide midfield players and a pair of central midfield players. This pair will play either as one attacking midfield player and one defensive midfield player, or as right-central and left-central midfield players who pivot on each other. If they use five midfield players, their formation will usually be two wide midfield players and a triangle of three central midfield players. This tri-

angle can take alternate forms: two stoppers and one attacking midfielder, or one stopper and two attacking midfield players. If they use six midfield players, their formation will almost invariably be two wide midfield players and a box of four central midfield players made up of two stoppers and two attacking midfield players.

When scouting teams, the coach's second biggest factor to identify is how the opposing team initiates its attack. Does it aim to get around, over, or through the opposing defense? The answer to this question will determine the method of defense that your team must use.

## Defensive Strategy

When preparing a scouting report, the scout should determine where the opposition decides to defend. Do they play a high-pressure game in the opponent's half of the field, or do they retreat nearer to their own goal? One player on each team usually organizes a team's defense. Knowing which player has this task is advantageous to your team because you can then preoccupy that player with a marking situation.

## Midfield Shape

As previously stated, the team that controls the setup area usually ends up winning the game. The scouting report should look closely at the opposition players who are deployed in the setup area. Do they use a single or twin stopper? Are there one or two playmakers? What are the qualities of the wide midfield players?

## Forwards

The scouting report should include information on the physical, technical, and tactical attributes of the opposing forwards. Are they big, fast, and powerful, or are they small, quick, and skillful? Do they come to the ball, or do they seek to run onto passes in the area behind the defense?

# Scouting Report

Team scouted_____ Date_____ Scout_____

Opponent_____ Score T.S._____ Opponent_____

Weather_____ Field conditions_____ Attendance_____

**System:** How many forwards?_____ How many at midfield?____ How many back?_____

Strengths of forward(s)_____

Weaknesses of forward(s)_____

Do they play over_____, through_____, or around_____? Which side do they favor?_____

Roles and effectiveness of outside midfielders_____

_____

Roles and effectiveness of center midfielders_____

_____

Midfield strengths_____

Midfield weaknesses_____

Do they use a sweeper?_____ How deep does the sweeper play?_____ Does the sweeper push up on their attack?_____

How far?_____ When does the sweeper drop back?_____ How far?_____ Do the sweeper's teammates trust him?_____

Tackling strengths?_____ Distribution strengths?_____ Temper?_____

What are the sweeper's weaknesses?_____

Do they favor player-for-player in the back or do they defend zonally?_____

Strengths of the marking defenders_____

Weaknesses of the marking defenders_____

If zonal, are there weaknesses?_____

Effectiveness of the stopper_____

Best way to beat their defense: over____ through____ around____ Why?_____

**Keeper:** Line_____ Sweeper_____ Strengths_____

Weaknesses_____

Where does the keeper like to distribute?_____

Name their key players:_____

**Set plays:** Corners. Who takes them?____ Near-post or far-post?____ How do they attack the post and who is involved?_____

Free kicks. Who takes them?_____ Do they take them quickly?_____ Describe the play they used:_____

When defending against a free kick is the wall set up quickly?_____ Who sets up the wall?_____ Do they allow defending players behind the wall?_____ If the free kick is from far out, where do they defend?_____

Who clearly leads the team?_____

**Additional comments:**_____

---

**Figure 13.1**  Sample scouting report form.

## Jimmy the Scout

In the early days of the North American Soccer League (NASL), my good friend Dave Jones was the coach of the Toronto Toros. Dave was a meticulous planner and organizer, and he would scout all league opposition and prepare comprehensive reports that he passed on to his players. Imagine his dismay when he found out that an exhibition game had been arranged between the Toros and Moscow Dynamo and that he would be unable to scout the Russians (the Toros had league matches on the days the Russians played their other exhibition matches).

Dave decided to send the assistant coach to watch the Russians in their exhibition games in Miami and Tampa Bay, but to Dave's consternation, the assistant coach fell ill the day before he was due to begin his long journey to Florida. Dave now had a problem. He wanted desperately to have a scouting report on the Soviets, but he had no coach available to travel. The only person seemingly available was Jimmy, an old-timer who had long ago played professional soccer in his native Scotland and now did odd jobs for the Toros. Dave decided that Jimmy should go because Dave needed certain knowledge and information about the Moscow Dynamo team.

Dave read in the newspapers that Moscow Dynamo had recorded impressive victories over both their Florida opponents, and he eagerly awaited Jimmy's return from his long and expensive trip. On Jimmy's arrival at the stadium, Dave assembled all the players and coaching staff to receive the scouting report. "Well, Jimmy," said Dave, "tell us about this Moscow Dynamo team." "Ehh!" said Jimmy, "They're a fine team." There was a long silence before Dave repeated his request for information on the Russians.

"Ehh!" said Jimmy again, "They're a fine team—a *real* fine team."

The players began to chuckle because it soon became obvious that Jimmy's brief summary was the extent of his report.

## Key Players

In the scouting report, coaches should identify the key players in the opposing team. Who leads their defense? Who orchestrates their midfield? Who threatens to score?

Most teams will have a leader in their defense. The goalkeeper or sweeper is usually in the best position to give defensive organizational instructions. As a coach, you should indicate in your report if either, both, or neither organizes the defense. If it is the sweeper, then your offensive plan should include some measure to fully occupy him in marking and covering one of your attackers. Do not allow the sweeper a free role with time to organize the defense.

Again, each team usually has a leader in the midfield. The opposing stopper normally assumes this role and is usually well positioned to accomplish it if allowed to play unopposed behind the midfield. However, if your team has a player in direct opposition,

The team leader needs to be responsible, hard working, and have a vision.

then their midfield leader will have less time to think and organize the midfield. Make the opposing stopper work defensively so that your team denies him the time to orchestrate the midfield offense.

Of course, the opposing goal threat must be stifled. Instruct your team to heavily mark the strikers on the opposing team, but be careful that you do not have a mismatch where your smallest or slowest defender is marking their biggest or fastest attacker.

## Set Plays

When preparing your team for a specific opponent, try to direct as much attention to the opposing team's set plays as to any other issue. Because developing a successful set play takes much practice to accomplish, an opposing team will unlikely change its set plays if they continue to be successful. The scouting report should therefore include details of how your opposition handles the following set plays.

### Corner Kicks For

- Who takes them?
- To which area do they serve the ball?
- Where do the attacking players line up?
- Where are the players not immediately involved in the corner-kick situation? What do they do?

### Corner Kicks Against

- How do they guard against a near-post corner?
- How do they guard against a far-post corner?
- How do they defend against a short corner kick?
- Do they mark on a player-to-player basis or in a zone defense?
- How does the goalkeeper perform against near-post and far-post crosses?

### Free Kicks For

- Do they take free kicks quickly?

- Do they have prearranged set plays at direct and indirect free kicks near the opponent's goal?
- If so, what are they? Who are the players involved?

### Free Kicks Against

- Who decides if a wall is required, and how many players are in the wall?
- Who lines up the wall?
- Who is the "keystone" player in the wall?
- Who are the other players in the wall?
- What do the other players do?
- What position does the goalkeeper take?

## General Conditions

The scouting report should also include information such as the nature of the field, its dimensions and surface, prevailing wind conditions, the sun, proximity of fans, and so on. The laws of the game in soccer require that the field be rectangular with a minimum and maximum length and width, and the laws stipulate that the length must exceed the width. Of course, the shape and dimensions of a field affect the type of game that is played. Defending on a small field with a bumpy surface is easier than attacking on one; likewise, building up solid attacking play on a large field with a quality surface is easier than defending on one. On a narrow field, goals are more likely to be scored from corner kicks and throw-ins than from wing play.

The prevailing wind and sun conditions should also help you determine which direction to play in the first half, provided you win the coin toss. Do you want to play with the wind at your backs and the sun in the opposing goalkeeper's eyes, or do you want to wait until the second half of the game for such advantages?

The proximity of fans to the field can affect the game as well by reducing the space for the run-up to a corner kick or the approach run to a throw-in. Unless they are prepared for it, the closeness of these fans can also adversely affect your players.

# PREPARING YOUR TEAM

In the prematch practices, the coach should focus on negating the strength of the opposition while making minimal changes in the team's style and method of play. For example, if the opposition plays with three forwards, a coach may find it necessary to adjust the regular 3-5-2 formation. Consequently, one of the stoppers would have to take on the role of a marking back. In another case, the opposition might have a wing back who likes to attack by overlapping the wide midfield player. You could then instruct one of the forwards to take a wide defensive position, thus forcing the play to the other side of the field. If the opposition has a star player, such as a playmaker or a striker, you should assign one of your players to mark this player tightly. Whenever possible, the marking player should get assistance from a teammate to double-team. If this star player favors one foot or a particular move, then instruct the marking player to force the star player to go to her weak side (usually the left foot).

Before actually meeting the scouted opponent, make sure your players run through such situations on the field in a practice situation. You will find it remarkable how many players fail to understand a chalkboard session but grasp the problem when the coach shows it on the field.

## Your Team's Set Plays

Devote some time during prematch practices to refine your set plays using the knowledge of your opposition's weaknesses. For example, do they only send one player out to defend against a corner kick? If so, then the team should practice short corners to develop goal-scoring opportunities from the initial two-on-one situation. Also spend some time perfecting the defense against the opposition's favorite set plays, particularly corner kicks or free kicks near the goal.

## Stop the Supply

Albert Finely was a giant of a man, six-foot-three-inches tall, weighing nearly 220 pounds, with wide shoulders, a narrow waist, and rippling muscles. He was a striker of immense power, and he terrorized the league, particularly with his heading ability.

After scouting Albert's team, I decided that the best means of defense was not to try to combat or stop Albert, but to cut off the supply of the ball to him. At the time, I had a marking player, Stan Allen, with amazing quickness, tenacity, and concentration. Stan's task was to stop the supply of crosses delivered to Albert by their right winger. It worked to perfection. We won the game, and Albert had a frustrating afternoon with hardly a touch of the ball.

The team will need to know the following information to defend well on set plays.

### Corner Kicks

- Who marks players and who covers space?
- How do they stop a short corner kick?
- What is the goalkeeper's position?
- Where do they clear the ball—high, far, and wide?
- How do they come out of defensive positions when the ball is cleared?
- Who takes the leadership role?
- What is the role of the team's forwards when defending a corner kick?
- How do they mount a counterattack?

### Free Kicks

- Is a wall necessary? Who decides?
- If so, how many players?
- Which players go into the wall?
- Who lines them up?

- Where do the other players position themselves?
- What does the goalkeeper do?

A team that you are scouting will often receive a penalty kick. The goalkeeper will find the following information useful:

**Penalty Kicks**

- Who takes the kick?
- What is the distance of the kicker's approach run?
- What is the angle of the kicker's approach run?
- What is the plant of the nonkicking foot?
- What is the strike of the ball—inside of foot or instep, or outside of foot, or even the toe?
- Does the kicker concentrate on power or accuracy? Where does the ball go?

Watching the opponent play before your match or studying a detailed scouting report is of immense value. Not having either, your team needs to be able to make adjustments when the match starts and as it progresses. You should have prepared them to make adjustments, on their own, to any system employed by the opponent. Identify dangerous players early. Defend against the opponent's set plays with extreme caution.

During the opponent's warm-up, you can often identify their shooters' strengths and their goalkeeper's weaknesses. By closely observing the early part of the match, you can then determine how to help your team make adjustments.

## SUMMARY

Consider the following points as you prepare your team for matches:

- Compromise between the two schools of thought regarding prematch preparation. That is, spend time perfecting your team's game and preparing to counter any major strengths in the opposing team.
- Consider the general conditions for play—the field (its dimensions and surface), the prevailing wind, the sun, the proximity of fans, and so forth.
- In prematch practices, focus on negating the strength of the opposition while making minimal changes in your team's style and method of play.
- Run through any adjustments you make to the team's formation or style of play in an on-the-field practice.
- Devote prematch practice time to refining your team's set plays based on knowledge of any opposition weakness.

# Chapter 14

# HANDLING MATCH SITUATIONS

Sports produce many types of coaches. Some excel at organizing fun-filled, physically demanding, and informative practice sessions. Others excel at recognizing talent; these coaches consistently put teams together that overachieve. Soccer also has coaches who can immediately identify the strengths and weaknesses of any team, including their own, and design situations and strategies to exploit such strengths and weaknesses. But, no matter how good you might be as an organizer of superior practice sessions or as a talent spotter, you will always struggle unless you can handle match situations—and that includes both prematch and postmatch situations.

Prematch situations include determining the starting lineup. During the match, your keen observation should tell you if your team is playing according to plan and if the plan is working. At the same time, it is your job to see what weaknesses the opponent may have. From your observations, you may have to adjust the match plan and make substitutions. Then, to ensure a better second half, make sure your instructions at halftime are explicit. Afterward, regardless of the match's outcome, make sure your postgame comments are well chosen so that your team is mentally ready for its next practice or match.

## SETTING THE STARTING LINEUP

The substitution rule for a particular match is a critical consideration in deciding the starting lineup. Is unlimited substitution permitted? Or is the match to be played according to FIFA rules, with a designated number of substitutes and no reentry after substitution?

If the match is to be played with limited substitution and no reentry, then you need to put the best starting lineup on the field. In that case, refer to your scouting report and prepare for the match in prematch practices. In matches where unlimited substitution is permitted, you should reward the players who have performed the best in previous matches or have shown the greatest dedication and determination in training. You run a risky course if you try to give all of your players equal playing time. Try to have a policy of equal opportunity, rather than a policy of equality. In matches against weaker opponents, I like to reward increased playing time to some of my weaker players who have displayed commitment, dedication, and determination in practice time.

## MATCHUPS

One of the greatest mistakes made by beginning coaches is that they allow mismatches to develop on the field. You will often see a team's biggest and fastest player marked by the other team's smallest and slowest player. In most instances, teams are punished for such mismatches. As a coach, don't allow mismatches to develop. Prepare for such events before the match and be ready to make adjustments during match play.

Of course, you should not only avoid mismatches that work against you, but you should also attempt to create mismatches that work in your favor. For instance, you may be able to create mismatches in the following situations:

- *The opponent leaves a big space between the goalkeeper and the last defender.* You may have an opportunity to play over the defense, especially if you have a fast forward.
- *The opponent plays the offside trap.* Can a deep player, such as a defensive mid-

fielder or stopper, dribble through the defense? Or, can you play the ball wide behind the defense to a wide midfielder who starts the run late?

- *The opponent has a slow defender.* You can attack this player with a quick player.
- *The opponent marks player-to-player at corner kicks, direct free kicks, and so forth.* Can you ghost in an open player? Can you pull the opponent into poor positions? To prepare your team for or against such situations is an easy task.

## DURING THE MATCH

Your immediate and primary objective during a match is to ascertain what your team is doing well and what weaknesses your opponent has. Be prepared to help your team solve any critical problem that arises. For example, does the opposing team play with three forwards? Have your players readjusted by using three marking backs? If so, has your central midfielder adjusted to the loss of one of the stoppers? Does the opposing team play with a deep-lying sweeper? If so, does your primary forward push up to make the opposing defense play flat across the field?

### Coach Conduct

A coach's conduct and demeanor on the touchline can have an impact on your team. In my experience, I have found that a coach who either sits on the bench or stands still (leans on something) has the most calming effect on the team. It is as if your body language oozes confidence to your players, who will then perform in a calm, confident, calculated manner. On the other hand, if you move up and down the touchline shouting instructions at your players, you're likely to have a nervous, underachieving team prone to moments of violent behavior. Your anxiety gets transmitted to your players, who will then perform with tension and insecurity.

To convey instructions to your players is permissible, on occasion, but you should do so calmly and quietly when the ball is at the other end of the field. To shout instructions to a player who is in possession of the ball is of little use to anyone. The player's attention should be on making a decision regarding the next move. As a coach, you should focus your attention on players far from the ball, who have the opportunity and the time to absorb your instructions.

## Coaching to Defeat

I made a causal analysis of coaches who had been ejected from matches in the English Football League between 1970 and 1982. These ejections were for a variety of reasons, but by far the most common was dissent by the coach and the use of foul language. I also made a causal analysis of players who had been ejected in the same matches in the same league. Player ejections were also caused by a variety of violations. But what was interesting was that when a coach was ejected, a player from his team was usually ejected, too. Invariably, that team lost the match. It was as if the coach's demeanor—anxiety, stress, or tension—had been transmitted to the players, who then underachieved.

## Player Conduct

Player conduct is often a product of coach conduct. Is it truly surprising that teams with coaches who scream and shout at their players, who rant and rave at the referees have the worst discipline record? No. Then should it be a surprise at all that teams who have calm, level-headed coaches who accept referee mistakes have the fewest discipline problems? No again.

Some players, of course, have discipline problems no matter which coach they play for. These players are usually prone to macho behavior, and they carry giant chips on their shoulders. I have found that I can help such players by giving them guidance and advice on the practice field. I try to explain to them the following ideas:

- Players who are repeatedly fouled are special because this is the only way that opponents can stop them. It is a mark of respect for their ability.

- A brave person will walk away from a confrontation, whereas the coward will enter into a war of words, ultimately falling afoul of the referee.

- The best answer to a provocative opponent is to score against him.

- Players should be yellow carded and red carded in practice matches, just as they would be in regular matches.

## Substitutions

The United States is one of the few places in the world where we find unlimited substitution in soccer. Elsewhere, only limited substitutions are allowed, which means that the main considerations for substitution are injury or tactical adjustment. When unlimited substitution is in force, injury and tactics are often not the primary considerations. Rather, playing time is what becomes the major issue.

Teams usually have between 15 and 18 players on the roster, and naturally, every player will demand some playing time during each match. Although you may plan your substitutions to give each player a certain number of minutes of playing time, you may have to change these decisions depending on the score. If your team is comfortably in the lead early in the match, then you can put in the weaker players earlier than planned. However, let's say that a match is even and that you put in your weaker players to give them their playing time. If as a consequence you lose the match, you can be certain of some criticism. In my opinion, unlimited substitution is a lose–lose situation for both coaches and players. No one likes to be substituted, and no one likes to be a substitute. Nearly everyone ends up disgruntled.

## Match Plan Adjustments

Even the best-laid match plans can sometimes go awry. A team can still trail in scoring despite total dominance in most aspects of play. A failed game plan can be the result of almost anything, such as superb goalkeeping, missed goal chances, and field and weather conditions. In cases such as these, you might find it necessary to push up an additional forward and risk being outnumbered in midfield; or, if the team is holding on to a narrow lead, you may need to add an additional defender. In addition, you may have strong winds blowing straight down the field or wet conditions at one end of the field. In such situations, the match plan may have to be adjusted, depending on which end a team is defending.

## Halftime

Most coaches make adjustments to a match plan at halftime. During this short interval, you can demand the total attention of all your players. Make sure your instructions are clear, concise, and to the point. All players must understand how any adjustment affects them and their roles on the team.

Remember, though, by being too general, you may miss the opportunity of making telling changes during the halftime talk. For instance, certain remarks are meaningless, such as "We must pick up in the midfield," "We must improve our marking," "We've got to talk more," or "We've got to move off the ball." Rather, you should say something like, "John, you must pick up your man in midfield," "Kristen, you must tell Gina which way to force the play," "Nicole, mark your player tighter and don't let her turn with the ball," or "Adam, take up a better support position that will allow Matt to pass the ball to you."

## AFTER THE MATCH

If the team and the players have performed well in a match, you should compliment them immediately. Reinforce the pleasant

Losing hurts. Be compassionate. Pick your players up.

memory of a successful play. On the other hand, if a player has failed or if the team has had a disappointing match, refrain from any immediate criticism. You don't need to add to any player's feelings of frustration.

## Postmatch Conduct

Immediately after the match, emotions are usually high. But no matter how frustrated or disappointed you might feel, refrain from making any negative comments to your players. Every coach should understand that players almost always try their best. When they fail or when the team loses, they will be insecure and disappointed. To blame or reprimand players in the immediate postmatch period serves no purpose. Rather, if disappointment and frustration prevail, coaches should make it a habit to simply inform the players of any immediate administrative messages and then leave.

The time to conduct the match postmortem is the next day when emotions have cooled and when everyone can discuss the match calmly and sensibly. But even 24 to 48 hours after the match, you will achieve little if you set out to blame any player or players for failure. Instead, point out the positive points in the performance and praise the players involved. If the loss can be directly attributed to a player's poor performance, then reassure the individual that he is still the same player who was on the team when they won some previous matches. Try to work with the player to identify the cause of the poor performance so that the athlete has the opportunity to correct the problem.

## Postmatch Lessons

If you and your team allow yourselves to learn from a match—win, lose, or draw—then you have gained. Ultimately, *the game* is the greatest teacher. Every player and every coach should commit this statement to memory.

The focal point of your practice session after a match should be the lessons learned in the match. If, for instance, the goalkeeper dropped some crosses in the match, then spend at least some of the next practice session on having the goalkeeper deal with crosses in realistic situations.

I am always amazed to see coaches who sincerely believe that they are addressing the problem that cropped up in the match by setting up drills without opposing players. To expect that doing so will yield positive results is not realistic. As a coach, you can only address the match problem by providing the player a similar opportunity in practice under match conditions.

## SUMMARY

Here are some basic guidelines to follow during a match:

- Consider the substitution rule for the particular match as you decide your starting lineup.
- Avoid mismatches that give an advantage to the opponent.
- Be in control on the touchline. Your conduct is transmitted to your players.
- Communicate only with players well away from the ball, when they have the opportunity and time to absorb your instructions.
- On the practice field, provide guidance and advice to your players about their match conduct.
- Be prepared to change your match plan during the match if things have gone awry.
- Make sure that every player understands the adjustments discussed at halftime.
- Refrain from making any negative comments to your players immediately after the match.
- Design your team's practice program on how the team performed in the previous match.
- Help your players improve on match problems by giving them an opportunity to solve the problem in practice under match conditions.

# Part VI

# COACHING EVALUATION

# Chapter 15

# EVALUATING YOUR PLAYERS

Observation and evaluation are important parts of coaching. When we are evaluating a player, we have to do more than just determine individual skill level. We must also evaluate how the player will fit into our program and contribute to the team's competitiveness and culture.

Player evaluations should start early. As a coach, you should try to learn as much as possible about a player long before the first practice. The more you know about a player, the better you can prepare to coach her. In preseason evaluations, try to observe a potential player under the pressure of match conditions. Go to competitive matches and observe. I also find it just as valuable to observe a potential player during training sessions. From there I can learn much about the player's attitude, social skills, concentration, motivation, work ethic, and willingness to learn.

Organizing evaluations is vital to any coach who wants to reap the benefits of conducting them. To help me with my evaluations, I developed some simple tools. They include a player evaluation form, a player profile form, and a player self-evaluation form.

Regardless of all preseason evaluations, your most critical period of evaluating occurs during the first days of practice before you make cuts. Unfortunately, the most traumatic part of coaching is making cuts. Doing so is hard on you, but it can be devastating for the player. You must therefore make sure that each player that gets cut has had a fair opportunity to prove himself or herself.

Once you have made the cuts, your evaluations should focus on technical ability and tactical awareness of the remaining players. From those evaluations, try to put the players into the positions best suited for them at the time. After a few practices with players in their assigned positions, you can begin to put the starting team together.

Keep in mind that evaluating doesn't stop after your first starting lineup. You should evaluate players before, during, and after every practice and every match. Through attentive observation and thorough evaluation, you can immensely increase your effectiveness and thereby your chances for success.

## PRESEASON EVALUATIONS

Players typically have experience playing soccer before trying out for high school or college teams. As a coach, you have numerous opportunities to watch potential players in action. For example, you could go to competitions for club teams, tournaments, and indoor centers. Try watching matches, especially those of the players that may try out for your program. By beginning to familiarize yourself with potential players, you are laying a foundation for a thorough evaluation.

## Watching Matches Before Tryouts

Coaches in high school programs do not recruit; they coach club teams. If such a practice is legal in your conference, by all means do it. It is a great way to see numerous players under match conditions. Many conferences and school districts, however, have ruled it illegal for a high school or college coach to coach other teams of the same age. In that case, watch matches and observe players who may be trying out for your team. In these early observations, you may want to evaluate only technical abilities, such as how well the player controls the ball, passes, shoots, heads, tackles, and dribbles. After doing so, you may want to figure out how to bring the player along and where the player might fit on your team. When watching, don't be position-conscious. For

instance, although the player you are watching may be playing defense, that position may not be his strongest.

## The Reluctant Forward

I looked at Kevin Mosher, a high school junior. His coach had told me that Kevin could probably make a contribution to our team. He looked impressive, but I felt that he didn't function all that well in his outside midfield position. His lack of speed over distance often caused him to be caught either too far up or too far back. When he had the ball, however, he was magic. He could screen the ball well; he was hard to get off the ball; he had excellent fakes; he was deceptively quick over a short distance; and he could shoot well with either foot. I recruited him and told him that I was going to play him at forward. Although somewhat reluctant, he cooperated. During Kevin's first season with us, he tied for the honors as the conference's leading scorer. He was selected to the conference all-star team, and he shattered a 15-year-old conference record for most goals scored by one player in a match.

I want to see as many players as possible before our actual tryout, especially those I am actively recruiting and those who have signed a letter of intent. I also want to see those who have interviewed and have said that they will be turning out. The reason I want to see them before tryouts is that I have never liked tryouts; I believe they don't really give the coach a true picture of a player's ability. Over the years, I have learned that many players just don't show well in a tryout. After one week of practice, we make our first cuts; we then make the final cuts one week later. So although our tryouts are long, I still believe that some players hold back or overdo it in a tryout atmosphere. Too many players equate self-worth with succeeding or failing in a tryout, and the stress defeats them. I have known players who could not eat or sleep during tryouts. I don't want to lose quality players before I have a chance to work on their confidence and hardiness.

The time to evaluate a player fairly is when the player is performing under match pressure, especially if the teams are of similar quality. The trick is not only to observe the player as a part of a team but also to evaluate the player's individual strengths and potential. When one of my assistants or I view a player in a match, we prepare a written evaluation. Our form is simple, but it gives me the information I need (see figure 15.1).

## Player Profiles

After the first contact with a new player, our college sends him a packet of information. That packet includes our player profile form (see figure 15.2). It is a simple form that gives me some basic information, but it is extremely useful if I'm not familiar with the player. For instance, if the player indicates on the profile that he has played select or premier soccer and was selected to an Olympic development team, I know that I'm dealing with an experienced player who is used to competitive soccer. The profile also provides me

## Player Evaluation Form

Name:_____

Age:_____ Date: _____

School or team:_____

Match versus:_____

Team coach:_____

Team coach phone:_____

**Rating Scale:**
5 - College caliber—starting
4 - College caliber
3 - Needs work; has possibilities
2 - Needs work
1 - Take a look next year

1. Overall technical ability in training (ball control, passing, dribbling, shooting, heading, tackling): **Rating_____**
Specific comments: _____
_____

2. Overall technical ability in a match:                                                                **Rating_____**
Specific comments: _____
_____

3. Tactical ability in training (awareness, transition, position, decisions, communication, use of space, support, vision):                                                                                        **Rating_____**
Specific comments: _____
_____

4. Tactical ability in a match:                                                                          **Rating_____**
Specific comments: _____
_____

5. Overall physical fitness (agility, flexibility, speed, endurance, strength): Height ____ Weight ____ **Rating_____**
Specific comments: _____
_____

6. Overall psychological wellness (attitude, concentration, motivation, confidence, courage, hardiness): **Rating_____**
Specific comments: _____
_____

Evaluator:_____ Overall rating:_____ Date:_____

**Figure 15.1**   Sample player evaluation form.

## Soccer Player Profile

Full name: _____

Home address: _____

City and state: _____ Zip: _____

Home phone: (____)_____ Social security number_____-_____-_____

Mother's name: _____ Occupation: _____

Father's name: _____ Occupation: _____

High school: _____ Coach's name: _____

Age:_____ Date of birth: _____ Height: _____ Weight: _____

Grade point average last 3 years:_____

Position played: _____ School uniform number:_____

Time 100 yards:_____ Time 1 mile: _____

Other sports played:_____ Positions:_____

Youth soccer experience (mark all applicable): Club_____

Select_____ Premier_____ ODP_____

Coach's name(s):_____ Phone(s):_____

Athletic honors received (captain, all-star, all-conference, etc.): _____

_____

What course of study are you interested in:_____

Have you applied for financial aid:_____

Uniform sizes: Shirt_____ Shorts_____ Warm-up_____

**Figure 15.2**   Sample player profile form.

with information about his speed, scholastic success, and financial needs.

## Player's Self-Evaluation

Most evaluations are done by me, an assistant, or one of the many club and school coaches who help our program by bringing talented players to my attention. In addition to our evaluation of them, I also find it useful to know what players think of themselves and their own ability. After the first cut, I schedule a self-evaluation session. I first talk to the players, then I tell them that I want them to be candid with their answers to the questions on the self-evaluation form (see figure 15.3).

The form asks players to address their strengths and weaknesses. If the player's view of strengths and weaknesses is the same as mine, we can go to work. If we differ, I'll have to alter my approach. By holding a private meeting with the player, I can ask him to tell me more about his reasons for feeling strong or weak in the areas we viewed differently. Eventually, we agree; but if not, it doesn't really matter. The self-evaluation form has told me that I need to approach this player differently than I do the others.

Constant evaluation is necessary. Some athletes look, talk, and walk like soccer players. But don't be fooled; performance is what counts. Like any coach, I have no difficulty at tryouts picking 20 players (out of 70 to 80) who look, talk, and walk like soccer players. The difficult part, however, is picking the 20 who are skilled, coachable, academically motivated, competitive, proud, honest, for-

## Self-Evaluation Form

Name:_____   Date:_____

In soccer, I feel that my three strong qualities are:

1.

2.

3.

I feel that my three weaknesses are:

1.

2.

3.

**Figure 15.3**   Sample self-evaluation form.

giving, team oriented, willing to work, and who have a sense of humor and can complement each other's capabilities.

## EVALUATING BEFORE CUTTING

During the early practices, most of our time is spent on conditioning. However, we do play a number of five-on-five games and have some full-field, coached scrimmages. Throughout these activities, my assistants and I are evaluating each player's technical and tactical development, fitness, and psychological characteristics. We are also looking at players who seem to work well together. Some players read each other well and can anticipate a teammate's actions, whereas others continually misread or miscue. Players who are tuned in to each other as practices begin are an immediate asset.

Although we evaluate every aspect we can during the early practices, the characteristic we look for more than any other is work ethic. As I said earlier, all of soccer's hard work is done in practice. A player who gives only 80 percent in practice will give a like effort in a match. I can encourage players to give their all in practice, but in the end, only the player herself can make the decision to be ready and go 100 percent. The player who can make that decision has the edge in my selection process. I have often picked a player less skillful than another because of his superior effort.

Coaching is the most exciting, challenging, and rewarding job I can think of. Every day is filled with positive anticipation . . . except for the two days when I have to make cuts. In fact, I find it difficult to sleep the night before the first cut, and I find it even more difficult the night before the last cut. I haven't been able to find the ideal way to do it—a way in which everybody understands and accepts the cuts, a way in which no one gets hurt. And you know what? There is just no easy way to do it. All I can really do is be as sure as possible about the cuts and then, somehow, attempt to ease the disappointment players feel when told they didn't make the team.

## Making Cuts

I don't believe in posted lists. They are cruel, uncaring, and impersonal. No player should find out that she didn't make the team when surrounded by peers. Some coaches will finish

202 Coaching Soccer Successfully

the tryout by informing the team that the players who made it will be called over the weekend. The phone call method is just as cruel, if not more so, because of the wait.

Although there is no easy way to do it, I still try to treat my players the way I would like to be treated in such a situation. First, I want to be sure as possible that I am making the right decision. For that, I thoroughly study all the evaluations we made. After that, I solicit the help of my assistants. Even though the final decision is always mine, their counsel is extremely important, especially when we discuss borderline players. My assistants may have seen or heard something that I missed. Before making a decision, I may even go as far as getting comments from team captains.

## Meeting With the Player

After I make final decisions, I schedule a meeting with each player who is being cut. Several already have a good idea that they will not make the team, especially during the first cut when I cut down to 30. But don't kid yourself. Not one has given up hope, and each player who gets cut is disappointed. They have dreams; they work hard; they come up through youth teams; they play for their high schools. Now they are being told that they are not good enough. It hurts. It hurts bad, especially for the last 10 who made it through the first cut. Some accept the decision stoically; others become angry; still others cry bitter tears.

When I meet with a player about to be cut, it's just the two of us. No assistant sits in because I don't want the player to feel ganged up on. I arrange the office so that we can sit down to talk without anything, such as a table or desk, between us. I want the conversation to be as open as possible. Although I know the player will be disappointed, I want to give myself every opportunity to help the player salvage his sense of self-worth. I don't want him to equate his setback with feelings of inadequacy. Although players may be

disappointed when cut, I want them to feel good about themselves when they leave my office.

I try to point out as many positive things as I can. I may say, "First of all, I want to compliment you on your work ethic in practices. You have a lot going for you. You are personable, a good leader, people like you, and I also noticed from your transcripts that you are a very good student. With all those qualities I know you will go far in your chosen major. I'm not saying that you won't encounter setbacks in life; they'll be there. But I feel that when they come, you'll be able to handle them. I hope that you will view what I'm about to tell you as just that, a temporary setback."

I then take time to point out areas that the player should be working on to improve and better prepare for next year's tryout. I also talk about some of our players who didn't make it the first year, but worked hard and came back a year later and won a starting position. If possible, I try to have a contact for the player. That contact is usually the phone number of a coach in the adult league who is looking for players. At the time of our meeting, the players may not be all that interested in the phone number, but I ask them to take it and hang on to it for a few days.

Making cuts is obviously an emotional time for me, but it is far more emotional for the player. I don't want those who are cut to leave the office feeling totally without recourse. Because we make the cuts on Friday, I ask them to take the weekend and think about everything that has happened and all that has been said. If on Monday they feel that I have made a mistake or if they feel that they want to talk some more, I will be available. I actually give each cut player a time to meet me should one or more be inclined to do so.

Again, I don't like tryouts, and I detest making cuts. I would hate them even more if in my heart I knew that I hadn't done everything in my power to be fair and to protect the player's self-esteem.

## The Jeff Colyar Story

Jeff Colyar, a defender, came to his Monday appointment with me after being cut. Jeff explained that he had been nervous throughout the tryout and felt that he really was better than what he had shown. He asked if he could keep coming to practices, even though he would not be competing. I gave my permission.

During the next few weeks, Jeff was far more relaxed, and he did indeed look better. His work rate was intense. Three matches into the season, Bryan Ruby, our right wing defender, broke his hand. We decided to activate Jeff because the player who would have taken Bryan's place was not working out too well. Jeff did an excellent job and was in the starting lineup when we played for the regional championship.

## EVALUATING PRACTICE

Once you have made all the cuts, it is time to start molding the players and the team. What you need to do now is determine how each player fits into the team structure. Naturally, every player on the field has attacking and defending duties. For instance, when the ball is lost, the forward closest to the ball becomes the first line of defense; the defender in possession should therefore attack. Every field player should be able to play every position on the field.

That a player will play certain positions better than others is a given. I like to compare the players to physicians. Every physician knows everything there is to know about medicine in general, but most of them specialize in a certain aspect. Of course, all of our players have to know the principles of play, but most of them specialize in certain positions. For example, players with a strong defensive awareness will probably feel most comfortable in defensive positions, and risk takers will prefer attacking positions. Regardless of preference, however, every player can't be strictly a defender or strictly an attacker. In today's soccer, all players on the field should be well rounded. With the recent play back rule changes, even the goalkeeper must have field player skills.

## Putting Players in Positions

After you have evaluated the players' overall abilities, you can begin to assess players for certain roles. To do so, you will need to evaluate defensive strengths, midfield characteristics, and forward capabilities. In other words, it's time to bring out the specialists.

Once you determine who the specialists are and what capabilities they have, you can start thinking about the style of play most suitable for the talent you have available. Next, you can begin to look for the strongest players in each of the three groups. After this, you will be able to begin assigning positions.

My friend Bobby Howe (former under-20 U.S. national team coach) likes to start by first selecting the strongest goalkeeper, then the strongest central defender, then the strongest center midfielder, and finally the most effective striker. He calls that the backbone of the team. After that, he fills the other positions based on evaluated strengths. This ritual creates the starting 11—for the moment. Remember, every coach needs to be flexible. The team you start in your first match never consists of these same 11 players in your last match. At least mine never has. Too many questions are still unanswered, such as the following:

- Are the selected players capable of playing the chosen style?
- How are the players responding to each other?
- How are they handling specific assignments?

- If we change the system, do all players adjust equally well?
- Does one system work better than another?
- How are individual players handling various degrees of pressure?
- Is this really the best position for this player?
- Is this really the best player for this position?
- Is there a good team culture?
- Who is communicating, and who is not communicating?

Only hard practices, keen observation, and honest evaluation can provide answers. Asking questions will force you to be flexible and open to adjustments or changes. And don't forget—flexibility is one of the keys to coaching soccer successfully.

## SELECTING THE STARTERS

One of the more sensitive issues you deal with is deciding who will be among the starting 11 and who will play the role of substitute. Keep in mind that most players equate playing time with self-worth. If you handle the decision improperly, the players on the bench will feel like losers. You can't be successful if a number of your players feel that way. Their discontent will eventually hurt the entire team.

All players on the team should know why they are starting or why they are not starting. At the same time, however, all players should know that they are an important part of the team. The nonstarters should at least have an idea under what circumstances you will bring them into the match. It is true that players earn their starting positions, but I don't believe in setting up players against each other because one will win and the other will lose. I shy away from any win–lose contest. I believe that by being candid, open, and honest, I can create win–win situations.

In most cases, I have a nonstarting player understudy one or two starting players. So, in case of injury, nonperformance, or any other tactical reason for substitution, the player is well prepared.

One of the tools I use early in the practices is a form that I call a sociogram, which asks for advice from the players. Although the decision of who starts is ultimately mine, the sociogram gives the players a feeling of having a voice in the decision-making process. It asks questions such as the following:

- Who do you feel is the best goalkeeper?
- Who do you feel is the best defender?
- Who do you feel is the best midfielder?
- Who do you feel is the best forward?
- If you had the opportunity to line up the team in a 4-3-3 system, who would you play on defense, at midfield, and as forwards?

## SELECTING THE TEAM LEADER

As I said earlier, soccer can't be coached during matches. Instead, a successful soccer team has to have a strong leader on the field. Without such a person, it is difficult to win consistently. Look at the world's successful teams, and you always find that one player who led them. Within your team, look for the player whom the team respects and whose positive attitude is infectious. A leader is one who has a sense of humor, is responsible and hardworking, stays focused, and has a vision. That player should be the captain of your team, the coach on the field. Because the role of the captain is so important, the coach should select her personally.

## Meeting With Assistants

During water breaks, my assistants and I briefly meet to discuss each segment of the practice. Because we frequently work in small groups (each with one group), we comment on our success rate—or lack thereof. Directly after practice, we meet again to discuss the practice. After consulting the practice plan for the next day, we may make some adjustments. However, we seldom veer far from the plan. If pertinent information comes out of the after-practice meeting, we enter it into our files. How much my assistants contribute to the success of our program and the welfare of our players always astounds me.

## EVALUATING MATCHES

Evaluating a match is hard work. It consists of constant observation and evaluation of the match and the players; then it involves making necessary adjustments. I have never understood coaches who seem to have time to yell and scream, argue with referees, or give a constant barrage of emotional advice to their players when there is so much other work to do during the match.

During the first half, I ask my assistant coach to observe our team and determine if we have any of the following: mismatches on the field; players who look tired or are not having a good day; a loss of team focus; problems with temper control. I observe the other team to find their strengths and weaknesses. Trainers look at the players who may not be totally fit or who may be recovering from injury. If we need information about shots on goal, corner kicks, or number of offside calls, we can quickly call the scorekeeper.

All the observations can be quickly evaluated and used to make tactical adjustments. During the second half, we observe if the changes, if any, were effective. The results are discussed in a brief aftermatch meeting.

## Staff Responsibilities

The stress that comes with match day is significantly reduced when everyone involved knows exactly what to do. Rick Harrison, our administrative assistant, watches the opposing team warm up and reports anything noteworthy, such as strengths and weaknesses

of the goalkeeper, the identity of the good shooters, and anything else that can benefit us. Another assistant visits with the officials to answer any questions regarding league rules, such as substitutions or overtime. He also asks the officials to stay after the match long enough to sign the match report. The scorekeeper doubles as statistician and keeps track of who starts, who enters later, who scores, who assists, who shoots, who saves, who fouls, who gets cautioned, who gets ejected, who gets a corner, and who takes it. A spotter helps the scorekeeper.

Even though we probably have a scouting report and have practiced accordingly, it is still my job once the match starts to evaluate weaknesses in the opponent's defense and their strengths on attack. I also look for obvious mismatches on the field of play. I carry a voice-activated tape recorder on which I can catch my comments and the comments of my assistants. Also during the match, I have one assistant who concentrates on the opponent to determine their style and tactics. He also looks for opposing players who are losing their concentration or becoming tired in the match. Another assistant concentrates on our team to determine the effectiveness of our tactics and game plan while viewing our players for fatigue and loss of temper. All report to me orally when they feel I should know about something. If at times I feel that I should have had an oral report but didn't, I may ask for it. Sometimes one of the observers sees something that has no immediate bearing on the match, but he jots it down on a notepad so that we can discuss it afterward or during the next prepractice meeting.

During the first half, Rick Harrison draws the movement of the ball on a small sketch pad for me. This little drawing shows who brought the ball up, who lost it, who shot, and who scored. He hands me the drawing every 15 minutes. It is a tremendous tool because it quickly gives me a two-dimensional overview of what occurred in the preceding 15 minutes. It shows who had possession and where on the field the opponent likes to have possession. Among other things, it shows where the opponent likes to attack and if we are using the field according to our game plan.

Figure 15.4 is a good example of one of these match drawings. It is Rick's sketch from a match we played against Shoreline Community College on October 11, 1995. It shows the action from the 15th to the 30th minute. We play from left to right. In the opponent's half, the sketch shows the action and numbers of our players only. The lines show the path of the ball. If the number of a player appears more than once on a line, it means that the player dribbled the ball to the point where his number appears last.

If a number is at the end of a line, the player lost the ball one on one. If a line proceeds to no particular receiver, then the shot was missed or a pass was intercepted. When a line has no number or starts without a number, it simply means that Rick missed that particular detail on that play. We show the action of the opponent in our half but not the players' numbers; there just isn't time. Besides, I already know who their dangerous players are, and I'm only interested in how they move the ball. Do they come through the middle? Do they attack wide? If so, which side do they favor? Do they play long or short? Where do they shoot from?

During those 15 minutes as illustrated in figure 15.4, we dominated, especially on our right side. That was pretty much according to game plan. The opponent's defender on our left side was strong. You can see that when we tried a few attacks on that side, our player was promptly fouled (F). We wasted the resulting free kicks. You can also see that we took seven shots at their goal during the period. Two were stopped by the goalkeeper. We were awarded one corner kick (C) and two throw-ins. The opponent had one good opportunity. It came from a throw-in to the top of the box from where it was crossed to the far post. A Shoreline player took a hard shot from there; however, our goalkeeper deflected it and gave up a corner.

Rick's drawings are a tool that usually confirms our observations. As such, they serve as an additional opinion to help us make decisions. I also find the drawings use-

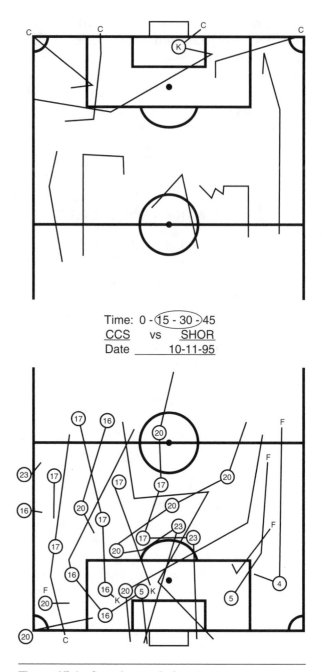

**Figure 15.4**   Sample match drawing.

ful at halftime. My instructions are more effective if I have a picture to back me up. For example, I can say, "You're not using Adam enough. Adam can beat the right outside defender. The goal Clayton scored came after we played the ball wide to Adam. He beat his man and short-crossed to Clayton. Goal. But since then, you have hardly used him. Here, let me show you on the drawing."

When I tell the stopper to shift a bit to the right because most of their attacking play is on that side, it helps when I can show him a picture of heavy traffic on the right and little on the left. He then understands better.

We instruct the trainers to watch for injuries and to know how they occurred. We ask them to have water ready for any player who needs it and has time during a stoppage to get it. One of our managers then watches the referee to see what is called, what and how much is let go, whether cooperation is established with the line crew, and how precise the line crew's offside calls are.

Starting with the opening whistle, we gather information and make tactical adjustments accordingly. For instance, we may have given one of our players instructions to mark an opposing player tightly. After a while, we find that the opposing player isn't all that dangerous. During the next stoppage in play, we may get a message to our player to ease up. Or, we may find that the opposing wing forward is just too fast for our outside defender. We substitute a quicker defender.

At halftime, we make final changes, and some of the players may get one or two new assignments. During the second half, all of us evaluate the effectiveness of our adjustments. If things are working out, I leave it alone. If not, I may have to make other changes. If we are behind late in the match, I may bring in an attacking midfielder for a defensive midfielder. If we are ahead, I may do the reverse.

I still maintain that soccer is not a coached sport. I call what we do during the matches observation, evaluation, and modification. We don't teach during a match. Instead, we take what we learn from the match to the next practice session.

## POSTMATCH EVALUATIONS

After a match is completed, I have a lot of information to sort through, such as the recorded notes, the videotape, the scoresheet with the stats, the match drawings, plus all the information that is still in our heads. To avoid losing the latter, the assistants and I meet directly after the match to discuss our observations. That discussion, combined with the hard information, determines the plan for the next few practices. During the next practice, we invariably walk the players through the problem situations we saw. We can show why it became a problem and what could have prevented it. We also walk through the areas where we had success, and we again show why it was successful. No matter what happens in a match, we gain from the experience. Because we always gain, we never lose.

## EVALUATION TOOLS

I feel that video recordings and a well-programmed personal computer are essential coaching aids.

## Video

All of our matches are videotaped. We also use video for specific coaching purposes. For instance, players develop faults over a number of years. I try to correct the faults in practice, but I am not always successful. Sometimes players think they have corrected it, but they haven't. To ease frustration, we shoot a video of the error. It's much easier for players to make corrections if they can see themselves committing the error.

I have found that video is also useful when you want to see an action in slow motion. For that reason, we often use it at goalkeeper practices, particularly when we are working on foot movement. Before a jump or dive, many goalkeepers have a tendency to move their weight to the wrong foot for a split second, thus wasting precious time. The movement is so quick, however, that they are unaware of it. Video, in slow motion, convinces them quickly.

We also use it during shooting practices. Again, the action of the shot is so fast that faults are difficult to detect and therefore almost impossible to correct. Using slow motion, I can clearly show a player who has been shooting high that she hits the ball too far below center. Seeing this, the player can start making corrections.

## Computers

We collect a tremendous amount of information before, during, and after a season. To keep track of it all and file it is difficult.

A tool I have found essential in helping me organize everything we do is a personal computer. I have one in my office and a compatible one at home. I find it helpful in updating mailing lists, keeping track of practice plans, laying out match schedules, providing accurate statistics, and writing form letters. All of the information and notes I gather are stored in easy-to-find files on a well-organized hard disk. The only thing it doesn't seem to do is brew my coffee, but I'm working on that.

## SUMMARY

To thoroughly, fairly, and expertly evaluate players is a crucial coaching task. I believe that the following suggestions help coaches become better evaluators.

- See players early. Observe them in competitive matches and at practice.
- Use tools like the player evaluation form, the player profile form, and the player self-evaluation form.
- Prepare yourself mentally before making cuts, and know in your heart that the player has had fair and meticulous evaluation.
- When making cuts, protect the player's self-esteem as much as possible.
- When putting players in positions, ask yourself constantly, "Is this the right player for that position, and is that the right position for this player?"
- Let players know why they are starting or why they are not starting.
- Don't neglect to have an in-depth post-match evaluation. Record information while it is still fresh in your mind.
- Make use of tools that can help you evaluate players, practices, and matches. Video and computers are essential to coaching and record keeping.

# Chapter 16

# EVALUATING YOUR PROGRAM

Regardless of what happened during the season, make sure that you promptly evaluate all aspects of your program as soon as the season ends. If it has been a bad season, you may want to step away for a few days and recover from your disappointment. If the season was great, you may be tempted to take some time off to come down from cloud nine. Neither one, however, is a wise idea. Evaluate everything while it is still fresh in everyone's mind, in yours and in those who will be giving the evaluations—the players, assistant coaches, and administrators. The next season starts the day after the current season ends.

## POSTSEASON EVALUATIONS

Only when you thoroughly evaluate the past season can you plan the success of the next season. You have to ask yourself the following questions: What happened during the past season? Did it progress the way you had anticipated? Was the progress satisfactory—considering schedules, quality of players, strength of competition, and performance of staff? Were there discipline problems? Would any area benefit by making changes?

Your evaluations are important, but they reflect only the impressions of one person. They may therefore be biased or limited in scope. To truly evaluate your program, solicit comments on the season from as many sources as you can. My athletic director, Dr. Maury Ray, also believes that immediate evaluations are crucial to the continued success of a program. (But then, Maury was a successful basketball coach.) He personally conducts several evaluation sessions—one with the head coach, one with the players, and one with the coaching staff. All sessions are scheduled and completed within five days of the end of a season.

The agenda for Maury's initial meeting with me is short. He solicits some general comments, and together we schedule a session with the players and a session with the staff. I usually make remarks about my satisfaction with the team's performance, my satisfaction with my coaching and support staff, budgets, recruiting plans, and suggested changes to the conference's code. If we had problems during the season, we discuss those as well. The purpose of the meeting is to give Maury the essential information he needs for his meeting with the players.

## Evaluation by the Players

When I was first told about being evaluated by players, I had some misgivings. When I found out that the evaluations were anonymous, my anxiety increased. I knew that it was difficult to please all players, and I feared their judgment whether it was biased or not. But over the years, player evaluations have become one of my greatest learning sources. The few negative comments have helped me pay more attention to the areas where I need improvement.

Maury leads the session, explains the importance of evaluation, and asks the players to be honest and fair in their appraisals. All evaluations are in writing. To ensure that they are candid, names or signatures are not required. The players are asked to complete a player evaluation form like the one in figure 16.1. After everyone finishes, the evaluations

## Postseason Player Evaluation Form

1. Was your coach (or coaches) well organized and prepared for each practice?

    Comments:_____

    _____

2. Were the practice sessions too long, too short, or about right?

    Comments:_____

    _____

3. Were there open lines of communication between you and your coach (coaches) so that you could solve problems together?

    Comments:_____

    _____

4. Did you feel your coach (coaches) had favorites, or did your coach (coaches) treat everyone fairly?

    Comments:_____

    _____

5. Did you feel there was enough discipline, too much, or not enough?

    Comments:_____

    _____

*(continued)*

**Figure 16.1**   Sample postseason player evaluation form.

6. Would you like more matches at home or away, if possible?

Comments:_____
_____

7. Was your coach (coaches) well organized and prepared for each match?

Comments:_____
_____

8. Did you enjoy the trips themselves, see new places, meet new people, and enjoy the company of your teammates and others?

Comments:_____
_____

What can be done to improve the trips?

Comments:_____
_____

9. Were your home matches well organized by the staff so that they ran smoothly from your point of view?

Comments:_____
_____

What can be done to improve match management?

Comments:_____
_____

10. Were you and your teammates and the opposing team treated well by match managers so that the home matches were first-class events?

Comments:_____
_____

11. Were the uniforms, equipment, and supplies furnished by the college adequate, more than adequate, or inadequate?

Comments:_____
_____

12. List the major strengths you see and like in the program. _____
_____
_____

13. List the major weaknesses you see and would like to change in the program. _____
_____
_____

14. Do you have a positive or negative feeling about your participation in the soccer program?

Comments:_____
_____

15. Do you have additional comments on strengths, weaknesses, and feelings about your coach and the soccer program?

Comments:_____
_____

**Figure 16.1**  *(continued)*

are collected and Maury studies them before meeting with the coaching staff.

Even if your athletic director does not require an evaluation by the players, I suggest you execute one on your own. Be prepared for some harsh criticism. Some of it will be unfounded, but some will have merit. Learn from it. You can only get better.

## Evaluation by the Assistant Coaches

A few days after the meeting with the players at the end of the season, my assistants and I will meet with the athletic director. Maury's questions mainly reflect team management. I need the assistants to evaluate the quality and effectiveness of our practices and our on-the-field performance. I require each assistant coach to write a detailed report that evaluates the overall season. The reports may include comments and suggestions on our physical condition, technical skill level, tactical understanding, practice and game management, coaching decisions, and efficiency of our trainers. I also ask them to analyze whether we were successful when we made style adjustments, changed the system of play, or reassigned players. Those reports become part of our permanent file and are a terrific tool for planning the next season.

The meeting with Maury is casual, and everyone has an opportunity to candidly discuss the good and bad points of the completed season. Because he has studied the player evaluations, he takes time to discuss some concerns the players may have expressed. Maury also requires all assistants to complete a written evaluation.

## Evaluating Your Assistants

I need to let my assistants know how I feel about them and their performance. Before we meet, I ask the assistants to list their coaching strong points and where they feel they need to improve. I also have made a list, and more often than not, our observations are relatively the same. As a coach, be sure to bring out all the positive points, but keep in mind that the assistant also has a right to know where you feel improvement can be made.

---

## Managing Stress

Kammie Jacobs is an excellent coach. She was, and still is, an exceptionally good player. She is also very competitive, and the team's performance is extremely important to her. There was one area where I felt she should try to make an improvement.

I felt for her during the moments right before a match and during the time it took to play the match. Her mouth would get tight, her eyes held a glare, and she would breathe at a rapid pace. During the match she would pace a lot. I could feel her stress. Interestingly, I could identify with her emotions because I used to do the same things.

When I confronted her about this and explained my old behavior to her, Kammie said, "That's hard to believe. You seem so calm."

I'm certainly not, but some time ago, a friend pointed out to me that if he could feel my stress, so could the team. I was most likely transferring some of my stress to the team, or at least showing them that I wasn't quite as confident as I said I was. That might cause them to doubt their preparedness. I have learned to manage my stress and purposely force myself to relax. I do that by doing deep-breathing exercises whenever I feel the stress coming on.

I offered to teach Kammie how to do these exercises and she took me up on it. She is now more relaxed and so is the team.

---

When making suggestions for improvement, choose your method and your words carefully. Don't trample on their self-esteem. When giving criticism, I find that the "sandwich approach" usually works best. Begin the conversation by pointing out the qualities you admire in the assistant. Next, discuss the area where you feel the coach could make improvements. Make suggestions and offer your help. Finish the discussion by again pointing out the coach's positive qualities and your overall satisfaction with his or her performance. If delivered properly, constructive criticism is appreciated by coaches who are eager to learn and improve.

We encourage our staff coaches to attend at least one clinic per year at the college's expense. After evaluating the assistants, I may suggest which clinics they should attend. First, I like them to get their United States Soccer Federation or National Soccer Coaches of America Association licenses. But because the USSF and the NSCAA teach little about coaching effectiveness, I suggest to our coaches that they study selected courses in that subject area. I also make them aware of other courses, such as sport psychology, sport management, sport marketing, physiology, and so forth.

## Evaluating Your Players

In a two-year system, the team is forever changing. Each year I lose about half of my players, so building a team is an ongoing challenge. Even so, I believe that any building (figurative or literal) will be strong if it stands on a firm foundation. Returning players become that foundation.

After coaching a competitive season, my assistants and I know our players well. We are then in the unique position of being able to fully evaluate each of them. Before the Christmas break, I ask my assistants to write an evaluation for every returning player, and I do the same. Once we have completed the evaluations, we prepare an off-season training program for each player.

All I'm really concerned with in the off-season is that the players succeed academically, stay fit, and take advantage of every opportunity to improve on their playing skills. We may recommend certain classes, such as strength training and other fitness activities. We make them aware of playing opportunities. A number of players take advantage of our own tournaments and camps to keep themselves in shape. I also conduct a technique development class in spring, and at this meeting, we discuss eligibility rules again.

In a short meeting with each player, I go over the evaluations and the newly written training program. I explain each item on the program and show how it will benefit him. I also schedule times for the player to report back to me to check his progress. This is time well spent. After all, these players are the foundation on which we build our dreams for the next season.

## Evaluating Yourself

The allure of coaching is that it is forever a learning process. Each year, each season, each coach will have new and different challenges. The challenge may be playing a formidable opponent, trying a new method or system, managing a difficult player, building a team culture, handling fatigue, or dealing with any number of other problems. Numerous challenges present themselves during a season of play, and we should evaluate all of them. Because I have evaluated practice and match performance challenges with the staff during season and postseason sessions, I don't need to evaluate them again. There is one significant area, however, that I still need to look at—the effectiveness of my own performance.

Within one week of completing a season, I evaluate my performance in areas other than practices and matches. I use a checklist with questions such as the following:

- Was I always physically and mentally prepared to perform my tasks?

- Did I separate my personal life from my life as a coach?

- If I became fatigued, did I maintain a positive attitude?

- Did I stay positive even after a defeat?

- Did I manage or lead?

- How well did I communicate, in groups and one on one, with players, staff, administrators, media, and community? Did I listen?

- When problems occurred, did I procrastinate or handle them immediately?

- How well did I handle confrontations? Did I listen?

- How patient was I when players or staff wanted to discuss personal problems with me? Did I listen?
- Did I stay performance-oriented throughout the season?
- Was I fair to everyone I met this season?
- Did I, at all times, consider the athlete's welfare first?
- What am I willing to do to improve?
- If I need to improve in any area, where can I go to learn?

I believe that giving honest answers to my questions will make me a better coach from season to season.

## After-Graduation Plans

The low cost of a community college education is attractive to many students and their parents. At a community college, the classes are usually smaller, and students have the opportunity to bring up their grade point averages in preparation for entering a four-year school.

Spokane has two excellent universities, and both offer varsity soccer for men and women. Many of our players apply to those schools, but some want to attend other universities as a result of certain soccer programs. Most often, they want to attend other colleges to specialize in their given major. Because we are distant from the more densely populated areas, we try to help our students find the schools that would be best for them.

For athletes who are trying to choose a college, youth and high school coaches can be of immense service. As a coach, you can help by finding out early the players who want to go on after graduation. With the student, prepare a profile that includes the player's background, statistics, cumulative grade point average, major, goals, a practice schedule, and a match schedule. To this package, add your own observations. Be candid and honest; don't oversell or undersell the athlete. College coaches will appreciate your information; and if you are consistent, they will look at your players.

The package and a cover letter should be targeted to the universities in which your student truly has an interest. The cover letter, written by the student, should be addressed to the head coach, using his or her name and title. The letter should give reasons why your student wants to attend that particular university. This letter is important.

## Building for the Future

My grandfather was a sea captain. As a child, I listened to his stories in fascination. One day, he took me to the harbor, and we went aboard his ship.

"She's a good ship," he said.

"Why, Grandpa?" I asked, and he said, "Because she's well built, she has an excellent crew, and she has a destination to go to."

Build your program well; surround yourself with ambitious, hardworking people; and set realistic goals. You'll have a good ship. Once you are sailing, stay on course.

To get to the top is not all that difficult, but staying there is. No matter how successful you become, keep evaluating each situation, each new plan, and each change in course. Keep listening to your players, your assistants, and your boss. Evaluate what they say because it may be important. Talk to and study other coaches, not just soccer coaches, but any successful coach. Learn from them, but in the end, be yourself. Only you can be the best you can be. Maintain your integrity, and always stick to your philosophy. It is your plan, your map to the future.

A man once said, "Winning isn't everything, it's the only thing." I agree. If by winning, he means taking a program from scratch and building it into a successful entity; if by winning, he means giving aspiring coaches an opportunity to develop; if by winning, he means taking a group of athletes and helping them play as close to potential as possible, then I agree. Winning is everything. As long as you care for your athletes and staff and as long as you stay focused on performance improvement, you'll never lose. Your efforts, by the way, will eventually be reflected in your win and loss record.

The most important part of your program is your athletes. They are your messengers. They look to you for guidance, leadership, values, integrity, and consistency. Be the role model they can emulate. Instead of just knowing many athletes, you will have hundreds of friends who fondly call you "Coach."

# SUMMARY

A stronger future can be built by evaluating the past. Next year's program will be better if you take the time to evaluate the strengths and weaknesses of the season just completed. Here are some suggestions for making the task easier.

- Do all evaluations within days of the season's completion.
- Allow administrators, players, and your assistants to evaluate your program.
- Don't let candid criticism bother you. Learn from it.
- Evaluate your players and assistants fairly and candidly. Be tactful.
- Do a thorough self-evaluation.
- Build the future of your program on the facts presented by your evaluations.

# INDEX

Note: The italicized *f* following page numbers refers to figures.

# ABOUT THE AUTHORS

**Roy Rees,** director of coaching for Southwest Soccer Club in Temecula, California, had a long career as a professional soccer player in the English Football League before becoming a full-time soccer coach. He has coached soccer at the youth, college, professional, and World Cup levels. From 1961 to 1982 Rees worked as an English Football Association staff coach at various national coaching schools in England. He also served as coach of the British Universities All-Star team, which played annually against Holland, Belgium, Germany, France, and Ireland.

While coaching in England, Rees led the Skelmersdale United team to F.A. (Football Association) Amateur championships in 1967 and 1971. During his years as head coach in Altrincham (1971 to 1977) the team won the Vauxhall Conference championship twice and the F.A. trophy once. Rees also coached the national teams in Iraq, Iceland, Sudan, and Algeria and was coach of the British team in the 1978 World University Games. From 1985 to 1993 he coached the U.S. national team under-17 age group.

Rees is the author of the best-selling book *Manual of Soccer Coaching*. He holds both a master of education degree and a master of arts degree from Liverpool University.

**Cor van der Meer's** involvement in soccer spans nearly 50 years and includes experience as a player, coach, referee, and administrator. He began playing soccer as a child in the Netherlands, where he was on the Dutch National Youth team for two years. In 1960 van der Meer emigrated to the United States and began coaching and working with soccer organizations in Vancouver, Washington. He not only helped organize the Columbia Youth Soccer Federation (which grew from 36 players to more than 6,000 under his leadership), but he also coached Team Vancouver, a semiprofessional team in the Pacific Northwest Soccer League. He also served the Washington State Youth Soccer Association (WSYSA) as district commissioner, vice president of organization, vice president of competition, and vice president of development.

In 1982 van der Meer moved to Spokane, Washington, where he coached the Spokane Youth Sports Association's elite Skyhawks Club. As head soccer coach for the Community Colleges of Spokane since 1985, he has led both the men's and women's clubs there to several successful seasons.

Van der Meer is the author of *Soccer Guide for Coaches* and *Keeper of the Goal.* He also writes two newspaper columns, *Nutrition for Athletes* and *Playing to Win.* Van der Meer was named Coach of the Year by the Northwest Athletic Association of Community Colleges (NWAACC) in 1989 and 1992. The Northwest Collegiate Soccer Conference also named him Coach of the Year in 1992.

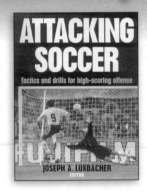
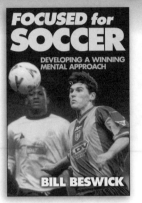

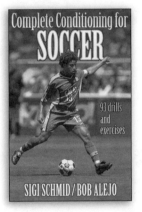